A Wonderful Work
of God

A Wonderful Work of God

Puritanism and the Great Awakening

Robert W. Brockway

Lehigh
University
Press

Bethlehem: Lehigh University Press
London: Associated University Presses

Associated University Presses
2010 Eastpark Boulevard
Cranbury, NJ 08512

Associated University Presses
16 Barter Street
London WC1A 2AH, England

Associated University Presses
P.O. Box 338, Port Credit
Mississauga, Ontario
Canada L5G 4L8

The paper used in this publication meets the requirements of the American National Standard for Permanence of Paper for Printed Library Materials Z39.48-1984.

Library of Congress Cataloging-in-Publication Data

Brockway, Robert W., 1923–
    A wonderful work of God : Puritanism and the Great Awakening /
Robert W. Brockway.
        p.   cm.
    Includes bibliographical references and index.
    ISBN 0-934223-72-6 (alk. paper)
    1. Puritans.   2. Great Awakening.   I. Title.
BX9323 .B76   2003
277.3'07—dc21   2002073027

To the Sacred Memory of My Mother
Edna M. Brockway

Contents

Preface

By THE OPENING DECADES OF THE EIGHTEENTH CENTURY, PURITAN zeal had waned among the Congregationalists of Massachusetts and Connecticut in New England and the Presbyterians of the Middle Colonies of New Jersey and Pennsylvania. Whereas doctrinal consensus prevailed, there were growing differences among Congregationalists and Presbyterians concerning preaching style. Some held that it should be highly intensive and touch the heart; others, that it should be scholarly and restrained. Most pastors were highly suspicious of religious fervor that, to them, smacked of "enthusiasm," a term much used at the time to mean extravagant emotionalism. In particular, there was controversy concerning sudden conversion experiences: were they genuine or not? were they essential or not? Many pastors emphasized the importance of what were called the "means," that is to say, orthodoxy of belief, regular church attendance, Bible study, prayer, and moral rectitude. Although the "means" in no way merited salvation, according to these ministers, they did indicate that a gradual process of redemption was being worked in the souls of those who exhibited them.

All Congregational and Presbyterian pastors welcomed signs of spiritual concern among their parishioners, but those who engaged in passionate preaching stressed the perils of damnation awaiting the unregenerate. Conservative ministers regarded this kind of preaching with suspicion, and it was earnestly discussed in meetings of synod because of the effects of such preaching in certain localities. Throughout the northern colonies there were sporadic upsurges of religious fervor in certain congregations, described in letters and pamphlets and reported in the press. As a result, there was general discussion of the nature of religious experience by late 1739, when a young Anglican divine by the name of George Whitefield arrived from England.

Whitefield had stirred up much religious fervor in Britain with his eloquent and highly persuasive preaching, which was reported in great detail in colonial newspapers, as well as in pam-

phlets circulated throughout the colonies. Consequently,
Whitefield was warmly welcomed when he arrived, and urged to
embark on an evangelical tour of the colonies. This he did, and in
the words of a prominent scholar, Perry Miller, "the lid blew off
New England."[1] Whitefield attracted large crowds which over-
flowed the churches and often resulted in outdoor meetings. He
also rallied a number of young Presbyterian and Congregational
ministers to his support who continued his work by engaging in
itinerant preaching. Many people were deeply moved by him; others became hysterical. Some, however, were skeptical. After his
tour of New England and the Middle Colonies, Whitefield and his
companions rode south to Georgia, but his effect in southern
communities was far less than it had been in the north. Here religious excitement reached flood tide during 1740–41. By late 1742,
it had abated.

By then, rancorous disputes had arisen among the clergy and
people of the northern colonies, and many congregations had become badly divided. The Friends of Revival, as they were initially
called in New England, became known as the "New Lights."
Their counterparts among the Presbyterians of New Jersey and
Pennsylvania were called "New Sides." These people asserted
that only those were saved who had undergone a sudden conversion experience. The so-called Opposers (or "Old Lights" in New
England and "Old Sides" in the Middle Colonies) did not necessarily reject experiential religion, but were disturbed by the bizarre behavior and disorder it seemed to cause in some quarters.
One prominent Boston Opposer, Charles Chauncy, titled a widely
read pamphlet, "Enthusiasm Describ'd and Caution'd Against."[2]

In the wake of the revival, schism shattered the unity of the
Presbyterian Synod of Philadelphia, and in Connecticut and eastern Long Island a number of separate congregations appeared,
some of which persisted as "Strict Congregational Churches."
This name implied a spiritual return to the original Puritanism
of the founders of the New England colonies. In later years most
of these congregations became Baptist, a sect that hitherto had
been represented by only five small congregations in Rhode Island. Baptist itinerant ministers traveled throughout the southern colonies during the 1760s and 1770s, making thousands of
converts among the unchurched people of this region. Other Baptist itinerants preached the evangelical message in the sparsely
populated communities of Nova Scotia, which had been settled
chiefly by migrant New Englanders.

In New England, revivalism triggered a lively debate among

learned members of the clergy concerning the nature of the conversion experience, religious affects (the psychology of religious experience), and doctrinal issues such as free will and predestination and the nature of God. These debates shattered the former doctrinal consensus in New England, and several schools of theology emerged. One was made up primarily of conservatives, another of evangelicals, a third revived Reformation doctrine, while yet another was made up of liberals who were called Arminians. It was this latter movement that gradually evolved into Unitarianism.

The religious excitement of the early 1740s was later called "The Great Awakening." Until recently most scholars had discussed it as a movement that had swept the colonies and transformed religious life. Because of the challenges in some quarters to ministerial authority and evidence of an emerging class struggle, a few scholars have cited the Awakening as a prelude to the American Revolution. This latter interpretation was revived and restated during the 1970s by revisionist historians. During the 1980s and 1990s another revisionist school emerged whose members cast doubt on the assumption that the Great Awakening happened at all, and argued that the whole phenomenon was actually a promotionalist invention on the part of George Whitefield. At the time of writing, this controversy continues.

The term "Great Awakening" may first have been used by Joseph Tracy, a New England Congregational minister, in *The Great Awakening: A History of the Revival of Religion in the Time of Edwards and Whitefield* (1841), published at the centennial of the event by an evangelical.[3] According to Tracy: "During the year 1840, public meetings were held in some places, and proposed in others, in commemoration of what [Jonathan] Edwards called 'The Revival of Religion in New England in 1740.'" This first suggested to the author the design of this work. Tracy had written the book during a time when there was much debate among evangelicals concerning the "new-measures" revivalism of Charles Grandison Finney during the 1820s and 1830s.[4] In his book, Tracy discussed the state of religion in New England during the early eighteenth century, emphasizing its decline; narrated the revivals of 1739 and 1740 in New Jersey among Presbyterians of New England origin; devoted seven chapters to the early life and evangelical activities of the Anglican divine George Whitefield; and assigned four chapters to Jonathan Edwards, and one to the revivalist minister James Davenport ("—His Rise, Progress, Excesses, Recovery, and 'Retractions.'— His Posthumous

Influence. . . "). He devoted two chapters to the "Opposition to the Revival in Connecticut" and the "Controversy in Massachusetts" and his final chapter to "The Revival continued at the South."[5]

In his preface Tracy lists his sources. All subsequent studies of the Great Awakening essentially have been based on the same documents, those that have survived from the early eighteenth century. The documents are as follows: Thomas Prince, Jr.'s multivolume *Christian History* (1743), a contemporary collection of accounts of the "Revival and Propagation of Religion In Great Britain and America"; Whitefield's seven volumes of *Journals;* Jonathan Edwards's *Thoughts on the Revival of Religion in New England in 1740* (1741); Charles Chauncy's *Some Seasonable Thoughts on the State of Religion in New England* (1743); letters by ministers preserved in the Boston Athenaeum and Massachusetts Historical Society; files of colonial newspapers preserved by the Massachusetts Historical and American Antiquarian Societies, church histories and town histories; Isaac Backus's "Ecclesiastical History of the Baptists in New England"; Benjamin Trumbull's "Ecclesiastical History of Connecticut"; and the Reverend Professor Hodge's "The Constitutional History of the Presbyterian Church." To date, Tracy's remains one of the few comprehensive discussions of the Great Awakening. In their bibliographies, most historians continue to recommend Tracy's book as a useful source. Although Tracy wrote his book from the evangelical point of view, he has dominated historical interpretations of the Great Awakening from his own time until the 1980s and 1990s.

During the early twentieth century professional historians became interested in Tracy's discussion of the "Great Awakening," called it by that name, based their own interpretations on research in the same sources he used, and, in general, followed his path without endorsing his religious views. Beginning with scholars of the 1920s, such as Herbert L. Osgood, specialists in the history of colonial America discussed the *Great Awakening* as an authentic historical episode. Osgood devoted fifty-three pages to a survey of the Awakening in Volume 3 of his multivolume *The American Colonies in the Eighteenth Century*.[6] Like Tracy's, his scope was vast, including as it did religious movements among the German Pietists of Pennsylvania between 1720 and 1755; early revivals among the Dutch Reformed and Scotch-Irish Presbyterians in New Jersey during the 1720s and 1730s; the revival fostered by Jonathan Edwards in the Connecticut River valley during 1733–35; the intercolonial evangelism of George White-field during 1739–40, that of Gilbert Tennent in the Middle Colonies and New England during 1733–40, the itinerancy of James Davenport during 1740–43, and the extension of the revival in Virginia during 1740–70. This meant that the geographical range of the Great Awakening comprised all of the colonies in the time frame 1720 to 1770. Neither Osgood nor Tracy discussed the Great Awakening in Nova Scotia between 1767 and 1791, but this was done later by other historians. Thus, by the Great Awakening, scholars uncritically and rather credulously accepted Tracy's lead in identifying it as a vast movement which constituted a "watershed" in early American history, and which occupied virtually the entire eighteenth century. This amazing time frame and geographical scope for the Awakening was standard among historians of Colonial America until the early 1980s. Textbooks in American history followed the same format in their brief discussions of the Great Awakening, so that on both the graduate and undergraduate levels what was essentially Tracy's interpretation was accepted as standard.

Few historians, however, discussed the Great Awakening in its entirety, but concentrated on the revival in New England, the Middle Colonies, or Virginia, with only limited references to revivalism elsewhere. Among the first of the latter was Charles Hartshorne Maxson in *The Great Awakening in the Middle Colonies* (originally published in 1920).[7] According to Maxson, the Great Awakening was the colonial American phase of a transatlantic revival which originated in German Pietism early in the eighteenth century and intersected with the Methodist Revival in Britain fostered by John and Charles Wesley and George White-field. During the early eighteenth century thousands of German settlers migrated to America, chiefly to Pennsylvania. They included Mennonites, Schwenkfelders, German Baptist Brethren (Dunkers), Moravians, and others.[8] Maxson emphasized the influence of the Moravians on the Wesleys and Whitefield in both Europe and America. He also mentioned a Lutheran cult called the "Order of the Woman of the Wilderness," whose members allegedly were borne across the sea by a great eagle to the wilderness where they were to await the millennium. They blended Lutheran doctrine with astrology and esotericism, practiced folk medicine, made amulets, and used divining rods to find underground springs. Maxson also discussed revivalism among the Mennonites in Germantown in 1722, the revivalism stirred up by the Dunker Peter Becker, and that of Conrad Beissel who established the commune at Ephrata, Pennsylvania.[9]

Maxson asserted that the Great Awakening began among the Pietists during the 1720s, and later among the Dutch of the Raritan River valley of New Jersey because of the evangelicalism of Theodore Frelinghuysen, a Pietist Dutch Reformed minister of German origins who arrived in New York in 1720. Frelinghuysen, in turn, had great impact on Gilbert Tennent, son of William Tennent, Sr., who founded a seminary derisively called the "Log College" at Neshaminy, Pennsylvania. William Tennent and his four sons became active revivalists among the Scotch-Irish. They, in turn, influenced Jonathan Dickinson, the Presbyterian minister of Elizabeth Town, New Jersey, who preached the necessity of second birth to transplanted New England Presbyterians, most of whom had originally come from Connecticut.[10]

The itinerary of George Whitefield during 1740 extended the local revivals among the German Pietists and Presbyterians into a general, intercolonial revival. This was the peak year of the Awakening. Thanks to Whitefield's evangelical tour of New England, followed by that of Gilbert Tennent, the revival swept New England and was later extended to Virginia and other southern colonies.[11] In 1930 Wesley Gewehr discussed the southern awakening in a published doctoral dissertation, *The Great Awakening in Virginia, 1740–1790*.[12] In it he focused chiefly on the proliferation of Baptist and Methodist congregations in Virginia during the middle and late years of the century.

In 1949 Leonard Trinterud wrote about the Great Awakening in the Middle Colonies, limiting himself to brief mention of Frelinghuysen but expanding at length on the work of the Tennents. His interest in the Great Awakening was subordinate to his theme, the early history of the Presbyterian Church in America, a church that had cut itself free of its European roots and was Americanized to an exceptional extent. He focused mainly on the schisms and conflict within the Philadelphia Synod and the forming of the revivalist New York Synod, his interest being primarily the early history of Presbyterianism in America as the title of his book indicates.[13]

During the late 1940s and early 1950s, several important studies of the Great Awakening were undertaken by notable Harvard scholars such as Perry Miller and Edwin Scott Gaustad. Miller's primary interest was Jonathan Edwards, and he attributed the Awakening to Edwards rather than to Whitefield,[14] devoting only one chapter to it in *Jonathan Edwards* (1949) in which he emphasized the importance of Edwards' *A Faithful Narrative . . .* (1737). This book, published in London, was widely read, and paved the way for Whitefield when, as Miller says, "the lid blew off New England."[15] Miller also discussed the Great Awakening in *Errand in the Wilderness* (1956),[16] but again subordinated it to other themes. The best history of the Awakening in New England is still Gaustad's *The Great Awakening in New England* (1956), a very brief book of 140 pages which describes the revival succinctly.

Two revisionist schools arose during the late twentieth century. The first, which could be called the "Revolution" school (my term), emerged during the late 1960s and 1970s, when interest in the American Revolution inspired several historians to link the Great Awakening to that event. The second school, which could be called that of the "debunkers," rose during the 1980s and 1990s.

The Revolution school includes Alan Heimert in *Religion and the American Mind* (1966), [17] Cedric Cowing in *The Great Awakening and the American Revolution: Colonial Thought in the Eighteenth Century* (1971),[18] Gary Nash in *The Urban Crucible: Social Change, Political Consciousness and the Origins of the American Revolution* (1979),[19] and Harry Stout in "Religion, Communications, and the Ideological Origins of the American Revolution" (1977).[20] Heimert argued that the Great Awakening unleashed egalitarian forces in prerevolutionary America, bringing about a translation of Calvinism into liberal revolutionary ideology during the 1760s. Cowing showed the impact of the Awakening in terms of links and continuities. Nash asserted that the Awakening involved urban social protest against the mercantile elite. All agreed that the unleashed individualistic and democratizing forces among the lower classes had become politicized during the 1760s and 1770s.[21]

Until the appearance of Jon Butler's "Enthusiasm Described and Decried: The Great Awakening as Interpretative Fiction" in the *Journal of American History* (1982),[22] scholars in the field of early American history confidently wrote of and discussed an event in colonial church history called the "Great Awakening." But according to Butler, twentieth-century historians in following the trail blazed by Tracy have created an "interpretative fiction" of a transformative episode which some historians insist was the origin of American individualism, democracy, and nationalism. Thus, in his startling article, the Purdue University historian tried to demolish 140 years of scholarship in a twenty-page critique.

Joseph Conforti, an historian at the University of Southern Maine, concurred with Butler that the Great Awakening was an invention. He disagreed, however, as to who the inventors were. In "Inventing the Great Awakening," the opening chapter of *Jonathan Edwards: Religious Tradition and American Culture* (1995),[23] Conforti argues that the term "Great Awakening" was a "cultural production" of the "Second Great Awakening" during the early nineteenth century. As such, it was the "invention" of New England Congregational ministers who adhered to the New Divinity, the theological system conceived by Jonathan Edwards, Samuel Hopkins, and others during the colonial era.

In *Inventing the "Great Awakening"* (1999), Frank Lambert of Purdue University agrees with Butler and Conforti that the "Great Awakening" is an invention.[24] However, he contends that "colonial revivalists themselves constructed the Great Awakening—not the term, but the idea of a coherent, intercolonial revival." According to Lambert, there was a "process of invention from small, scattered local 'great awakenings' beginning in the Connecticut and Raritan river valleys in the mid-1730s [leading to] the interconnected revivals of the 1740s known to contemporaries as 'the remarkable Revival of Religion' and to most historians as the Great Awakening."[25]

In light of these criticisms, was there a coherent movement that could be identified as the Great Awakening? Was it a significant forerunner of the American Revolution? Was it limited to a few places and a few years? Was it crucial in the growth of egalitarian democracy? Did it enhance class conflict?

Gaustad limited his discussion of the Great Awakening to New England Congregationalists in the neighborhood of Boston and the Connecticut River valley during 1740–43, while Trinterud discussed only the revivals among the Dutch Reformed and Presbyterians of New Jersey and Pennsylvania between 1720 and 1746. Neither included within the temporal and geographical limits of the Great Awakening Solomon Stoddard's "harvests" at Northampton during 1692–1727, or Jonathan Edwards' awakening in the Connecticut River valley during 1733–35, though Gaustad calls these "ripples of revival." Neither includes the proliferation of Baptist and Methodist congregations in Virginia and the Carolinas during 1750–70, or the "Great Awakening" in Nova Scotia of 1767–91. Both assigned very limited consequences to the Great Awakening, did not claim that it was the "first round of the Revolution," or that it even resulted in significant increases in church attendance. Gaustad *did* contend that it shattered the Puritan consensus in New England and caused separations in church congregations. Trinterud says that the Awakening caused much controversy and schism among Middle Colonies Presbyterians. Both maintain that it introduced extempore preaching. In his article on "Evangelicalism" in volume 5 of *The Encyclopedia of Religion* (1987), George M. Marsden states: "The character of American Evangelicalism began to take shape during the Great Awakening of the eighteenth century."[26] I agree. I also agree with Conrad Wright that New England Unitarianism originated among the Arminians who were Opposers, or "Old Lights," during the Awakening.[27]

However, I concur with some of the correctives applied by Butler, Conforti, and Lambert, though I have serious reservations concerning others. In my view, Lambert's chief contribution is his emphasis on the promotionalist aspects of the Awakening, especially on the part of Whitefield, admirably stated in his *"Pedlar in Divinity": George Whitefield and the Transatlantic Revivals, 1737–1770* (1994).[28] Although the economic prosperity of the early eighteenth century is not news, Lambert has made a very important contribution in showing how the evangelicals exploited the new promotional techniques of the day derived from the business world. As Lambert shows, Whitefield, Edwards, and others made much use of the media to extend the scope of their evangelical messages.

I agree with the revisionists that the Great Awakening may have been much more limited in time and geographical scope than has been thought, that its long-term effects were much more limited than those in the Revolution school contend, and that many of the effects of the Awakening were essentially transitory. There is no supporting evidence justifying the claim that it was a cause of the Revolution. However, there is some evidence that it enhanced class conflict. For example, Rhys Isaac has shown that the social protests in Virginia were based on religious rather than political grounds.[29]

Lambert maintains that there were no radicals involved in the Great Awakening. I disagree. He underestimates the extremism of the small group of evangelicals of whom James Davenport was the most conspicuous representative. In this respect I am in agreement with the Revolution school, that is, with the class struggle arguments of William McLoughlin, Gary Nash, Harry Stout, and Rhys Isaac. However, while there was social unrest, no competent social leader arose to focus and structure the discontent which was in any case very transitory and only occurred within the context of religious revivalism. In 1933 John C. Miller published one of the few discussions of social protest in New England, "Religion, Finance, and Democracy in Massachusetts," in the *New England Quarterly*.[30] His arguments were countered in 1971 by J. M. Bumstead in an article entitled "Religion, Finance, and Democracy in Massachusetts: The Town of Norton as a Case Study."[31]

The latter typifies historical research in the area of colonial New England during the 1970s and 1980s. It is a highly focused study of a specific community based on town records. Studies such as this have shattered many earlier generalizations concerning early New England. Invariably, these studies fail to show evidence of class conflict until the very eve of the Revolution, and strongly suggest that, in most communities, the effects of the revivals were transitory.

Concerning the legacy of the Awakening, I am inclined to concur with Gaustad in his concluding chapters of *The Great Awakening in New England*. Whereas, as Gaustad states, the revival did not result in an appreciable growth in church membership, it did have considerable effect on New Englanders individually, causing much personal concern as evidenced by the records of ministers engaged in counseling. The Awakening shattered theological consensus in New England, as has been asserted by all of the earlier historians of the revival; enhanced the Proto-Unitarian tendencies; and also, at the opposite extreme, the more extreme forms of evangelicalism. Clarence C. Goen has shown that one important consequence of the Awakening was the emergence of a new sect, the Strict Congregationalists, and that it also resulted in the proliferation of Separate Baptists.[32] As well, the Awakening led to a change in preaching style which has persisted. There is much merit in Harry Stout's discussion of pulpit rhetoric, of the popular preference for extempore preaching as opposed to the prepared sermon in literary style delivered from notes that was the common pattern prior to the revivals of the 1730s and 1740s.[33]

At the same time I agree with Patricia Bonomi's more conservative discussion of the Great Awakening in *Under the Cope of Heaven* (1986), in which she does not agree with Butler that the revival was an "interpretative fiction."[34] I believe that a careful study of the available sources fully justifies discussing the Great Awakening as a movement in American colonial history. However, I believe that the southern awakenings and the Nova Scotia awakenings are aftershocks of the main movement which lie beyond the scope of any discussion of it. The Awakening, I contend, was the American phase of a transatlantic evangelical revival of the first half of the eighteenth century. If the discussion is restricted to this, then I think we can meaningfully discuss the *Great Awakening,* using that term. The most useful service the debunkers have provided is to prune the tree of the movement. What is left can scarcely be characterized as a "watershed" of American colonial history, and was most certainly not vital to an understanding of the American Revolution. Nevertheless, this is not to deny the importance of the Awakening within appropriate bounds. It happened; it caused certain changes, some transitory and others not; and it is worthy of discussion. I deny that the Great Awakening was either an "interpretative fiction" or an "invention."

Finally, it is my conviction that all historians, myself included, inevitably form their opinions about the past and write history under the influence of the ambiance of their own times. I believe this is inevitable, though usually unconscious and unintended rather than deliberate. The older school of historians of the Great Awakening, writing from the 1890s to the mid-1960s, attempted to be scientifically objective, and believed this was possible. This ideal stemmed from the impact of German intellectual attitudes of the turn of the century in which the physics model was adopted by scholars in the humanities and social sciences. Beginning with Johns Hopkins University, American graduate departments in history adopted the German approach in doctoral studies. Subsequently, the counterculture had great impact on universities and, in that context, scholars from the mid-1960s through the 1970s often reflected the radical attitudes of at least part of that era. These attitudes are easily detected both in choice of topics and in the interpretations that followed. This does not mean they were wrong. It only means that they viewed historical events, such as the Great Awakening, from perspectives influenced by the counterculture and the Vietnam War. In the 1980s and 1990s, a new school of historians has arisen which also reflects their times. In addition to deflating the claims made by Heimert and others, Butler, Conforti, and Lambert show the strong influence of the growing obsession with business of these decades. This, too, does not mean that they were therefore wrong in their appraisals but is only to assert that they, like the rest of us, invariably make value judgments.

Acknowledgments

I WOULD LIKE TO TAKE THIS OPPORTUNITY TO THANK MY COLLEAGUES in the Religion Department of Brandon University for their continuing encouragement and support. I also wish to thank the Brandon University Research Committee for research funds. I particularly wish to thank Alice Brancewicz of interlibrary loan for obtaining certain books and articles that I urgently needed in the process of revision. I wish to thank Dr. Philip Metzger and Judi Mayer of Lehigh University Press for their encouragement and help during the various stages of producing this book. As ever, I want to thank my wife, Katie, my best friend and my collaborator, as copy editor. And as always, I wish to express my gratitude to Little Guy, our Shetland sheepdog, just for having been.

A Wonderful Work
of God

1

The Augustan Age

THE AUGUSTAN AGE

THE BRITISH HISTORIAN GEORGE TREVELYAN CALLS THE DECADES IN which the Great Awakening took place the "Augustan Age," based on the pacific reign of Emperor Augustine, founder of the Roman Empire, a time of comparative tranquillity, prosperity, and stability. The comparison was appropriate. This was one of those good times to be alive, especially in the British colonies in America. However, there were actually only twenty-five years of peace during the first half of the eighteenth century, and prosperity in the colonies slumped after 1740.

The European Augustan Age began either with the Peace of Utrecht of 1714 which ended the War of the Spanish Succession or on 26 August 1715, when Louis XIV died. The Sun King's long reign had been a time of constant warfare between Britain and France on the high seas and in the colonies, with prostrate Germany the battlefield of the continental powers. Mindful of his errors, the dying monarch summoned his grandson and successor to his bedside: "Try to keep the peace with your neighbors," he told him. "I have loved war far too well; do not copy me in this, nor in the lavish expenditures I have made."[1]

The Peace of Utrecht ushered in twenty-five years of prosperity which ended in 1739 with the War of Jenkins' Ear, so named because a Spanish naval captain lopped off the ear of a British smuggler and thus started a war between Britain and Spain. The next year the conflict broadened into the War of the Austrian Succession (1740–48) which was accompanied by an economic slump in the colonies because of the attacks on British shipping in the Caribbean.

During this twenty-five-year period of comparative tranquillity, Britain and her American colonies enjoyed unprecedented prosperity. The effects were to create a new breed of entrepre-

25

neurs, and to encourage manufacturing and commerce, expansion in overseas shipping, and the proliferation of newspapers and journals, the first mass medium. The new promotional opportunities, as Lambert argues, were adopted by evangelical preachers and were the means by which they and other evangelicals "invented" the Great Awakening.[2] This was particularly true of Jonathan Edwards, the Congregational minister of Northampton, Massachusetts, on the Connecticut River, and of George Whitefield, the Anglican divine, whose revivalism was chiefly responsible for its being a transatlantic as well as an intercolonial phenomenon.

Communications between continents were, however, very slow, though by 1700 there were regular shipping routes between Europe and the Americas. As a result of maritime commerce and European colonization, a new *Atlantic Civilization* was being born during the early eighteenth century.[3] That civilization was ethnically and religiously pluralistic, but dominated by Europeans and European values. It was also highly elitist. A tiny minority of wealthy, privileged people ruled in both Europe and the overseas European colonies, a dominant minority made up of monarchs, courtiers, landed aristocrats, merchant princes, and ecclesiastics in Europe, and of merchants and large landowners in the colonies.

GREAT BRITAIN

In 1707, the Act of Union between England and Scotland created the United Kingdom of Great Britain. Political instability persisted, though not nearly as much so as during the previous century. Some outstanding issues were settled in 1688 when the autocratic James II was deposed by Parliament, thus establishing parliamentary supremacy. That body, however, was made up of privileged wealthy property owners, and the common people of Britain still enjoyed very little representation. This created an unstable social situation which was to continue throughout the eighteenth and nineteenth centuries.

George I, who assumed the throne in 1714, spoke no English, preferred to spend most of his time in Hanover, and left British affairs to the chancellor of the exchequer, Sir Robert Walpole. George II ascended the throne in 1727, and kept Walpole on as chancellor. The latter was a pragmatist who lived by the maxim "let sleeping dogs lie." On these grounds, he adopted the policy of "salutary neglect" where the colonies were concerned. This meant that he did not urge the enforcement of navigation acts and restrictions on colonial manufacturing. Thus, to all intents and purposes, the colonies became self-governing dominions.

The regime was notoriously corrupt, with aristocrats and great landowners and merchant princes having their own way. The life-style of the wealthy was hedonistic, self-serving, and self-indulgent. There was often little difference between the merchant princes and pirates like Henry Morgan. Indeed, many a colonial governor and merchant prospered from the proceeds shared with the pirates.

Lambert argues that the revivalism of the early eighteenth century was determined by economic factors. He discusses the commercial revolution in some detail in *"Pedlar in Divinity."*[4] Despite political instability and corruption, Britain enjoyed great prosperity during the peaceful quarter century between the Peace of Utrecht and the outbreak of the War of Jenkins' Ear. Visitors to London were astounded by the vast variety of goods for sale in London shops. Indeed, Britain was well on her way to becoming a "nation of shop keepers." Vast quantities of British goods were shipped to America, which also enjoyed great prosperity during these boom times. It was a time of plenty.[5]

Theoretically, the British system, like that of other European countries, was mercantilist. Mercantilism was the economic theory that export trade produces wealth if a favorable balance of trade is based on restrictions on manufactured imports. In accordance with mercantilist theory, colonies were founded to provide sources of raw materials and markets, but were to be so regulated that they did not compete with the mother country in the production of goods. As mentioned, the system did not work where the British were concerned because of "salutary neglect," so that, in effect, free trade flourished between Britain and her colonies. What is more, the colonials did not hesitate to trade with the French and Dutch West Indies, even in times of war. The effects of mercantilism, despite its shortcomings, did produce prosperity to an unprecedented degree for the upper classes. Those who enjoyed the consumer society of the early eighteenth century were members of the rising middle class, which included Whitefield and the Wesleys, the great landowners, the gentry, the burgeoning mercantile class in the towns, and the aristocrats, many of whom were investors.

There was astounding population growth both in Britain and in the colonies during these years. There had been much clearing of the land in Britain; swamps were reclaimed; and, thanks to innovations in agricultural technique, yields were much higher than ever before. By 1740 a squirrel could no longer leap from tree to tree from John O'Groat's to Land's End. As a result, the prices of agricultural products fell even while demand grew.

More people meant not only a larger workforce, but also more customers for the increasing volume of manufactured goods. Also, the enlarged economy created a taste for imported goods on the part of the affluent classes able to afford them. Therefore, there was a growing market for tea, coffee, chocolate, wine, spices, silk, and other imported luxuries.

Shipping improved as well, with the development of regular shipping lines between Britain and her colonies. But in Britain, as well as the colonies, the roads were deplorable, and, thanks to highwaymen like Sixteen String Jack, dangerous as well. However, the traffic was enormous and growing. By 1724 new turnpikes were appearing in Britain; around eight a year. There was also much canal building, soon to produce a comprehensive network of inland waterways. The once isolated counties became integrated with the metropolis. Lambert quotes Arthur Young, an inventor of new agricultural techniques. The latter applauded the increased "circulation [of] new people—new ideas—new exertions—fresh activity to every branch of industry—which flow with full tide . . . between the capital and the provinces."[6]

THE AMERICAN COLONIES

By 1715 Britain held twelve continental American colonies which historians divide into three sections: New England, the Middle Colonies, and the South. There were also the vast territories of the Hudson's Bay Company, occupying most of what is now Canada, and the recently acquired Acadia, which became Nova Scotia.

The American colonies were then chiefly restricted to the coastal areas, with settlement extending westward in New England to frontier settlements just beyond the Connecticut River, such as Stockbridge. New England was cut off from further westward expansion by the French and the Six Nations, as well as by the Province of New York. Consequently, northeastward expansion occurred in the area that now includes Vermont, New Hampshire, Maine, and Nova Scotia. The Province of New York was confined to Manhattan, western Long Island, and the Dutch set-

tlements along the Hudson as far north as Albany. The Jerseys
were united into the royal province of New Jersey in 1704. The
Quaker proprietor William Penn had founded Pennsylvania in
1681. It included the former Swedish colony called Delaware.
Maryland, Virginia, and the Carolinas were royal colonies with
sparse, scattered populations, mainly engaged in tobacco plant-
ing. The youngest of the colonies was Georgia, founded by the
benefactor George Ogelthorpe and his associates as a refuge for
impoverished Londoners.

The southern coastal areas are called the "tidewater" by historians, referring to settlements up to the limit of navigability of
rivers. The hinterland from there to the Appalachians is called
the "Piedmont."

During the opening decades of the eighteenth century, the colonial population increased very sharply from around two hundred
thousand in 1700 to two and a half million by 1740. The inhabitants of New England were chiefly descended from grandparents
and great grandparents who migrated to the Massachusetts Bay
Colony during 1630–40 (the "Great Migration"), many from the
northwestern counties of England where evangelical Puritanism
prevailed, with its emphasis on second birth. The Middle Colonies
had a multiethnic population of Dutch, Swedes, Germans, transplanted New Englanders, and Scotch-Irish (Scottish Lowlanders
settled in Northern Ireland during the Commonwealth era).

By 1730 the British colonies in North America had undergone
considerable expansion and development. There was a broad
band of settlement from what is now Maine to South Carolina,
with backwoods Scotch-Irish and German settlers pressing westward to the foothills of the Appalachians and down through the
valley of Virginia. America was becoming a land of scattered
farms, hamlets, villages, and towns. In some areas, settlement
was more than a century old and was already attaining maturity.

Whereas at least ninety percent of colonials were subsistence
farmers of modest means, there were wealthy planters throughout the tidewater South, *patroons* (Dutch landowners) along the
Hudson, and wealthy merchants in the four colonial seaport
towns of Boston, New York, Philadelphia, and Charleston. In
South Carolina the slave population outnumbered whites, and
slaves were to be found in all of the colonies, both north and
south. There were also demoralized remnants of the Pequods,
Wampoags, Narragansetts, Mohegans, Montauks, and other Atlantic Native American tribes, most destitute and culturally de-
prived.

Although there were few titled aristocrats in the colonies, there *were* wealthy planters and merchants who aped the manners and lifestyle of the English upper classes. Most American historians call them "patricians." They included merchants, shipbuilders, shippers of the northern seaport towns, and tobacco planters in the South. There was also an artisan class of what were called then "mechanicks," craftsmen who constituted the lower middle class. In addition, there were small shopkeepers who enjoyed the same status. The ninety percent of the population engaged in subsistence agriculture were considered lower middle class. At the bottom of the social pyramid were the laborers, seamen, squatters, indentured servants, and slaves. Women and children, as in the rest of the world at that time, had few rights, and enjoyed status only in terms of their families. This is significant in that they formed an overwhelming proportion of those responding to the revivalist message, possibly because of their state of repression.

Although colonial manufactures were forbidden by Britain, the restrictive acts, as we have seen, were not enforced. There were profitable iron foundries in New England, many prosperous shipbuilders, and many businessmen profitably engaged in the textile industry. Shipping was a particularly lucrative enterprise for New Englanders. Around a thousand ships visited Boston every year. Yankee shipbuilders also built and sold hundreds of seagoing vessels.

In America, Whitefield exploited the print network created by the newspapers, all of which were founded during the early eighteenth century. Readers were confined to the wealthy classes who could afford to subscribe. Consequently, Whitefield's evangelical message was largely addressed to the upper classes in the colonies, and only later to the masses by means of his open-air meetings. The same was true of Jonathan Edwards. His *Faithful Narrative* (1737) affected chiefly the literate transatlantic middle and upper classes, as was the case with the printed sermons of Dr. Benjamin Colman and other divines. Through correspondence and the printing press, the Evangelicals of the early eighteenth century widened their influence beyond the pulpit and the lecture hall.

THE COLONIAL TOWNS

According to Gary Nash in *The Urban Crucible: Social Change, Political Consciousness, and the Origins of the American Revolu-*

tion (1979),[7] the most impressive effects of the Great Awakening were in the towns rather than the countryside. A small minority of colonial Americans, fewer than ten percent, lived in coastal towns such as Boston, Newport, New York, Philadelphia, and Charleston. Of these, Boston and Philadelphia concern this narrative. The Great Awakening had comparatively little effect on the others. Boston, which had a population of sixteen thousand, was the largest town in the colonies. The wealthier of its merchants lived in commodious brick mansions in pleasant residential districts; imported fashionable clothing, household furnishings, books, and journals from Britain; had close commercial contacts with the West Indies; and engaged in foreign trade in defiance of the navigation acts. In most respects, they were transplanted upper class Europeans. They lived among townspeople of middling means: shopkeepers, artisans, and craftsmen, who lived comfortably enough in frame houses near the waterfront.[8] There were also many of the "poorer sort" who worked for wages, as well as numerous indentured servants and African slaves. Class distinctions in Boston were sharply drawn by the beginning of the eighteenth century. Many of the wealthy property-holders corresponded with friends in Britain, and some, such as Timothy Cutler, a Puritan divine who took Holy Orders and became an Anglican priest, made occasional crossings to Europe.

The chief base of the Great Awakening in the Middle Colonies was Philadelphia, laid out in blocks and squares by William Penn and his associates in 1681. By the time of the Great Awakening it was still a very small town of around eleven thousand. The original settlers were chiefly Quakers (Friends), but they were swamped by newcomers from the other colonies as well as by Germans and Scotch-Irish. Philadelphia was a thriving commercial port, and the Quakers formed the elite in its society, wealthy landowners and merchants who now lived very comfortably, even owning slaves in some cases. They remained, however, people of social conscience, at least where pacifism was concerned. By the end of the seventeenth century they had become very exclusive, staid, and conservative.

The Quakers were almost unaffected by the Great Awakening, to them a bewildering affair, having long ago forgotten their own radical roots and their own original emphasis on second birth. They no longer made many converts, but were becoming families for whom Quakerism was an inheritance passed on to their descendants. Though outnumbered by the more recent immigrants, they continued to dominate the political life of the colony because of the support of the equally conservative German Pietists.⁹

THE RURAL POPULATION

According to Lawrence Gipson, the vast majority of colonials were farm families in New England and the Middle Colonies in the early eighteenth century. Most were subsistence farms, rather than plantations dependent on a single product. The farms were small enough to be worked by the family with the help of a few hired hands. Crops were diversified, as were animals. There were usually sufficient cash crops to enable the purchase of a few manufactured goods. Most farm families, however, depended on their own handicrafts for clothing, farm buildings, household utensils, and tools.¹⁰

The New Englanders

In New England farm families originally had clustered into villages surrounded by fields, pastures, commons, and woodlots. By the beginning of the eighteenth century the best land had been taken and there was considerable land hunger in New England, expansion being effectively blocked by the French and their Native American allies. During the course of the late seventeenth century, some Connecticut families migrated to the neighboring province of New York and also to New Jersey.¹¹ Other New Englanders migrated northeast to occupy the young colony of New Hampshire and what later became the states of Vermont and Maine. Still others settled lands evacuated by the deported Acadians in Nova Scotia.

Those New Englanders who migrated to New Jersey reproduced their New England villages in communities such as Newark and Elizabeth Town. The only significant change they made was the adoption of Presbyterian polity in the place of their traditional Congregationalism. However, Presbyterianism and Congregationalism were virtually interchangeable in theology at that time, though not in polity. Although Jonathan Dickinson of Elizabeth Town played a prominent role in the Awakening, most transplanted New England Presbyterians in New Jersey were only marginally affected by it, and these chiefly because of evangelical preaching during the 1730s, prior to the arrival of Whitefield.

There were no large towns in New Jersey, formerly a proprie-
tary colony which became a royal province in 1704. East New Jersey was populated by a mixture of the aforementioned migrant
New Englanders and the Dutch. The latter were descendants of
the colonists of New Netherlands which the English had seized in
1664. The Dutch population had expanded considerably by the
early eighteenth century. Most were rural folk who lived on scattered farms in such areas as the Raritan River valley, in which
the largest town was New Brunswick. At the time of the Great
Awakening, there were also resident Scotch-Irish and a Presbyterian Church in that community.[12]

The Germans and Scotch-Irish

During the years between 1720 and 1755 there was a mass migration of Germans to Pennsylvania, chiefly from the war-devas-
tated Rhineland. Much more will be said about them in later
chapters. Suffice it to say here, most were Lutheran, German Reform, or else members of small Pietist sects. They were so numerous that, by 1750, they constituted half the population of
Pennsylvania.

During these same years there was also a mass migration of
around one hundred thousand Presbyterian Ulster Scots, called
the *Scotch-Irish* by American historians of colonial history. Most
settled in the frontier areas of the Middle Colonies, usually in
scattered farms or in hamlets where they built their own Presbyterian meetinghouses and conducted services as best they could
without benefit of clergy. The latter were very few in the colonies
compared to the size of the Scotch-Irish population.

CLASS CONFLICT IN THE COLONIES

Some historians maintain that there is clear evidence of class
conflict in the colonies at the time of the Great Awakening.[13] Others disagree.[14] The former argue that social protest played a significant role in the Great Awakening. Upper class colonials, like
their counterparts among the gentry of England and their ladies,
wore powdered wigs, elegant coats, knee breeches, hose, and
buckled shoes, while their ladies wore coiffeured hair and gowns
of the latest London fashion. The gentry were witty, sophisti-
cated, cosmopolitan, and very proud. Most regarded themselves
as being too good to damn. They assumed a virtual monopoly of

political privilege in all of the colonies, based on the assumption that they and they alone were qualified to make decisions. The consequence in the colonies, as in Britain, was a system chiefly based on croneyism and confidentiality, and riddled with corruption. Few members of the privileged classes on either side of the Atlantic had much social conscience; few were above enriching themselves at public expense.

Writing in 1977, a year after the bicentennial of the Declaration of Independence, William G. McLoughlin characterized the Augustan Age as an era of ruthlessness and greed:

> Neighbor vied with neighbor, merchant with merchant, in aggressive competitive ways. Normally decent people cut moral corners, abused their offices, engaged in sharp dealings for private profits. This, in turn, produced an increasing number of lawsuits over alleged frauds or violations of contract. Town meetings became bitter, quarrelsome affairs.[15]

The poor attacked the rich master class for their style of life, and, because most clergymen sided with the upper classes, there was growing hostility against them on the part of people of the lower orders. McLoughlin thinks that the Great Awakening was precipitated because of repressed guilt feelings on the part of the wealthy, and that some, at least, suffered pangs of conscience for having departed so far from the Puritan ideals of their grandparents and great grandparents. Among the upper classes, who were both educated and articulate, there was increasing concern over the decay of family values, and the general loss of respect for the clergy. There was concern, as well, for the decay of the sense of community, the decline of old ways of believing, sharing, and trusting.[16] Some were nostalgic for Winthrop's "Citty on a Hill," a dream that had never been realized.[17] However, the golden aura usually cast over the past distorted collective memories in New England, and gave the people a feeling that something precious had been lost. McLoughlin thinks that this had much to do with the readiness with which the upper classes initially responded to revivalist preachers such as Jonathan Edwards.

According to what I have called the "Revolution" school of revisionists, these were reasons why the Great Awakening happened. They were also the reasons why the Evangelical Revival occurred in Britain. The conversion experience did not require an intermediary; God could act on and through anyone without the need for clergy, the educated, or the upper classes.[18]

Evangelicalism was a populist religion. It was also apocalyptic. But as McLoughlin observes with a new twist, "The guilt which had been internalized prior to 1735 and had caused much turmoil during the Awakening was projected outward after 1765 upon a common enemy."[19] This bicentennial historical thesis (now challenged by revisionists like Butler and Lambert) does at least have validity in one respect. Revivalists such as Edwards denounced not only the moral and religious decay of the colonials in New England, but that of the upper classes in Old England as well. Edwards attacked the "river gods" of the upper Connecticut River, ruthless merchants who exploited the farmers with small holdings, denouncing them for their greed and citing them as exemplars of the moral decline of the day. Edwards and others held that the millennium was soon to be realized in America; that the Americans would be converted and become the means for the salvation of humanity.

There is evidence that the Awakening initially cut across class lines in all the northern colonies affected by it. In its early stages the Awakening was strongly encouraged by ministers such as Dr. Benjamin Colman of the fashionable Brattle Street Church in Boston, who played a principal role in fostering revivalism through his correspondence with Isaac Watts and John Guyse. They, in turn, published an expanded 136-page book by Jonathan Edwards, originally a personal letter to Colman, called *A Faithful Narrative of the Surprising Work of God* (1737), which most scholars think touched off the Great Awakening.

Indeed, the pastors of all fifteen of Boston's Congregational churches were initially supporters of the Awakening, including even Charles Chauncy of First Church, who was soon to become its harshest critic. Only the rectors of the three Anglican churches viewed George Whitefield with strong reservations when he first arrived. However, by the time Whitefield departed some seven weeks later, disenchantment and concern was felt among conservatively minded people of the upper classes. However, people of the lower orders were captivated both by Whitefield, and, soon after, by Gilbert Tennent. Tennent arrived during the cruelest winter in memory, followed during 1741 by James Davenport. It was not until the deportation of the latter that class conflict surfaced, with Tennent and Davenport having become champions of the lower classes, at least in their own eyes. (Whitefield was by then also regarded with some hostility by the upper classes because of the publication of his latest *Journal* containing some unflattering comments about his distinguished Boston hosts.)

The Great Awakening was therefore a religious movement, which, in its opening stage at least, cut across class lines. Whether or not it continued to do so, however, is open to question. Here I agree, but only in part, with Heimert, McLoughlin, Harry Stout, and other members of the Revolution school. What began as a purely religious movement, emphasizing second birth, utimately became a class conflict, though without precise political implications. No revolutionary leaders arose. There was little cohesiveness among the evangelicals; little or no organization and structure, but instead, personal evangelical ministries in which charismatic preaching was the chief feature. Patricians were disturbed by the outcries, writhing, screaming, and fainting that accompanied Whitefield's meetings, and which were even more pronounced in those led by Tennent and Davenport. However, there was never much fear of a popular uprising against the people of property, and there was no social dimension to the revivals other than attacks against the "unconverted ministers," which may have implied social discontent. Class conflict was in any case exacerbated by the depression that followed the outbreak of the War of Jenkins' Ear in 1739, and especially when this war against Spain broadened into the War of the Austrian Succession (1740–48). Shipping was subject to privateers and naval attack on the high seas; markets, such as the French islands of Guadeloupe and Martinique, were closed, or at least difficult to access, and the declining fortunes of the gentry had their effect on the lower classes.

The revisionists reject the assertion of the Revolution school that the Awakening was a *major* cause of the American Revolution. I agree that the evidence does not support the contention of historians such as McLoughlin and Alan Heimert. My view is that the Awakening was a *factor* in the American Revolution, but an indirect one.

THE GREAT AWAKENING: FACT OR FICTION?

The revisionist "debunkers" (my term) claim that the Great Awakening was nothing more than a number of local revivals blown out of proportion by self-serving promoters; an invention of preachers who were no less ambitious than the people whom they denounced.[20] I do not agree. Although the revivals were local and scattered in time, a coherent impulse underlay them all, justifying the designation, the Great Awakening.

But the Great Awakening did not sweep through the colonies as those of the Revolution school assert. Instead, the revivals were local and confined to limited geographical areas: the neighborhood of Boston; Rhode Island; the Connecticut River valley; the Raritan River valley in New Jersey; Philadelphia and environs; northeast Maryland to a very limited degree; tidewater Virginia; Charlestown, South Carolina; and Savannah, Georgia.[21] Seeds sown during the Awakening also later blossomed in parts of the South, the Old West, and in Nova Scotia. But the connection between the revivals was more subtle than those of the Revolution school maintain.

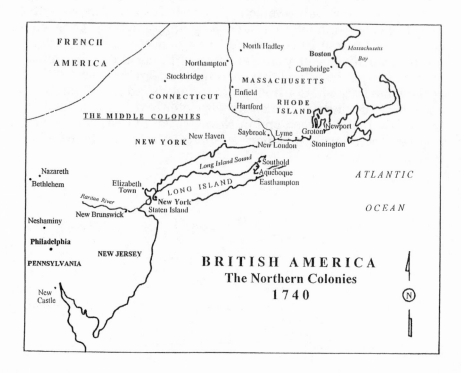

FRENCH

AMERICA

THE MIDDLE COLONIES

North Hadley

Northampton

Stockbridge

Boston

Massachusetts
Bay

Cambridge

MASSACHUSETTS

Enfield

Hartford

RHODE
ISLAND

CONNECTICUT

NEW YORK

New Haven

Saybrook

Lyme

Groton

Newport

New London

Stonington

Nazareth

Bethlehem

Elizabeth
Town

Raritan River

New Brunswick

Long Island Sound

LONG ISLAND

New York

Staten Island

Southold

Aqueboque

Easthampton

ATLANTIC

OCEAN

Neshaminy

Philadelphia

NEW JERSEY

PENNSYLVANIA

New
Castle

BRITISH AMERICA
The Northern Colonies
1 7 4 0

N

2

The State of Religion in Colonial America

FROM THE EARLY SEVENTEENTH CENTURY ON, THE CONTINENTAL British colonies were religiously pluralistic. This was particularly true of the Middle Colonies, but also applied, to a lesser degree, to New England. From north to south, Congregationalism (or Independency) prevailed in New England. It was the established church in both Massachusetts and Connecticut. Rhode Island was unique. Here religious freedom flourished. Not only were there Congregationalist and Anglican churches, but Friends meetinghouses, and five Baptist churches, almost the only houses of worship of that sect in the colonies prior to the Great Awakening. Elsewhere, dissenters were tolerated at best.

In the Middle Colonies, there were the Quakers of the Jerseys and Pennsylvania, the German sects which grossly outnumbered them, and the Presbyterians, most of whom were Scotch-Irish and some of whom were transplanted New Englanders. There were also Dutch Reformed people in New York and New Jersey, around six hundred Swedish Lutherans in Delaware, and rapidly increasing numbers of Anglicans, thanks to the activities of the Society for the Propagation of the Gospel.

Some historians of the past have grossly overstated the alleged moribund state of religion in New England and the Middle Colonies in the early eighteenth century. Later historians contend that the unchurched increased chiefly because population growth was so rapid that churches could not be built fast enough to accommodate them, nor ministers recruited to serve them. Church *membership* and church *attendance* were not identical: full members (those who were accepted as converted) were in a declining minority; general attendance, however, was on the increase.[1] This suggests that only fervent belief was weakening.

NEW ENGLAND CONGREGATIONALISM

As mentioned, all of the Congregational churches in Massachusetts and Connecticut were established. The church building was the property of the town and the business of the church was an indistinguishable aspect of town affairs. Each parish was independent. However, all of the parishes together constituted what was called the "standing order." Every citizen of the parish was bound by law to pay taxes for the support of the church, an imposition from which Quakers, Anglicans, and Baptists were finally exempted in 1715. Church attendance was mandatory, but imposition of this had become relaxed by the end of the seventeenth century. The service was austere, the sermon being the central feature. The only music was the oral chanting of psalms. The general behavior of the congregations was decorous and the atmosphere formal.[2]

In recent years, scholars such as Kenneth Lockridge have studied the town and church records of certain New England communities, and, on the basis of these records, reconstructed a three-stage model of the social history of these settlements from their founding early in the seventeenth century to the Revolution.[3] Lockridge, for instance, studied the history of Dedham, a community in eastern Massachusetts not far from Boston. He found that the Puritan pioneers who founded the settlement in 1636 were mostly English peasants who were deeply moved by Puritan idealism. Theirs was a "unified social organism," a corporate community based on Christian piety. Lockridge was amazed by the high degree to which they achieved the Puritan ideal of a "Wilderness Zion" or John Winthrop's vision of a "Citty on a Hill." By mid-century, Dedham had become a secure community, since the fear of "Indians" and wild beasts had passed. The forests had given way to fields and pastures.

However, an increasing number of people in villages like Dedham could not profess to having experienced a personal religious crisis. Ability to testify to such to the satisfaction of the congregation was essential for church membership. Accordingly, they were denied full membership in the church because they could not prove they had been saved. This also meant they were denied full political rights as citizens of the community.[4] Lockridge was interested to note the absence of resentment on the part of the unregenerates.

So few were eligible to partake of the Lord's Supper (Holy Eucharist) in communities such as Dedham that the rite was usually held very infrequently, and then only after most of the congregation had departed following Sabbath worship. To solve part of this problem the Synod of 1662 adopted an accommodation known as the Half-Way Covenant, under which those who were not counted among the saints could be granted limited membership. The ministers who urged the laity to adopt the Half-Way Covenant, which will be discussed in more detail later, did so in fear of losing their congregations.

Lockridge was interested to note that by 1688, the beginning of the second stage, there was a notable transition from a corporate and communal spirit to individualism in Dedham. Public life became more contentious than it had been. The traditional leaders, the magistrates and ministers, gradually declined in both status and authority. The citizens became more self-assertive. However, despite these changes, Dedham remained in essence a peaceful, stable, and closely knit community of relatives, friends, and neighbors, who usually interacted with one another cooperatively, and who continued to observe the decorum of their forefathers.

During the years from mid-century to the Revolution, Lockridge's third stage, Dedham became increasingly closed, socially speaking, with clearly structured class lines. It had become highly stratified, and land was distributed on a very unequal basis in terms of rank as well as size of family. Here, and elsewhere in New England, social status had become the basis of seating arrangements in the church, with saints and the wealthy occupying the best pews. Stability and order were the priorities, and the citizenry accepted as a matter of course their status in the community. By then, wealth was becoming more important than the state of one's soul as a determinant of social status. He refers to the last stage as a "Europeanized" society, meaning that the town was more like a rural community of its size in England (or elsewhere in Europe) than had been true during the previous decades.[5]

Not all investigators agree with Lockridge. In *Peaceable Kingdoms* (1970), Michael Zuckerman attempts to "comprehend the culture of provincial Massachusetts whole." His researches in the records of certain Massachusetts communities convinced him that the original patterns of the founders continued up through the Revolutionary era, and that communal consensus was as strong in 1750 or 1770 as it had been in 1700 where values and attitudes were concerned. Zuckerman's thesis is "that the consciousness of community, in Massachusetts, continued at least three quarters of the way through the eighteenth century as a prime value in public life." [6]

The Half-Way Covenant

By the late seventeenth century church membership in New England had become a problem because of its demands. The candidate must first satisfy the minister that he or she had experienced conversion, then testify to the entire congregation, narrating the experience and submitting to their judgment. Even that was not enough, because rigorous examinations by minister and elders followed before the person was considered to be a fit candidate for full membership. To accommodate the children of people who could not profess to having had religious experiences, but led upright lives, a compromise known as the Half-Way Covenant was adopted in 1662 as an amendment to the Cambridge Platform (1651).[7] It allowed the children of unregenerates to be baptized, if the parents accepted a partial form of church membership, the Half-Way Covenant. A person who was affiliated with the church through this covenant was not permitted to participate in the Lord's Supper, but was expected to support the church. The Half-Way Covenant thus created two kinds of church membership: full membership, called "owning the covenant," enjoyed only by regenerates, and partial membership for the remainder (the unregenerates). Soon most people in every congregation held membership on the basis of the Half-Way Covenant. They consented to abide by the discipline of the church, to be taught doctrine, and to profess the orthodox tenets set forth in the Cambridge Platform. If, at any time, they experienced the saving grace of conversion and became "visible saints," they became full members and were allowed to participate in the Lord's Supper.[8] As mentioned, becoming a saint was not a purely private matter, but required public witness. Either because they were embarrassed to do this, or because in the course of self-examination they could not profess to having undergone a spiritual crisis, only a minority made such professions.

Questions then arose concerning the nature of religious experience. Must conversion *necessarily* occur during a crisis, or could it be gradual? Both pastors and laity differed on these questions. In the neighborhood of Boston, an increasing number suggested that there could be a variety of religious experiences, including the quiet and gradual. In the Connecticut River valley, however, most tended to be more traditional and rigid, and to insist that to be a visible saint one had to have undergone a highly emotional public conversion experience.

By the beginning of the eighteenth century churches were growing in number. Boston, for instance, had eighteen by 1740. To an increasing extent, as has been said, class distinctions prevailed. Thus, New North Church had a congregation largely made up of artisans, small shopkeepers and their families, whereas the Brattle Street Church was the most prestigious church in Boston.

The Brattle Street Church

In 1698 a group of wealthy and influential Harvard College trustees founded an independent congregation in Boston which they called the Brattle Street Church, named for the wealthy Thomas Brattle, who was one of the most prosperous men in New England. Brattle spent several years in England. He was highly educated, cosmopolitan, and an accomplished astronomer and mathematician in an age when it was possible for amateurs to reach the outer limits of virtually any science. In 1692 he had opposed the witchcraft mania initiated by Increase and Cotton Mather. Brattle had a brother, William, who was minister of the church in Cambridge, and a tutor at Harvard.

Along with other businessmen, Brattle invited Benjamin Colman to be minister of the new congregation. Colman was a Harvard graduate who went to England where at Brattle's suggestion he was ordained by the London presbytery. This made him independent of the Boston Ministerial Association dominated by Increase Mather.

Colman was a highly learned minister who attracted a prosperous congregation of wealthy businessmen and their families. His doctrines were those of the Westminster Confession, and were completely orthodox. He subscribed to predestination and election, and to most of the other Puritan tenets. However, the Brattle Street Church did not require those who "owned the covenant" to relate their inner experiences to the congregation. Instead, the candidate had only to satisfy the minister that he or she was spiritually of the elect by having had the conversion experience. This practice set a precedent which liberalized church membership.

The Brattle Street Church was, to use a phrase of the Canadian writer Pierre Berton, a church of the "comfortable pew." By that,

Berton does not mean quality of seating, but absence of religious intensity. Once a week, Colman's prosperous parishioners listened to a well-prepared and learned sermon extolling the sovereignty of God, the depravity of humanity, the need for repentance, and the urgency of conversion. However, while Colman's eloquence was stirring, and his sermons were rich in content, the Sabbath service had more the character of a refined form of entertainment than of worship. Brattle Street Church became a society of nominal Christians who paid lip service to the Westminster Confession and who professed faith and obedience to Christ as a matter of common decency. An anonymous wag wrote of the Brattle Street Church:

> Our churches turn genteel
> Our parsons grow trim and trip
> With wealth, wine, and wig,
> And their heads are covered with meal.

But by the beginning of the eighteenth century other churches in the neighborhood of Boston were emulating the Brattle Street Church. Puritan practice was becoming more relaxed, much to the distress of the small conservative minority. It became even more so because of the effects of the reforms of Solomon Stoddard.

Solomon Stoddard and Northampton

Solomon Stoddard, minister of the Congregational Church of Northampton on the Connecticut River in western Massachusetts, was one of the most prestigious clergyman in the province.[9] He was a Puritan of the old school and much disturbed by the decline in church attendance, and of religious concern generally. Arminian tendencies were particularly troublesome to him.

He was also concerned with the worldliness of so many of his parishioners, especially the young. During the late seventeenth and early eighteenth centuries it was common practice for families of the gentry in Northampton to meet socially on Sunday evenings instead of going to church. Young people were given the freedom to meet without the supervision of their elders. There was also much "tavern haunting" and "night walking" in Northampton. It is not quite certain what was meant by the latter but those who indulged in it were suspect.

A further problem was the lack of experiential commitment on the part of so many of Stoddard's parishioners. For that reason, beginning in 1692, he exhorted his congregations on at least five occasions, and reaped what he called "harvests," which is to say, spiritual renewals. These were called "revivals." Stoddard's "harvests" were among the ripples preceding the "great and general awakening."

"Stoddardeanism," as it is sometimes called, marked a sharp departure from traditional Puritan usage, but there was no intent to relax Puritan spiritual demands. In no way should Stoddard be regarded as a liberal or quasi-Arminian, or thought to be weakening or undermining Calvinist orthodoxy, although his critics accused him of it at the time. It is rather that Stoddard sought more effective means of encouraging conversion. He, like Colman, did not require public confessions of religious experience as a requirement for full church membership. Nevertheless, most of his congregation were of the Half-Way Covenant. He considered the Lord's Supper to be a *saving* sacrament, a means for the Holy Spirit to bring about conviction and conversion, and rather than exclude the vast majority of his congregation from it, made it available to all whether or not they had "owned the covenant." Effectively, this eliminated the Half-Way Covenant by granting the privileges of full membership in the church to all. Those who had not "owned the covenant" were still not saints, but they enjoyed all the earthly benefits of membership. Because participation in the sacraments, as channels of grace, are soteriological rites in Roman Catholicism, the pastors who adopted Stoddardeanism were sometimes accused of "Papism."[10]

Connecticut and the Saybrook Platform

Since neither the Half-Way Covenant nor Stoddardeanism arrested the growing secularization of New England, some ministers complained that these practices were in themselves the causes of the problem. There were also complaints about *Arminianism*, which, to them, meant being liberal in any way. Some thought congregations were assuming too much power in the churches. In 1679, a "Reforming Synod" was held in Boston which addressed itself to these matters and passed resolutions demanding a tightening of ecclesiastical discipline. At the time, these resolutions were ignored, and in Massachusetts congregational polity continued to prevail during the late seventeenth and early eighteenth centuries. This was largely because in eastern

Massachusetts, which was cosmopolitan with many highly educated people, printers, and newspapers, Latitudinarian, or liberal tendencies predominated.

A different situation prevailed in conservative Connecticut. From the founding of New Haven and Connecticut, the churches of these colonies had depended on one another for mutual aid, whereas those of Massachusetts were highly independent of one another. As a result, while congregational polity prevailed as stated in the latter colony, a system was adopted at Saybrook in 1708 which added some of the features of Presbyterianism. The Saybrook Platform provided for consociations to which pastors and laity sent delegates, and for a general synod which exercised a supervisory role. The consociations did not have as much authority as presbyteries, but they did impose some limitations on congregational freedom, which was resented by many laymen, though not by the clergy. Essentially, the Platform provided a way of enhancing the authority and status of ministers. Reaction to it contributed to the Great Awakening, and especially to the schisms within congregations, and separations.

The Congregational Church of the first half of the eighteenth century was very different from the Puritan Church of the previous era. The new Massachusetts Charter of 1691 did not disestablish the church, but did weaken it. The prestige of the church was further weakened by the Salem Witchcraft trials of the following year which ended in scandal. Magistrates and ministers, such as the Mathers, were discredited in many quarters during the rationalist reaction which followed. By 1715 belief in witchcraft had waned, as, indeed, it had in Britain and continental Europe generally. The dawn of the Enlightenment was accompanied by religious toleration. Anglicans, Baptists, and Quakers were granted freedom of conscience, and, by 1730, were no longer obliged to support the Standing Order.[11]

Gipson cites the appearance of the *New England Courant* as a sign of the times, and of changed attitudes toward the church and clergy. The new journal was edited by James Franklin, elder brother of Benjamin. Between its founding in 1721 and its demise six years later, the *Courant* published diatribes against both the clergy and the Establishment. At the same time, the press began to replace the pulpit as the chief medium. The first American newspaper was *Public Occurrences Both Foreign and Domestic,* beginning in 1690. Richard Prince, the printer, published but one issue and was then silenced. In 1704 Postmaster John Campbell founded the *Boston Weekly News-Letter* which continued publication until the Revolution. Another postmaster, William Brooks, founded the *Boston Gazette* in 1719. It was printed by James Franklin, and continued publication until absorbed by the *New England Weekly Journal* in 1727. The *Boston Weekly Rehearsal* began as a literary journal in 1731 and became the *Boston Weekly Post* in 1733, with Thomas Fleet as proprietor and publisher. Two years later it was renamed the *Boston Evening Post* and continued to publish under that name until the Revolution. In 1734 Postmaster Ellis Huske started the *Boston Weekly Post-Boy* which published for the next two decades, when it became the *Boston Weekly Advertiser*.[12] All of the Boston newspapers articulated the viewpoint of the conservative power elite, which included the ministers of the Boston churches. They became principal vehicles for the assault against the radical New Lights during the Awakening. For this reason, their accounts, though among our chief sources for the revival, are suspect, as are sources such as Charles Chauncy's *Seasonable Thoughts on the State of Religion in New England* (1743) which is countered by the revivalist *Christian History* (1744) of Thomas Prince.

New England Congregationalism was united at the beginning of the eighteenth century. The ministerial associations preserved the consensus, and there was little dissent. This situation prevailed through the first three decades of the century. Jonathan Edwards did not threaten it with his *A Faithful Narrative* (1737) which had the imprimatur of Benjamin Colman, who, at sixty-two, was the dean of Boston clergy. Not until the appearance of Whitefield was there so much as a hint of dissent.

Although the Great Awakening was a movement among Congregationalists and Presbyterians, by no means all colonials were of these two persuasions. During the early eighteenth century the church making the most impressive gains was the Anglican, especially in the Middle Colonies and New England. On the other hand, the Quakers, always few in number, were becoming even scarcer, even in Pennsylvania. There they were swamped by vast numbers of German Pietists and Scotch-Irish Presbyterians between 1720 and 1755. Whereas the Scotch-Irish are definitely within our area of concern, the Quakers and Pietists are not, nor are the Dutch Reformed of New York City, New Jersey, western Long Island, and the Hudson River valley. I mention these other groups only to indicate the religious pluralism of the colonies during the time of the Great Awakening, and to emphasize the fact that there were many in the colonies who were only slightly affected by the movement if at all.

THE PRESBYTERIANS OF THE MIDDLE COLONIES

During the course of the late seventeenth century some Connecticut families migrated to the neighboring province of New York, and also to New Jersey. Here, as mentioned earlier, they founded communities such as Elizabeth Town and Newark which were identical to those in New England.[13] These people, though originally Congregationalist, became Presbyterians in order to strengthen the order and discipline of their churches. The most prominent minister among them was Jonathan Dickinson, minister of the Presbyterian church of Elizabeth Town.

In contrast to the Congregationalists, who originally demanded proof of conversion to qualify for membership, Presbyterians held that the state of a person's soul was known only to God. Those who sought membership had only to satisfy the ministers and elders representing the congregation that they were orthodox in belief and upstanding in moral character. The new member thus admitted was eligible to partake of the Lord's Supper (Holy Eucharist). Admission to a Presbyterian Church meant membership in the whole Church of Christ. Presbyterians ordained ministers to serve the Church Universal. They could serve as such in any congregation, and were ministers for life. They expected recognition of their ministerial status by all other Christian churches whether Presbyterian or not.[14]

Most of the Presbyterians of the Middle Colonies were Scotch-Irish immigrants from Ulster. Their forebears were Lowland Scots who were settled in that county during the seventeenth century. They are sometimes called Ulster Scots. Their situation became difficult after the Restoration in 1660. The restored Stuarts were hostile to Presbyterianism, and discriminated against the Scotch-Irish on religious grounds. To make matters worse, the English government also imposed restrictions on the Ulster textile industry which embittered the Scotch-Irish even more. Early in the eighteenth century many of them decided to emigrate to the New World. Between 1720 and 1750 around one hundred thousand migrated to America. Here they were further beset because of their poverty. They were unmercifully exploited by the colonials, and, in desperation, most of them moved to the dangerous frontier areas where they carved clear-ings in the forest and squatted on land that they did not own. The one cohesive institution in their lives was the church. Those who settled in the older communities joined the Presbyterian congregations of the transplanted New Englanders, not always finding a warm welcome there when they did so. Those who settled on the frontier built crude meetinghouses, and, since ministers were comparatively few among them, conducted their own worship services.

In 1716 the transplanted New Englanders and Scotch-Irish founded the Synod of Philadelphia which became their governing body. It was wholly independent of Old World connections from the beginning. Thus, from its very founding in colonial America, Presbyterianism was distinctively American in character.[15] The Scotch-Irish Presbyterians were staunchly orthodox, with most subscribing to the Calvinist tenets of the Westminster Confession. Scotch-Irish ministers tended to be highly conservative.

William Tennent

Among the Scotch-Irish immigrants was William Tennent, an Anglican priest who brought his family to America because of his discontent with episcopacy and Anglican ritual, chiefly on scriptural grounds. On arrival in America, Tennent became a Presbyterian minister, was welcomed as such by the Philadelphia Synod, and was settled at Neshaminy just north of Philadelphia. Here he founded a one-room seminary which his enemies derisively dubbed the "Log College."[16] He did so, in part, because of the acute shortage of Presbyterian ministers, but primarily to educate ministers in Evangelicalism. His tiny student body consisted of his sons, Gilbert, William, Jr., Charles, and John, as well as one Samuel Blair. He was a highly effective tutor and taught his students Latin and Greek, in which he was proficient, and some Hebrew, in which he was not. He also taught rhetoric, logic, and other standard courses which prepared divinity students for the ministry. The Log College caused considerable controversy among the Scotch-Irish clergy, all of whom were educated in Edinburgh, Glasgow, or Trinity College, Dublin. They particularly deplored Tennent's emphasis on experiential religion which they deeply distrusted. As strict subscribers to the Westminster Confession ("subscriptionists") they insisted on doctrinal orthodoxy. *That* caused no problems. The Tennents did so as well. However, the subscriptionists also discouraged emotional preaching, and interpreted salvation (as had Calvin) in terms of gradual infusion of divine grace rather than as the result of a sudden conversion crisis.[17]

However, the conflicts among the Middle Colonies Presbyterians were not at all about doctrine, and by no means altogether about evangelical preaching. The chief source of division was the perceived weakness of the Philadelphia Synod and its feeble discipline. Tennent deplored the lack of authority and control, and it was that more than any other factor that set him at odds with fellow ministers.

On the eve of the revivals, the situations in New England and the Middle Colonies were very different, and so were the issues. Whereas New Englanders who later responded to evangelical preaching were disturbed by the state of their souls, the Scotch-Irish Presbyterians were preoccupied by the challenges faced by impoverished immigrants in the New World. In New England those who were initially impressed by evangelical preaching included a considerable number of wealthy, well-established men and women who felt guilty because of their prosperity. The Scotch-Irish, on the other hand, were chiefly concerned with the preservation of their church in the wilderness, order and church government being the most pressing issues. Paradoxically, those most disturbed about these issues were not the conservatively minded subscriptionists who were to become the "Old Sides" during the Middle Colonies Awakening, but the "New Sides" Evangelicals who deplored the moral state of the ministers and laity and demanded more effective control.

As for doctrine, New England Congregationalists and Presbyterians both subscribed to the same creeds, especially the Westminster Confession, and professed the same doctrines. This was Calvinism, but not precisely that of the Reformation. Instead, the standard form of Calvinism, from the early seventeenth century on, was what theologians and church historians have called the "federal" or "covenant" theology. The alternative was Arminianism. This was a form of Calvinism that, without formally denying predestination and election, emphasized faith as a free choice in response to divine grace.

THE FEDERAL THEOLOGY

Federal Theology originated in Switzerland and the Rhineland because of the importance of corporate contracts. Towns, guilds, and all other medieval and early modern corporations enjoyed rights and liberties because of their charters, which were contracts between kings and feudal lords with the towns. The individual dealt with superior powers of all kinds through representatives rather than directly. The laity therefore readily understood the meaning of divine–human compacts in which there were obligations on both sides, and also penalties in the event the terms of the contract were violated. They also understood representative government. By translating Reformed theology into these comprehensible terms, the theologians and clergy ensured the continuance of the established church.

During the second half of the sixteenth century Federal Theology appeared in the writings of John Preston (1587–1628), William Perkins (1558–1602), and William Ames (1576–1633), who were taught by continental theologians. Covenant theology was incorporated into Chapter 7 of the Westminster Confession adopted by Parliament as the creed of Puritan England.[18]

The idea of covenant, or foedera, had its biblical warrant in texts such as Isaiah 42:6, Hosea 6:7, Luke 22:20, and Hebrews 9:15–17. It also occurred in patristic literature, especially in the writings of Irenaeus. Thus, there were early Christian precedents for the doctrine. It was "an uneasy blend of incompatible elements,"[19] made up of components drawn from medieval scholasticism, Calvinism, humanistic rationalism, and legalistic tenets. This theology resulted partly from the application of medieval insights: that reason is completed by revelation, nature by grace, and man's works by the supplement of divine power.[20] Thus, according to Dudley Fenner's *Theologica* (1585), there was first the "covenant of works" which God made with Adam at his creation, and which applied to all of humanity, his progeny. Adam's disobedience nullified this covenant and therefore the efficacy of works in obtaining salvation.[21] After the Fall came a series of interim covenants, such as those with Noah, Abraham, and Moses, culminating in the "covenant of grace" based on the perfect obedience of Jesus.

According to the tenets of Federal Theology, God did not deal with humanity on an individual basis, but only through his federal representatives, Adam and Christ. Adam's sin of disobedience broke the first covenant, and alienated the primal couple and their descendants from God. Because of this original sin, all human beings are born in a state of depravity. Thus, if a person dies before conversion, he or she is eternally damned. No one is innocent, not even those who are baptized as infants. Until the coming of Christ, the covenant of works defined God's basic relationship to humanity, and all who lived before that time were damned because they were compelled to sin (apparently, this included all the Old Testament prophets and covenanters). The compulsion to sin was the habitus (innate lifestyle) of what was called "natural man" or "the old Adam."[22] In time, God became man in Jesus Christ, rendered Himself perfect obedience, and by so doing, ransomed those whom God had predestined to be saved and who are therefore of the elect. Christ did so as the second federal representative of the human race, and, by so doing, established the covenant of grace. In keeping with Calvin's teachings, Puritans held that those predestined for salvation experience *conviction of sin*, that is to say, an awareness of their depravity and the perilous state of their souls roused in them by the Holy Spirit. If they are predestined for salvation, conviction is followed by the joyful experience of *conversion* in which their sins are forgiven and they are no longer alienated from God but are in Christ. They are now saints, which does not mean that they are perfect, but rather that they have been given a new habitus which enables them to live as God intended and to enjoy eternal bliss after death.[23] Federal Theology was legalistic and contractual. This disturbed ministers like Edwards, who held that God could not be bound by any agreement, but was omnipotent. In his view, the foedera created false security based on assurances that decency in human terms sufficed to guarantee salvation. Federal Theology gave rise to Arminianism, which Edwards viewed with great concern.

ARMINIANISM

Arminianism, a Reformed theology, was named for its founder, the Dutch theologian Jacobus Arminius (1560–1609). It originated in that country, and subsequently spread to England and Scotland, as well as among Calvinists in other Protestant countries. Arminius studied theology in Geneva under Theodore Beza, Calvin's successor, who extended the doctrine of predestination with what was called *supralapsarianism*. (Latin: *supra lapsus*, literally "before the fall.") According to Beza, God decreed that Adam and Eve would sin. When he returned to Holland, Arminius taught this doctrine first as pastor in Amsterdam, and then as a professor of theology at the University of Leyden, until it was challenged by Dirck Coornhert. In the course of the debate that followed, Arminius became doubtful not only of supralapsarianism, but of many other aspects of orthodox Calvinism as well. According to Dr. Fairbairn, as quoted in the *Encyclopaedia Britannica*, "He [Arminius] held that it (the doctrine) made God the author of sin, that it restricted his grace, that it left multitudes outside without hope, that it condemned multitudes for believing the truth; viz., that for them no salvation was either intended or provided in Christ, and it gave an absolutely false security to those who believed themselves to be the elect of God."[24] The issues of the debate were widely published, and, as a result, the Dutch Reformed Church was split between those who supported Arminius and those who defended orthodox Calvinism.

At the time, Holland, engaged in the Eighty Years' War with Spain, was consequently in tumult. The orthodox Calvinists supported Prince Maurice, who was attempting to unite the Seven Provinces which had risen up in revolt against their Spanish overlords. Wealthy Dutch merchants, who were republican and favored provincial autonomy, supported Arminius. The rise of Arminianism was thus not only a religious matter but an aspect of a fierce social and political struggle. To resolve the controversy, the States General, the governing body of Holland, called a synod at Dort in 1618 which met for seven months. The delegates came not only from Holland but from parts of Germany, Switzerland, England, and Scotland as well.

The Arminian party tried to have their views heard, but soon learned that they were actually being tried as heretics. They rallied under the name *Remonstrant*, meaning "a reproof" or "a correction." They presented their views in a document entitled "Five Articles of the Reformed Church of Holland." These articles summarize Arminianism. Arminius himself, sickened because of the controversy, and having never produced a systematized theology, died soon after the synod closed in 1619. The five articles are as follows:

1. that the divine decree of predestination is conditional, not absolute;
2. that the Atonement is in intention universal;
3. that man cannot of himself exercise a saving faith;
4. that though the grace of God is a necessary condition of human effort it does not act irresistibly in man;
5. that believers are able to resist sin but are not beyond the possibility of falling from grace.[25]

The Calvinists retaliated by proclaiming five articles which re-affirmed the orthodox Calvinist position:

1. Fallen humanity is depraved;
2. Election is unconditional.
3. Christ's atonement is only for the salvation of the elect.
4. God's grace is irresistible.
5. Those who are born again persist in the faith and cannot fall.[26]

The Arminian position on the relative importance of faith and works is a subtle one. Man must be born again to do good works; therefore "good" works alone cannot suffice. Being born again depends only on God's grace, but His grace can be resisted. Being born again is not a permanent guarantee of salvation; falling from grace is possible (by behaving badly? losing faith?). God in His omniscience has foreknowledge of what man's actions will be, putting a "condition" on predestination. Jesus died for all mankind, not only for the elect.

Arminius argued that "He [God] cannot will to do . . . that which He cannot do of right. For His will is restricted by justice." Because God is omniscient, He knows in advance that people will sin. He does not, however, *will* them to do so. Arminius emphasized humanity's freedom of choice: those who are "ready for the conflict, and desire His (Christ's) help, and are not inactive" are kept from falling.[27] Although this does not mean that salvation is attained by human merit alone, it did lead to a practical emphasis on works on the part of later Arminians who were tolerant and humane in spirit. Indeed, critics of Arminianism accuse it of encouraging man's faith in himself and his works rather than in God's grace. Arminius provided a crack in the door of orthodox Calvinism, which ultimately resulted in the emergence of humanism.

The issues argued at Dort crossed to England, where the dispute continued. At stake were the doctrines of predestination and election, essential, in the view of the orthodox, to the sovereignty of God. The Arminian argument was confused and inconsistent from a purely logical point of view, but those who held it were convinced that the passages in Scripture on which predestination is based were subject to more than one interpretation; and that the deity is basically benevolent. During the late seventeenth century, Arminianism gave rise to Latitudinarian tendencies among those Anglicans who were influenced by the liberal teachings of

Daniel Whitby and Jeremy Taylor. Educated colonials of the upper classes read their writings, and those of other Arminians and Latitudinarians, and many were persuaded. Although there does not appear to have been outright public espousal of Arminianism prior to the Great Awakening, the viewpoint was widely held and discussed.[28]

Perry Miller asserts that the Puritans who migrated to the Massachusetts Bay Colony during the early seventeenth century subscribed to the Federal Theology rather than to pure Calvinism as set forth in *The Institutes of the Christian Religion.* Miller contends that this doctrine softened Calvinistic predestination and election by emphasizing "preparation," the doctrine that every person is capable of predisposition for grace.[29] Miller argues that while the Puritans retained Calvinist rhetoric, they actually professed a form of Arminianism, albeit unofficially and perhaps unconsciously, with full awareness that Arminianism was a heresy to be condemned. However, since they held that the human will cooperates with the divine in the work of salvation, their position was close to Arminianism despite their avowed opposition to it.[30]

Samuel Eliot Morison disagrees with Miller, and argues that the Puritan founders of New England professed Calvinist orthodoxy in its strict predestinarian form.[31] However, he concedes that Puritan Calvinism in New England developed into a quasi-Arminian doctrine in which there was emphasis on the human capacity to predispose oneself for divine grace.

Both Miller and Morison have been challenged by Gerald J. Goodwin, who argues that they created an academic myth which Goodwin calls *Arminian-Calvinism.* (This term appears to be Goodwin's invention.[32]) He argues that not only were the original Puritan founders of New England pure Calvinists, but their descendants were as well until the mid-eighteenth century. Miller, according to Goodwin, ignores the development of Calvin's doctrines after his time, and asserts that at the time of the Synod of Dort (1618–19), the strict Calvinists stated their position very clearly in five principles: (1) unconditional election, (2) limited atonement, (3) total human depravity, (4) irresistible grace, (5) perseverance of the saints. Expanding upon these points, Goodwin holds that the Calvinists at Dort averred that the Fall left humanity in a state of such corruption and helplessness that Adam and Eve and their descendants could do nothing of worth in aid of their own salvation. Christ only atoned for the elect by his sacrifice on the cross. Those few from each generation who were of the elect were predestined to be so from before the creation of the world. Grace is in no way dependent on humanity. What is more, those who have undergone conversion and become members of the elect could not lose the benefits of grace despite sins subsequent to conversion. These, according to Goodwin, are what New England Puritans referred to as "Our Doctrines of Grace." Goodwin contends that the Puritans who founded New England subscribed to these doctrines, as did their descendants, until the appearance of Arminianism during the mid-eighteenth century.[33]

Goodwin disputes Miller's chapter on Arminianism in *Jonathan Edwards*,[34] asserting that Miller failed to prove that there were Arminians in New England prior to this time, and that he based his case on the alleged influence of two Anglican Latitudinarian theologians, Daniel Whitby and Jeremy Taylor. Goodwin correctly maintains that the two leading Arminians, Charles Chauncy and Jonathan Mayhew, did not become so until after the Great Awakening.[35] Even so, this did not mean that they repudiated predestination and election, or preached salvation either by works or by the combination of faith and works. This position, the early form of American Unitarianism, was not taken until the early years of the nineteenth century, and, even then, very tentatively and cautiously.

Goodwin emphasizes the sharp distinctions made between Calvinists and Arminians in New England, and states that this division was perpetuated by the growth of Anglicanism. The latter subscribed to and published Arminian principles to the great distress of the Calvinists. For instance, an Anglican layman, John Checkley, made the first open attack on Calvinism in his *Choice Dialogues* in 1720. Checkley attacked the theory of divine decrees, predestination, and limited atonement.[36] Thomas Walter, who had connections with the Mathers, retorted that Calvin's doctrine was the "true ancient and primitive Doctrine of the Church of England."[37] In 1722, there was a second attack, this time by Joseph Morgan, which was answered by Cotton Mather. Goodwin finds that between 1722 and the beginning of the Great Awakening (1739), Anglicans were the only exponents of Arminianism in New England. In his interpretation the religious controversy between Puritans and Anglicans proves that the former retained their Calvinism. This is further indicated, according to Goodwin, by Cotton Mather's *Ratio Disciplinae* (1726), in which the author asserted that "there is no need of Reporting what is the Faith professed by the Churches in New England; For every one knows, That they perfectly adhere to the CONFESSION OF FAITH, published by the Assembly of Divines at Westminster." More explicitly, Mather stated: "I cannot learn that among all the Pastors of the Two Hundred Churches, there is one Arminian: much less an Arian, or a Gentilist."[38] Goodwin also cites the Westminster Assembly's Catechism which contained the official doctrine of New England, and the *Assembly's Shorter Catechism,* used for religious education of children, both explicitly Calvinist. Both catechisms reiterate that after the Fall, humanity "wholly lost all Ability of Will to any spiritual Good accompanying Salvation, so as a natural Man, being altogether averse from that Good, and dead in Sin, is not able by his own Strength to convert himself, or to prepare himself thereunto."[39] Augustine, let alone Calvin, could not have said it more definitively.

Goodwin accedes that Jonathan Edwards, Thomas Prince, William Cooper, and other godly divines constantly complained about the state of religion in New England. Their dismay, however, was not because of heterodoxy, but lack of religious intensity. He cites numerous other examples to prove his point. The Congregational ministers of Boston, for instance, endorsed William Cooper's *Doctrine of Predestination* when the Great Awakening was in full flood in 1740.[40] This doctrinal principle was explicitly upheld by the tutors of Harvard College and by the New England clergy generally. The latter frequently described themselves as "Predestinarians and Calvinists." Repeatedly, as Goodwin avers, there were Puritan expressions of alarm concerning the Latitudinarian Anglicans such as Daniel Whitby of Cambridge, England, and warnings about their errors.[41] Goodwin's argument is convincing. If there were Arminian New England divines during the first half of the eighteenth century, they must have been exceedingly discreet, as much or more so than Charles Chauncy prior to 1784, when the latter published his first open avowal of Arminianism.

Was there *unconscious* Arminianism among New England clergy during the second half of the seventeenth century and the first half of the eighteenth? Goodwin argues that there was not. He disagrees with the interpretation that the Great Awakening was an attempt to suppress "unwitting" Arminianism.[42] He asserts that the New and Old Lights during the Awakening did not divide over doctrine even though the Friends of Revival often accused their opponents of being "Arminians." The context, he argues, clearly indicates that this was simply name-calling, as today when people of the radical right accuse liberals of being "communists."

Goodwin emphasizes explicitly asserted doctrinal public statements in making his case. This, however, does not rule out the private entertainment of Arminian opinions on the part of some New England ministers prior to Mayhew's explicit advocacy of them from the pulpit. The chief authorities concerning New England Puritanism, Miller, Morison, Wright, Heimert, and Gaustad, all agree that there was no *formal* abandonment of the Augustinian/Calvinist doctrines of predestination and election prior to the Great Awakening.[43] They also agree that Mayhew was the first to openly profess Arminianism, and that few ministers openly preached Arminian doctrines until after the Revolution. Conrad Wright identifies these ministers as Proto-Unitarians, and argues that New England Unitarianism evolved from Arminianism during the post-Revolutionary era.

As we have seen, Goodwin maintains that the Federal Theology of the early eighteenth century was strictly predestinarian. This theology supposedly precluded the Arminian assertion that the achievement of salvation is a cooperative process between God and humanity. Once again, however, it must be stressed that Arminianism is not based on "convincing oneself" or "preparing oneself for salvation," but acceptance of divine grace. There was no formal denial in Federal Theology of election limited to a chosen few, of the irresistible nature of divine grace, and of the belief that conversion is wholly the work of the Holy Spirit. However, predestinarianism tended to be marginalized and emphasis was placed instead on the "means": church attendance, prayer, Bible study, moral uprightness, and other pious practices. While they were not formally deemed to be guarantees of salvation, people tended to behave as though they were.

In my view, however, Goodwin does not sufficiently acknowledge the subtle reinterpretations of Calvinism in both Old and New England during the late seventeenth and early eighteenth centuries. I suggest that the term "Arminian-Calvinism" aptly identifies a *de facto* emphasis on "preparation for salvation" even though virtually all Puritan divines officially continued to profess predestination and election. The problem lies in the logical contradiction inherent in the Augustinian/Calvinist assertion that human effort is of no avail in the attainment of salvation. If so, there is no reason to do anything but to await divine grace, preparations of any kind being futile. Without openly challenging orthodox doctrine, virtually all ministers of the time treated what they called "the means" as ways to make oneself a fit candidate for conversion.

With the passing of the original generation of Puritan settlers, many of whom were saints, clerical emphasis shifted from exhortations for renewal and enhancement of the spiritual life of the already sanctified to persuasion addressed to the unregenerate. Without maintaining that *anything* done by a human being could merit conversion and sanctification, all Protestants, including Calvin, placed great store by baptism, strict moral behavior, prayer, Scripture reading, and regular church attendance. They were what a person must do to be predisposed for grace. But those who were saved had not earned it by their spiritual and moral merit: salvation was entirely in God's hands, and "the means" in no way diminished God's sovereignty or guaranteed conversion. It was rather that divine grace often manifested itself through such channels. God foreknows all that is to happen, being above time/space. However, since human beings do not know God's will, they must act within the limits of their humanity.

Since what is known best is not God's will in this or that situation, but what can be done by human beings, the stress is naturally on the latter. This was the narrow crack in the Calvinist door which was widened by the Arminians and then thrown open by the Unitarians. Calvinist adherents of the Federal Theology were careful to keep this door shut, but not tightly so. If they had locked the door, there would have been no point whatsoever in doing anything. It was not necessary even to question predestination and election in order to open the door just wide enough to allow for preparations for salvation.

PIETISM

The origins of Evangelicalism lie in Reformation doctrine, Anglo-American Puritanism, and German Pietism. (For more detail on the antecedents of Puritanism in the writings of Paul, the church fathers, and Augustine, see Appendix I.) Pietism was a religious movement founded by Jacob Spener of Frankfort in 1670, when he established devotional societies called *collegia pietatis* within Lutheran and German Reformed churches. These groups engaged in intense Bible study and spiritual exercises. Spener's approach attracted many who were dissatisfied with the perfunctory religious observances of the day. In large measure, Pietism was a reaction against the strident sectarianism that had caused the Thirty Years' War which so devastated Germany that the much divided country did not recover for a century. Germany suffered further devastation because of the Wars of Louis XIV during the second half of the century.

German Lutherans were acrimoniously divided among themselves during the late seventeenth century, and the Duke of Brandenberg (which later became Prussia) invited Spener to Berlin as a peacemaker. He was successful in this, and thanks to his influence in court, he then founded the University of Halle with a Pietist faculty.[44]

After Spener's death in 1707, leadership of the Pietists passed to August Hermann Francke who, among other achievements, founded an orphanage at Halle which provided a model for like institutions in Britain and the colonies. Pietist writings had much impact on John Wesley and George Whitefield.[45] The Halle model was adopted by George Whitefield for his Bethesda orphanage in Georgia. Francke continued to work for the revitalization and reform of Lutheranism, opposed dogmatism and formalism, and insisted on the necessity of the sudden conversion experience for redemption.

There were many Pietists in the Rhineland principality known as the Palatinate, an area fought over during the Wars of Louis XIV, and consequently devastated. Here a number of small Pietist sects became important to the Awakening, including the Mennonites, founded by Menno Simons in Holland; the Schwenkfelders; and the "Dunkers," or German Baptist Brethren. All were originally Anabaptists during the Reformation, but were moribund until revitalized by Pietism. Another seminal sect was the Unitas Fratrum, or Moravians, which originated in Moravia prior to the Reformation. Its founder was burned at the stake for heresy by the Council of Constance in 1415. Uprooted from Moravia, the survivors of the Unitas Fratrum were reorganized by Count Nicholas Zinzendorf and settled on his estate in Herrnhut, Saxony. The Moravians were a highly organized, disciplined people, with cooperative business enterprises, and were active in social reform, founding orphanages and schools for the disadvantaged. They were famous for their religious emotionalism, their devotional music which had much impact on the emergence of hymnology during the Great Awakening, and as pioneers in overseas missions.[46]

In 1683, two years after Penn founded his colony, a group of Mennonites came to Philadelphia and later founded Germantown. In 1694 they were followed by a very interesting band of around forty German mystics. These were Lutherans who formed a society called the Order of the Woman of the Wilderness, so called because they believed that they had been carried overseas by the "wings of a great eagle" to settle in the wilderness. They were apocalyptic in belief, on the basis of astrological calculations. They used divining rods to locate underground springs of water, practiced folk medicine, and manufactured amulets.[47]

A large company of destitute Pietists from the Palatinate arrived in the colonies in 1709. Most were brought to New York by the British government. However, soon after their arrival, some of them made their way down the Susquehanna River to Pennsylvania, the most liberal of the American provinces. They were followed in 1717 by six or seven thousand Lutherans, German Reformed, and Pietists, driven from Germany by persecution, who migrated directly to Philadelphia. In 1719 twenty families of Dunkers joined the foregoing. In 1729 Alexander Mack, their founder, brought another company to Germantown. They were followed by Schwenkfelders in 1734. In that same year, a few Moravian evangelists arrived.[48] Therefore, from around 1700 to 1755, thousands of Germans migrated to Pennsylvania. By 1740 they constituted about half of the population.[49] Most lived in self-contained communities in southeastern Pennsylvania, preserving their language, religion, and customs. They supported the Quaker ruling elite and thus dominated the Pennsylvania assembly. Known as the *Pennsylvanische Dütsch,* the Germans of Pennsylvania became the Pennsylvania Dutch of today, not Holland Dutch, but Germans.[50]

Life on the frontier was difficult for the pioneer Germans, and most were wholly preoccupied with the struggle to survive in the wilderness. Pietism, however, though threatened by this, prevailed. Evangelical Pietists arrived from Europe, where Pietism was on the ascendance, to strengthen the faith. Revivals were led by mystics such as Conrad Beissel of the Dunkers. Beissel founded a commune at Ephrata, which served as a center for evangelical activity.[51]

There was little contact between the Germans and the Scotch-Irish Presbyterians. Indeed, the latter were constantly enraged by Quaker and Pietist pacifism, and the failure of Pennsylvania to defend its frontier Scotch-Irish settlements from French and Indian attack.

The religious movements among the German Pietists were

quite separate from that which should be identified as the Great Awakening. The Pietists chiefly affected this movement through the influence of Peter Böhler on John Wesley, and Count Nicholas Zinzendorf and other Moravians on George Whitefield.

Whitefield, the major evangelist of the Great Awakening, was an English Anglican priest who made a trip to Georgia in 1738 to found an orphanage, modeled after the Pietist orphanage at Halle. He deeply admired the Moravian settlers in Georgia, and was keenly sympathetic to their plight when the War of Jenkins' Ear, mentioned earlier, broke out in 1739. Moravian pacifism did not endear them to their English neighbors, and they found themselves caught between the belligerents.

Whitefield also acquired a tract in Pennsylvania which he named "Nazareth." Here he intended to build a school for the education of blacks. He encouraged the Moravians in Georgia to come to Nazareth and build his school, which they did. However, Whitefield and the Moravians had a falling out over doctrine, and the latter acquired a nearby tract of their own which they called "Bethlehem" because they founded their settlement on Christmas day.[52] Because of persecution in Saxony, Count Zinzendorf brought hundreds of Moravians to Bethlehem, and it soon became a flourishing community. Both Nazareth and Bethlehem continue to exist today. The schoolhouse built for Whitefield also remains, as a museum called Whitefield House.

The German sects, though as stated above not a part of the Great Awakening, did have in common with it an evangelical religious orientation which will now be discussed.

EVANGELICALISM

In his article "Evangelical and Fundamental Christianity" in Volume 5 of *The Encyclopedia of Religion,* George M. Marsden defines *Evangelicalism* as "a largely Protestant movement that emphasizes (1) the Bible as authoritative and reliable; (2) eternal salvation as possible only by regeneration (being "born again"), involving personal trust in Christ and in his atoning work; and (3) a spiritually transformed life marked by moral conduct, personal devotion such as Bible reading and prayer, and zeal for evangelism and missions."[53] According to Marsden, while the origins of evangelicalism are in the Reformation and seventeenth-century Puritanism, Evangelicalism is "largely an Anglo-American phenomenon" which began during the eighteenth century with the Holy Club founded by John and Charles Wesley in England, of which George Whitefield (1714–70) became a fervent adherent. Called "Methodists" by their detractors, the members of the Holy Club were distinguished by their emphasis on the conversion experience and their strict adherence to biblical teachings. Because John Wesley was influenced by Count Zinzendorf and the Moravians (Unitas Fratrum) at Herrnhut, Saxony, there was a strong German Pietist component in Methodism from the outset. Whitefield and the Wesleys parted company later over theological differences: while the Wesleys and their followers were Arminian in that they emphasized that Christ's atoning death could save all of mankind, Whitefield became a Calvinist and emphasized predestination and election.

According to Marsden, "The character of American evangelicalism began to take shape during the Great Awakening of the eighteenth century. This movement, really a series of revivals throughout the middle decades of the century, brought together several movements." The Great Awakening specifically refers to the intercolonial hallelujah of revivals between 1739 and 1745, in which Whitefield, Jonathan Edwards, Gilbert Tennent, and James Davenport played leading roles.[54]

The central feature of Evangelicalism is the sudden conversion experience, whereby the natural man or woman becomes born again as a spiritual person. According to William James in *The Varieties of Religious Experience* (1902), the word "conversion" suggests the act of "turning around," in this case a spiritual about-face.[55] The word seldom appears in the Bible, but has the same meaning as scriptural terms such as "repentance," "regeneration," and "being born again." In modern parlance, "to be converted is like making a 'U-turn.' It is 'starting at square one again' or 'back to the drawing board.'"[56]

> To be converted, to be regenerated, to receive grace, to experience religion, to gain an assurance, are so many phrases which denote the process, gradual or sudden, by which a self hitherto divided, and consciously wrong inferior and unhappy, becomes unified and consciously right superior and happy, in consequence of its firmer hold upon religious realities.[57]

For Evangelicals, the classic case of conversion is that of Paul on the Damascus Highway.[58]

The Great Awakening, whether interpreted as an intercolonial revival or as the name erroneously given a series of eighteenth-century revivals, was about sudden conversion, the most distinctive feature of the Evangelical message. "Conversionist evangelicalism," as Lambert terms it, is distinguished by belief in "periodic extraordinary outpourings of God's grace."[59] According to Lambert, while Calvin regarded salvation as preordained, English Puritans were divided into two soteriological schools, one of which flourished in the southeastern counties from the Wash to Bristol and the other in the north and in Scotland. According to many of the northern school, regeneration occurs at a precise moment which the person can recall, giving specific time and date. If not, he or she has not experienced the New Birth and is not a New Creature in Pauline terms. By emphasizing religious crises, divines such as Perkins and Sibbes developed a form of Calvinism that the founder of that movement would have repudiated. According to them, conversion is an "experience of the heart" rather than an intellectual awareness. Perkins maintains "fiery sermons" are the channels of redemptive grace and are absolutely necessary for the work of salvation and a necessary preparation for the "inner witness of the Spirit."[60]

Lambert shows that during the early eighteenth century, British Evangelicals emphasized the supreme authority of the Bible and the individual or personal nature of the New Birth, and focused on the redemptive work in the heart by Christ. By so doing, Lambert identifies the specific theological strand within Calvinism from which revivalist theology and soteriology emerged. The "conversionist evangelists," according to Lambert and his sources, predominated among the Puritans who settled in the Massachusetts Bay Colony during the Great Migration of 1630–40. Therefore, there was considerable fervor among the first generation of Puritan colonists. Quakers, too, belonged to this northern school of English Puritanism, as did, during the Commonwealth era, Ranters, Muggletonians, Fifth Monarchy Men, and other sectarians. Their spiritual descendants became the New Lights.[61]

Conversion is the work of the Holy Spirit, who appeared for the first time to the disciples at Pentecost, the Jewish harvest festival held on the fiftieth day of the second day of Passover in the cycle of the Jewish year. According to Acts 2:1–3:

> And when the day of Pentecost was fully come, they were all with one accord in one place. And suddenly there came a sound from heaven

as of a rushing mighty wind, and it filled all the house where they were sitting. And there appeared unto them cloven tongues like as of fire and it sat upon each of them. And they were all filled with the Holy Ghost, and began to speak with other tongues, as the Spirit gave them utterance.

The Holy Spirit or Holy Ghost, the mysterious third member of the triune Christian deity, was promised by Jesus at the time of the Last Supper. In Evangelical theology, the Holy Spirit both guides the ministry and mission of the Church and manifests himself in extraordinary outpourings of grace, such as prophecy and speaking in tongues. Evangelicals of the eighteenth century held that the second "extraordinary outpouring of the Holy Spirit" had been during the Protestant Reformation, especially among the more radical of the reformers such as the Anabaptists. The third manifestation of the Holy Spirit, they claimed, was the Evangelical Revival, or Great Awakening.

Evangelicalism is best understood by reading accounts of personal conversion experiences such as those of George Whitefield, Jonathan Edwards, and David Brainerd, all of them important revivalist figures during the Great Awakening. They are also discussed in considerable detail in Edwards' *A Treatise Concerning Religious Affections* (1746).[62] This important pioneer study in the psychology of religious experience was not superseded until William James' *The Varieties of Religous Experience* (1902) appeared. Between the publication of these two important works, Evangelicalism became recognized as a distinct form of mystical experience which, though related to Paul's vision of Christ on the Damascus Highway as well as to the experience described by Augustine in his *Confessions,* nonetheless assumed a peculiar character which particularly appealed to Americans.

Evangelicalism did not originate during the Great Awakening, yet it acquired certain characteristics at that time which have distinguished it ever since. There are three distinct stages in Evangelical religious experience: *conviction, conversion,* and *sanctification.* The first refers to a sudden inner awareness of sin, an awakening, according to evangelical doctrine, by the Holy Spirit. This characteristically causes anguish of spirit, deep emotional distress, terror at the prospects of damnation, and horror, as well, over one's own tendencies to lust, greed, envy, and other such personal shortcomings. This does not take the form of self-reproach alone. Instead, these guilt feelings are contrasted with the perfection of the divine, resulting in a sense of deep unworthiness. Edwards, who was fascinated with spiders and insects when young, later compared sinners to both of these low forms of life. He emphasized self-loathing in the context of God's revulsion, an extreme form of disgust convincing the person that he or she is so depraved as to be deserving of eternal hellfire. Therefore, conviction, which is the work of the Holy Spirit, is not a natural emotional experience, to be explained in psychological terms, but the dark night of the soul. In some instances, the terrors may excite the person to writhe in agony; to shout, cry out, weep, or even to faint. In other cases they may result in withdrawal, brooding, deep melancholy, and dread.

There is no guarantee that the person will experience the second stage, redemption. However, if the person completely surrenders to the divine, abandons all worldliness, all hope that anything whatsoever can be done to merit salvation, and affirms that salvation comes from God and God alone, those whom God elects then experience inner joy, also usually a sudden experience. This is accompanied by deep love of God, gratitude for the redemptive sacrifice of Christ on the cross, and the inner realization that one is among those whom the Savior has not passed by but chosen to be one of his own. This joy may be expressed in exultant hymn-singing, praise, and/or shouts of ecstasy. The person feels deep love for everyone and concern for the souls of those who have not been saved, and can forgive his or her worst enemies. S/he becomes a man or woman in Christ, united with him in the kingdom, and assured of everlasting bliss in the life to come.

The person who has been saved is a saint in the third, or sanctification stage. However, the effects of conversion may not last. Although the saint is still among the redeemed, he or she may not continue to experience the ecstasy of deliverance from the bondage of sin. The person who has been redeemed may well slip back into old ways of thought, feeling, and behavior, and will not always continue to live on the high plane of ecstasy experienced during conversion. For that reason, the saint must continue to struggle, and having been redeemed by God in Christ, there are now behaviors he or she must follow in order to grow in the Spirit. These include what New Englanders called "means": regular church attendance, family devotions, intense Scripture study, reflection, and efforts to live the morally upright life. Unlike unregenerates, however, the twice-born is enabled to continue to live the good life because of the constant infusion of divine love, a wholly undeserved spiritual energy. This persists, despite backsliding, throughout life; and at death, the saint passes serenely into the life of the spirit, and enters heaven, which is not a place but a state of the soul.

The Great Awakening introduced a strong emphasis on the power of inspired preaching. Therefore, when the fervent Gilbert Tennent or the quiet Jonathan Edwards terrified their audiences with vivid, highly imaginative descriptions of the lake of fire, the agony of the damned, and the meaning of eternity, it was because the Holy Spirit flowed through their hearts and minds to be expressed in the rhetoric of the sermon. Charismatic preaching, therefore, was a major means of securing conviction and conversion. Some, however, like George Whitefield, experienced conversion by reading devotional books; others, like John Wesley, while listening to a lecture on a passage by Luther. Conviction can occur with or without the medium of the preacher. However, it was the view of Evangelical ministers that it was most frequently effected through preaching.

Thus, in the colonies during the 1730s and 1740s, conversion was experiential, that is to say, inwardly felt, like *satori* in Zen. It became the Evangelical way, moreover, for it to be effected most frequently in group experiences rather than in solitude. Therefore, the preacher tried to reach as many people as possible with the sound of his voice, and in any location whatsoever: the meetinghouse, preferably, but if that was not possible, the streets of the town, the fields in the countryside, or wherever people gathered. Those who underwent conversion in this way became in their own eyes changed persons even though it might not always be apparent to others.

People of the early eighteenth century believed in Satan, and were constantly warned of his wiles, deceptions, and false promises. Just as Satan could quote Scripture, so he could counterfeit the conversion experience. Therefore, Edwards, Chauncy, Whitefield, and other divines of the early eighteenth century were very preoccupied with the problem of identifying the "distinguishing marks of a Work of God," frequently a sermon topic in those very words. These "marks" referred to the "fruits of the Spirit" which included the capacity to forgive one's enemies, a major test. True saints were known by their "distinguishing marks," none of which were achieved by anything for which they could take personal credit, but which were outpourings of divine grace. The saints were also given the power to "know one another."

Since conversion gave the twice-born strength to meet and overcome Satan, they claimed to be able instantly and confidently to recognize the differences between true and false religion as well as to detect the sly, subtle works of the devil. Others who had not been twice born might not recognize these distinguishing marks, but the redeemed could.

LOCAL REVIVALS IN AMERICA

A network of correspondence linked the British and American Evangelists, and the Anglican Evangelical George Whitefield was at the center. During the years between 1739 and his death in Philadelphia in 1770, Whitefield wrote no fewer than fifteen hundred letters which were published during the early 1770s, made seven journeys to America, and fourteen to Scotland. He sent huge quantities of letters from the colonies to England. Whitefield's journals were also published. A new religious community based on Calvinist Evangelicalism appeared. Ministers on both sides of the Atlantic regarded themselves as co-workers, "friends in God." They located each other through revival publications. In this way, a correspondence network was created, the core of which included three leading New England ministers: Benjamin Colman, Jonathan Edwards, and Thomas Prince; and in England, Whitefield, John Guyse, and Isaac Watts. The principal Scottish correspondents were James Robe, William McCulloch, John McLaurin, and John Erskine. "Their interlocking and overlapping connections made them a close-knit group."[63]

Just beyond the inner circle was another large company of ministers, lay Evangelists, financial backers, and printers, all of whom were in touch with Whitefield and other leading lights. This new community of transatlantic correspondents was part of the seventeenth-century Puritan letter-writing network. However, "its spirit of evangelism marked a point of departure."[64] Many of the letters dealt with practical matters, such as arrangements for meetings, but most were concerned with ways of converting the unsaved. The correspondence in general during the two years between 1740 and 1742 tended to be narrative and descriptive. Many of the letters express the excitement of the revival preachers with the many conversions made.

Those of Edwards, especially, chiefly dealt with religious experience. Some of these letters were five thousand words long. Correspondence was a principal means by which the Friends of Revival promoted their Evangelical cause, and the circulation of letters was thus an important means of disseminating religious ideas.[65]

George Whitfield (1714–1770). Courtesy of the Harvard University Portrait Collection, Gift of Mrs. H. P. (Sarah H.) Oliver to Harvard College, 1852.

3

Transatlantic Revivals

THE ENGLISH EVANGELICAL REVIVAL

As MENTIONED PREVIOUSLY, THE ENGLISH EVANGELICAL REVIVAL began with the "Holy Club" founded in 1729 by Charles Wesley at Oxford and presided over by his brother, John. Both were High Church Anglicans, called "Methodists" by their enemies because of the systematic nature of their intense religious devotions. They were joined by George Whitefield, who became known as the *Grand Itinerant* or wandering evangelist *par excellence.* Indeed, it was because of Whitefield's ministry in America that the Great Awakening occurred at all. Without him there would have been local revivals in New England and the Middle Colonies, but not a mass movement.

Whitefield was born in the Bell Inn in Gloucester, England, on 16 December 1714. He said: "This, with the Circumstance of my being born in an Inn, has often been of Service to me in exciting my Endeavours to make good my Mother's Expectations, and so follow the Example of my dear Saviour who was born in a Manger belonging to an Inn" (*GW*, 37).[1]

As a boy he loved to read plays, and in retrospect he recalled exclaiming to his sister "God intends something for me which we know not of" while he was reading a play aloud to her (*GW*, 42). When he was ten his mother entered what was to be an unhappy marriage. When he was twelve, his mother sent him to a grammar school, St. Mary de Crypt. In his spare time the boy continued to read plays and also to secretly indulge in "abominable secret Sin," probably masturbation (*GW*, 37). Since his mother could not afford to give him a university education, George left school, initially against her will, and became a tapster. After many vicissitudes, alternating between religious impulses and worldly occupations, he went to Oxford University, where he met John and Charles Wesley and became a member of the Holy Club.

Whitefield threw himself into the ascetic ways of the Holy Club. Although he had been exceptionally fastidious, and once remarked that "he did not think he should die easy, if he thought his gloves were out of place," he renounced pride in his appearance.[2] He stopped powdering his hair, dressed in rough woolen clothes, and wore a patched gown. He also gave up eating the fruit he enjoyed, and donated the money he would have spent on it to the poor. Indeed, he lived a rigorous life and ate little of only the poorest sort of food. Recalling those lean times, he wrote in his journal that "though I was then convinced that the Kingdom of God did not consist in Meats and Drinks, yet I resolutely persisted in these voluntary Acts of self-denial, because I found them great Promoters of the Spiritual Life" (GW, 52).

The rigorous disciplines did nothing for Whitefield, however, except to cause him misery. As he wrote in his journal, his "soule was barren and dry." He felt himself like a "[m]an locked up in iron armour." He suffered, as he later recalled, great distress in mind and body, spent nights groaning in his bed, and "[w]hole days and weeks lying prostrate on the ground, and begging for freedom from . . . proud hellish thoughts" (GW, 52). Nothing he tried to do helped. He could not "take Heaven by storm." It was then that he learned that "a man may go to church, say his prayers, receive the sacrament, and yet . . . not be a christian."[3]

During the spring of 1735, after seven weeks of anguish in which he suffered feelings of "unspeakable pressure both of body and mind," a passage from the gospels occurred to him: Jesus on the cross crying out, "I thirst" just before he died. Whitefield threw himself on his bed crying out, "I thirst!" and soon after he felt that he "was delivered from the burden that had so heavily oppressed [him]. The spirit of mourning was taken from [him], and [he] knew what it was truly to rejoice in God [his] Saviour, and, for some time, could not avoid singing psalms wherever [he] was." He adds, "Thus were the days of my mourning ended. . . . Now did the Spirit of God take possession of my soul" (GW, 58). What was most important to Whitefield about his conversion experience was that he seemed to have so little to do with it himself. To him it was a wonderful work of God, and all the glory belonged to him. During June he wrote enthusiastically about his conversion. Thereafter, full of joy, he talked about his experience to anyone who would listen.

During the spring of 1735, on his physician's advice, he returned to Gloucester. There he formed a small society of worshipers, and stayed until March 1736. He spent many of his days

praying, studied the Bible and other sacred texts, visited prisoners in the jails and preached to them, and called on the sick. From
the time of his conversion on, nothing was as important to him as
the experience of being twice born. It finally gave meaning to his
existence (*GW*, 61).

His piety impressed his friends, who urged him to take holy orders. The Right Reverend Martin Benson, the Bishop of Gloucester, was so impressed with him that he ordained him a deacon in
the Church of England on 20 June 1736 in the Gloucester Cathe-
dral despite his youth.[4] Shortly afterward, Whitefield completed
his studies at Oxford, earning the Bachelor of Arts degree.

Whitefield remained in London until mid-November, preaching
in prisons as well as in churches. He was then appointed supply
pastor to the parish of Dummer, and it was while he was there
that he received letters from John Wesley inviting him to go to
the new colony of Georgia in America, where Wesley was evangelizing (*GW*, 35–36).

Whitefield became a very popular itinerant preacher in London
and the counties. He preached to large congregations in the
Tower, and while returning to Gloucester from which he was to
sail for Georgia, he preached at Bath and in Bristol. People of all
classes were entranced by him, from aristocratic fops to grimy
colliers, and he raised a great deal of money for his missionary
work. A great crowd came to hear his last sermon before his departure to America on 28 December 1737. "I took my last fare-
well at Bristol," he confided to the world in his journal (which
was published later). "But when I came to tell them, it might be,
that they would 'see my face no more,' high and low, young and
old burst into such a flood of tears, as I had never seen before"
(*GW*, 85).

John Wesley had gone to the new colony of Georgia to evangelize and had failed. Deciding to emulate the Pietist Francke at
Halle, Whitefield decided to go there himself to found an orphanage. He sailed to Georgia by way of Gibraltar, arriving in the raw
port of Savannah on an evening in May 1737. His reputation as a
preacher had preceded him. Readers of the *Virginia Gazette* in
the southern colonies knew that Whitefield was very popular in
England, and that he packed churches in London with overflow
crowds. The rude colonists of Georgia were very responsive to his
preaching, and unlike Wesley, he soon became very popular in the
young colony.[5]

He stayed in America until August 1737, then returned to England, arriving in London on 9 September 1737. During his ab-

sence, the first of his seven *Journals* was published in which he was, in part, highly critical of Latitudinarian Anglican priests and bishops. The latter were enraged, and from then on, Whitefield was persona non grata among most clergy and laity of the Church of England. Unperturbed, he became a celebrity by preaching out-of-doors to large crowds throughout England and Wales. During these occasions he collected funds for the proposed orphanage in Georgia. According to almost certainly exaggerated newspaper reports, he sometimes preached to crowds estimated at from twenty to as high as fifty thousand people in such places as Kennington Common and Moorfields.[6] Kennington, with its elm-lined walks, taverns, and gardens, had become a favorite recreation ground. Vast numbers of people of all classes flocked to hear Whitefield over and over again.[7] In time they built him a tabernacle, a temporary shelter, there.[8]

Because of his continuing interest in founding the orphanage in Georgia, however, he decided to return to America. He sailed on 14 August 1739, arriving in Savannah, where Mr. Habersham "whom I left schoolmaster of Savannah, was directed, I hope by Providence, to make choice" of five hundred acres on which to establish Whitefield's orphanage (*GW*, 395). This time he stayed in America for two years and began the itinerant preaching that was to knit purely local revivals into the Great Awakening.

As we have seen, John Butler, in his 1982 article "Enthusiasm Described and Decried: The Great Awakening as Interpretative Fiction," denies that there was any meaningful connection between the local revivals of this time.[9] He holds that these were all separate phenomena, only occasionally intersecting because of contacts among revival preachers, but otherwise having little more in common than coincidence in time. Even at that, the time frames overlap. Therefore, even if we restrict our temporal references to 1739–45, we have to separate out the evangelical phenomena among the German Pietists from that which may or may not have occurred among the Dutch of the Raritan River valley, and both of these from what I identify as the essential "Great Awakening," namely, the revival among the transplanted New England and Scotch-Irish Presbyterians of New Jersey and Pennsylvania and the Congregationalists of Massachusetts and Connecticut between 1739 and 1745.

The issue is further complicated because George Whitefield made evangelical tours both in Great Britain and in all thirteen of the colonies. Some scholars, including Butler and Lambert, insist that there were no fewer than four revivals at about the same time, and identify that of George Whitefield as the fourth. Looked at this way, Butler's argument that the term "Great Awakening" should be dropped since it adds only confusion is well taken. Abandoning it does not, however, give full recognition to the unique character of the Middle Colony and New England revivals which were highly integrated, linked together by Whitefield and Gilbert Tennent. For that reason, I hold that the older term "Evangelical Revival" is appropriate for the religious activities of the Wesleys and Whitefield in Britain, that the Pietists should not be included in any discussion of the Great Awakening, save for their influence on Whitefield, but that Frelinghuysen's evangelicalism among the Dutch should be discussed.

THEODORUS JACOBUS FRELINGHUYSEN

Edwards spoke of Frelinghuysen with approval in *A Faithful Narrative,* and Whitefield also mentioned him in his *Journal.* Chiefly on those grounds, Maxson and Trinterud both credited him with beginning the Great Awakening. However, recent studies insist that his was a purely local revival, important to the Great Awakening chiefly because of his personal influence on Gilbert Tennent who was the newly appointed minister of the Presbyterian Church of New Brunswick. I agree with Maxson and Trinterud: though local, Frelinghuysen's revivals were clearly part of the movement as a whole.[10]

The Raritan River valley of New Jersey was an isolated area in which travel was difficult, involving the fording of streams and making one's way through wilderness areas on horseback. Here, ministers, called dominies, such as Bartholf and Freeman, gathered four Dutch Reformed congregations to serve the people of the frontier villages: rustic folk of little education, typical of Dutch *boeren,* or farmers. Most spoke only their own language and were boorish in behavior, and there were many complaints about moral delinquency. While most of the original Dutch settlers in New Netherlands had been imbued with Reformation zeal, their children and grandchildren were not. A situation prevailed very much like that in New England, in that there was a distinct decline of piety during the second half of the seventeenth century.

The Dutch Reformed Church, a Calvinist denomination, was structured much the same as the Presbyterian. The congregations elected delegates to consistories, which, in turn, elected delegates to the local *classis*, a governing body corresponding to the Presbyterian general assembly. Dominies were authorized by a body known as the *Coetus*. Because there was a shortage of dominies, many of the churches were led by elders. The Dutch Reformed churches in America were under the authority of the Classis of Amsterdam.

Reformed Church Calvinism was essentially Federal, or covenant theology as modified by the Synod of Dordrecht in 1607. Baptism, church attendance, and creedal orthodoxy were considered sufficient for salvation. Religious observances tended to be perfunctory and formal. Dominies and Elders encouraged decent moral behavior, but discouraged emotionalism because it smacked of Antinomianism.[11]

Early in the eighteenth century, Dominie Freeman of Long Island, one of the founders of the Raritan River valley Dutch Reformed churches, received a call for a pastor and delegated the task to a dominie in Holland who happened to be an Evangelical, a young divinity school graduate by the name of Theodorus Jacobus Frelinghuysen who lived in Lingen, a German border town under Dutch occupation. Though of German birth, Frelinghuysen identified with the Dutch, spoke that language, and was ordained as a minister of the Dutch Reformed Church. He called himself a Pietist but his actual orientation is controversial. What is certain is his evangelicalism.[12] Frelinghuysen readily accepted the call of Dominie Freeman and took ship for New York. He had been under considerable restraint in Holland by the conservatives of the church and welcomed the opportunity.

During the crossing from Holland to New York he told the ship captain that he intended to stir up a new reformation in America. He landed in New York in January 1720, and was immediately invited to preach. In his very first sermon he made a fervent emotional appeal which offended many of the elders and also Dominie Boel, the junior pastor of the Dutch Reformed Church in New York, who rebuked the young man. Frelinghuysen was called to New Brunswick on the Raritan River in New Jersey to serve the Dutch Reformed church there as well as three others in nearby neighborhoods.

Undeterred by the opposition he had raised in New York as soon as he was ashore, Frelinghuysen rode south to the Raritan River valley and preached to his scattered congregations. Unlike the conventional dominies, he made highly purposeful parish calls in which he inquired about the religious experiences of his parishioners. He also founded schools for the religious education of children, and, in his sermons, denounced perfunctory religious practices, asserting that God demanded spiritual regeneration of those whom he intended to save, and that true conversion had to be a dramatic episode. This message caused both doctrinal and generational schisms in his congregations, as well as class conflict. The conventionally orthodox prosperous farmers were offended by Frelinghuysen; poorer people found his sermons inspirational. Younger people were drawn to Frelinghuysen; their elders were repelled. No doubt much of his popularity among the young and poor was because he fearlessly attacked the elite, accusing them of the outward performance of religious observances devoid of inner experience. He also leveled attacks against the complacent dominies of New York, like Boel, and for the same reason. The targets of his attacks, of course, were angry and reacted accordingly.

Outraged parishioners rushed to New York to lay their complaints before Boel, who accused Frelinghuysen of heresy. Boel's brother, who was a lawyer, drew up a *Complaint* and sent it to the Classis in Holland, hoping to have Frelinghuysen recalled. When this failed, they tried, with equal lack of success, to have Frelinghuysen removed by the courts and the governor.

Dominies Freeman and Bartholf rallied to Frelinghuysen's defense, judging his sermons to be "learned, well digested, and thrilling" and also "highly sound and scriptural."[13] Dominie Boel visited the Raritan River valley, where he met with the disaffected, and organized resistance against Frelinghuysen and his admirers and defenders. The Dutch Reformed folk of New York and New Jersey became deeply divided between the conventionally orthodox and the Evangelicals.

There were also local revivals among the Presbyterians during the 1720s. One of these was because of the evangelical preaching of Jonathan Dickinson of Elizabeth Town, New Jersey. He was one of the few among the New Englanders of the Middle Colonies to be affected by revivalism.

JONATHAN DICKINSON

In 1722 Jonathan Dickinson preached a sermon to the newly founded Synod of Philadelphia in which he stated that Christ is the only lawmaker of the Church, and that the synod and presbyteries therefore have only administrative functions. Only Scripture is authoritative, and even the Westminster Confession is but a guide. He urged that wide latitude be left to the individual who may dissent from this or that article of the confession on grounds of conscience. Dickinson also urged that candidates for the ministry be strictly examined concerning not only doctrinal orthodoxy but also inner experience. The conservative Scotch-Irish argued that inquiries concerning a candidate's inner experiences were intrusive, and that it was enough that the candidate be orthodox in doctrine and have the necessary educational qualifications. Dickinson's sermon thus created a division between the more rigid Scotch-Irish and the New Englanders. However, the moderate Scotch-Irish joined the New Englanders to form a significant faction in support of Dickinson.

The conservative Scotch-Irish faction eventually became known as the "Old Sides," and became "Opposers of Revival."[14] The "New Sides," who became "Friends of Revival," included Dickinson and other New Englanders such as Aaron Burr of Newark. They were evangelical in approach, though never taking an active role in the Awakening; certainly not as itinerants. Instead, they supported the moderate faction of Scotch-Irish led by William Tennent, Sr.

THE LOG COLLEGE MEN

Little is known about William Tennent, Sr. He was, for a time, a priest of the Church of England in Ireland, but becoming dissatisfied both with prelacy and Arminianism, embraced the religion of his wife, Presbyterianism. When the Tennents came to America in 1718, as mentioned earlier, they settled first in parishes in New York and Pennsylvania before acquiring acreage in the latter colony near the village of Neshaminy. Here, in 1726, Tennent built the aforementioned "Log College" where he trained twenty-one young men for the Presbyterian ministry, including his four sons. The "Log College" became the prototype for other private academies in the New World, and was itself the beginning of Princeton University. There were many such academies started in England and Scotland after the Restoration, when Non-Conformists were banned from the universities.

Tennent was a highly competent teacher, and his students were well grounded in Latin, Greek, and some Hebrew, also in logic. There was less emphasis placed on literature and philosophy. Although Tennent's "Log College" was scorned by some of his university-educated brethren, his ministerial candidates were licensed as ministers by the Philadelphia Synod.[15]

GILBERT TENNENT

William's son, Gilbert Tennent, who was to play a major role in the Awakening, was born in 1703 in County Armagh in Ulster, Northern Ireland. During the crossing to America with his family, Gilbert had a profound religious experience. As he wrote later, "It pleased God to give me the light of the knowledge of His Glory in the face of Jesus Christ."[16] However, although he attended the "Log College" of his father in preparation for the ministry, he did not at first experience a call, and later studied medicine. He ultimately decided on a ministerial career, and studied further for this at Yale, where he earned the degree of Master of Arts in 1725. In that same year the Presbytery of Philadelphia licensed him to preach.[17]

He first served as a supply pastor to the Presbyterian Church in New Castle, Delaware. Although the congregation then called him, he declined "rather unceremoniously" and for reasons unknown, and was reprimanded by the presbytery for doing so. Subsequently, the presbytery authorized him to gather a congregation in New Brunswick, on the Raritan River. He did so, and was ordained in 1727.

He had a difficult start, partly because of feelings of inadequacy. Frelinghuysen, dominie of the local Dutch Reformed Church, was at first not pleased when Tennent recruited and organized his congregation. However, they soon became good friends, and Frelinghuysen very hospitably shared his meetinghouse with the Presbyterians. Sometimes both ministers preached at joint services of the two congregations.

Tennent soon fell ill, and, during his recovery, received an encouraging letter from Frelinghuysen with advice concerning his ministry in general and his preaching in particular. It came while Tennent was agonizing over his perceived lack of effectiveness in the pulpit, and convinced him that he should become more forceful in his preaching, and go among his people as an evangelist.

On his recovery, Tennent began an intense ministry which his parishioners found disconcerting. His first sermon, after rising from his sick bed, was "A Solemn Warning to the Secure World." In this and subsequent sermons he attacked spiritual complacency, warning that those who had not experienced conversion were in danger of damnation. He discovered that he had a gift for extemporaneous emotional preaching, which had great impact on his congregation. Older members of his congregation were disconcerted and shocked by his vivid depictions of hell and the agonies of the damned; younger people, however, were deeply affected.[18] Following the example of Frelinghuysen, Tennent also called personally on all of his parishioners and subjected them to close scrutiny concerning their religious experiences. Not surprisingly, he found that only a few could testify to having experienced conversion.

Gilbert Tennent lacked refinement. He dressed in a coarse manner, his behavior was rustic, and his preaching loud and aggressive. This suited his younger rural parishioners, and soon he was attracting large congregations. Like the Dutch Reformed, the Scotch-Irish Presbyterians were accustomed to doctrinal orthodoxy, but not to fervor. As Tennent's reputation reached elders in the presbytery, conservative members were disturbed. What was required, in their view, was strict subscription to the Westminster Confession as the standard of orthodoxy, regular church attendance, study of the Scriptures, and uprightness in moral life. They did not approve of emotional preaching.[19] Furthermore, many of the Scotch-Irish ministers had never had the conversion experience themselves and had scant regard for those who claimed they did.

Gilbert's evangelicalism was soon shared by his short-lived brother John, as well as by his elder brother William and his father, William, Sr. By 1730 the Tennents and a few other young candidates for the ministry such as Samuel Blair had become well known for the new style of preaching.

A similar move toward evangelical fervor took place in western Massachusetts in the neighborhood of Northampton on the Connecticut River because of the preaching of young Jonathan Edwards. His revival of 1734–35 was another local episode that was a harbinger of the Great Awakening.

4

Jonathan Edwards

Turning now to New England, the Great Awakening was preceded by several religious developments among the people of the Connecticut River valley during the years between 1721 and 1740. Included were scattered revivals in certain communities such as Windham, Connecticut, and above all, Northampton, Massachusetts. Jonathan Edwards, the pastor of the Northampton Church, described the revival in that congregation in detail in *A Faithful Narrative of the Surprising Work of God in the Conversion of Many Hundred Souls in Northampton and the Neighboring Towns and Villages* (1736), one of the most significant promotional tracts of the Awakening. This account, and later revisions of it, was widely read and discussed throughout the colonies and in Europe.[1]

Next to Whitefield, Edwards was the most prominent figure in the Great Awakening. However, the two Evangelical ministers differed very sharply from one another. While Whitefield was a showman and celebrity, a charismatic preacher who swayed vast throngs with his dramatic oratory, Edwards was a quiet intellectual who preached prepared sermons from closely written notes in a moderate tone of voice. Whereas Whitefield had no interest in theology, much less philosophy, Edwards was highly learned in both, as well as in science. He kept abreast of the latest developments of the Enlightenment, and was as knowledgeable as any of the *philosophes,* although he remained orthodox in religious belief and did not share their skepticism. Whereas Whitefield traveled extensively throughout the colonies to spread his message, Edwards confined his ministry mainly to the communities of the Connecticut River valley, though he influenced ministerial colleagues elsewhere through correspondence.

Edwards became aware of the evangelical work of Whitefield through newspapers and his network of correspondents. The same sources, in addition to his brief sojourn in New York in 1726 as a student, and his occasional return visits, had made him aware of the evangelical work of Frelinghuysen and the Tennents. Beginning in 1731, he was also in direct contact with sympathetic ministers in Boston, such as Benjamin Colman.

In his own Connecticut River valley, there was in 1721 "a remarkable concern . . . among the people" in Windham during which the whole town was affected by religious fervor, an outpouring of "love, joy, thanksgiving, and praise,"[2] which resulted in a sharp increase in church attendance. The religious excitement lasted for six months before abating.

On Sunday night, 29 October 1727, there was an earthquake, a rare geological phenomenon on the Eastern Seaboard of North America. Many took it as a portent of Judgment. However, the emotional effect soon faded, and with it, the religious concern it aroused. A diphtheria epidemic in some communities shortly after also triggered apocalyptic fears. However, though the effects of both of these happenings were transitory, they nevertheless made people more receptive to the revivalist message Edwards was later to deliver.

Edwards was among those ministers who stressed the significance of these events as signs of the Second Coming. He and other New England ministers also saw such portents in reports describing luxurious living and pleasure-seeking among the British aristocracy, the greed of London merchants, and the lawlessness and drunkenness of people of the lower classes there. He predicted that the new age would dawn therefore in America, and not in the decadent Old World. However, Edwards also saw signs of imminent Judgment in the moral laxity of many of the young people in and around Northampton, which, to his distress, was treated indulgently by their elders, and the greed, worldliness, and complacency of some of the local landowners and merchants.

JONATHAN EDWARDS: EARLY LIFE

Edwards was a prolific writer from boyhood on, and a few of his childhood essays have survived. These give us interesting clues concerning the development of his ideas. He was born on 5 October 1703 in a parsonage in the village of East Windsor, Connecticut, on the shore of Long Island Sound. The area, though long settled, contained abundant woodlands. Jonathan was of the fourth generation of his family in Connecticut, the only son among eleven children. His father, Timothy, was the second member of the family to become a minister. He was often away during Jonathan's boyhood, so that the prime influence on him in his early years was his mother, Esther Stoddard, daughter of Pastor Solomon Stoddard of Northampton. She was a very strong willed woman who personally attended to her son's elementary education. She taught him Latin, arithmetic, and composition. His father once wrote his mother from New Haven cautioning her not to let the boy " 'Loose W^t he hath Learned . . .' or to be too free with his time."[3] The precocious Jonathan, growing up in solitude despite his large family, spent a great deal of time wandering about the countryside, studying nature with a boyhood zeal, and writing little essays on his observations.

We have at least five of these which he wrote when he was a young schoolboy. They include one which he entitled "Of Insects," written when he was twelve. Most deal with natural philosophy; all have strong theological themes. "Of Insects" is not about insects at all but *arachnidae*—spiders. Jonathan was chiefly fascinated by how they spun their webs and how they seemed to fly. "Of all Insects," he wrote, "no one is more wonderfull than the Spider especially with Respect to their sagacity and admirable way of working" (*JE*, 3).[4] Far from being repelled by them, he found spiders very "Pretty and Pleasing." He acknowledged that other people did not agree with his opinion, and in later years frequently drew on the image of the spider in his sermons to illustrate God's revulsion against sinners.

Jonathan exhibited an understanding of the scientific method in his study of spiders, as well as other natural phenomena such as rainbows and colors. In "Of Insects," he reports:

I Repeated the triall Over and Over again till I was fully satisfied of his way of working which I Dont only Conjecture to be on this wise viz they when they would Go from tree [to tree] or would Sail in the air let themselves hang Down a little way by their webb. (*JE*, 4)

The essay is illustrated with a crude little drawing of a stick, thread, and spider, with steps one and two showing its movements. Pious young man that he was, he added a theological corrollary: "We hence see the exuberant Goodness of the Creator Who hath not only Provided for all the Necessities but also for the Pleasure and Recreation of all sorts of Creatures. And even the insects and those that are most Despicable" (*JE*, 7). That he should have grasped the essence of the scientific method, that is to say, experimentation and verification, is remarkable in a twelve-year-old minister's son living at the beginning of the eighteenth century in an impoverished village in a backward province.

Jonathan's musing concerning the relationship between nature and the divine led him to write "On Being." In this essay, Jonathan addressed himself to the ontological problem without having, as yet, read Plato, Aristotle,Thomas Aquinas, Bacon, or Descartes. Suppose, he reasoned, we could abolish resistance, solidity, and differentiation between objects, and conceive of an infinite nothing. "That there should absolutely be nothing at all is utterly impossible[.] [T]he Mind Can never Let it stretch its Conceptions [,] ever so much bring it self to Concieve of a state of Perfect nothing[.] [I]t puts the mind into mere Convulsion and Confusion. . . . So that we see it is necessary [that] some being should Eternally be . . . this necessary eternall being must be infinite and Omnipresent" (*JE*, 18).

There have been other precocious boys like young Jonathan; children who were fascinated with nature and who drew theological or philosophical conclusions from their studies. Unfortunately, few have left writings that survived, and few have recalled in later years what they thought when they were very young. The Swiss psychiatrist Carl Gustav Jung was one of the few who did the latter. Since he and his secretary, Aniéla Jaffe, did not write *Memories, Dreams, Reflections* until Jung was in his eighties, his recollections are probably not reliable. However, that problem aside, his reminiscences of his youth are interesting when compared to the childhood writings of Edwards. Both boys were sons of Calvinist ministers, and reared in parsonages. Both loved nature and spent much time roaming around the countryside, studying plant and animal life with remarkable intensity. Both realized from their boyhood rambles that the apparently gentle and attractive features of nature such as spring flowers and bird song are a veneer covering savage struggles for survival. Both Edwards and Jung therefore evolved concepts of deity that emphasized the ruthlessness of the divine.[5] In the context of different ideational systems, both Jung and Edwards apprehended *mysterium tremendum et fascinans,* the tremendous yet fascinating mystery of the divine in nature as well as in the depths of the soul.[6]

Given his background and boyhood predilections, there was no question but that Edwards was destined for the ministry. In October of 1716, at the age of thirteen, Jonathan was sent to the new Collegiate at New Haven. Founded in 1701, it was later

named for its chief benefactor, Elihu Yale. The tutors were ministers who prepared boys for the ministry. The curriculum included
arithmetic, algebra, Latin, Greek, Hebrew, rhetoric, logic, recita-
tion, and a rational analysis of religious faith largely based on *Me-
dulla* by Ames, who was one of the Puritan exponents of the
Federal Theology. The ancient languages studied enabled ministerial students to read not only the Bible in the original tongues,
but also the Greek and Latin classics, the writings of the Church
Fathers, and the works of European scholars of all nationalities
since, at that time, virtually all such works were written in Latin.
The student's mind was disciplined by mathematics and logic,
and his verbal self-expression by rhetoric. These studies gave him
great powers in the world of learning.[7]

Yale students were specially privileged because of the gift of a
library by a benefactor by the name of Jeremiah Dummer in England. The collection included one each of the few copies of John
Locke's *Essay Concerning Human Understanding* (1700), George
Berkeley's *Essay Toward a New Theory of Vision* (1709), and the
Principia of Sir Isaac Newton. Edwards probably read them during his second year at the Collegiate since, during the first, he and
ten other boys were removed to Wethersfield, where they studied
under a brilliant minister by the name of Elisha Williams. Some
dispute among the tutors, long forgotten, seems to have been involved in this move. The dispute, whatever it was, was settled by
the Connecticut Assembly in 1719, and the boys returned to New
Haven for the rest of their education.[8]

Yale tutors tended to be formalistic and abstruse. Edwards may
have learned more from reading the books in Dummer's library
than from his instructors. Indeed, Yale had a poor reputation
among Evangelicals. Nevertheless, Edwards emerged from his
studies as an exceptionally learned young man, having mastered
ancient languages, philosophy, mathematics, and physics.

While at Yale, Edwards began keeping a diary, and also set
forth a set of resolutions for his daily guidance:

> Being sensible that I am unable to do anything without God's help, I
> do humbly entreat him by his grace, to enable me to keep these Reso-
> lutions, so far as they are agreeable to his will, for Christ's sake. (*JE*,
> 38)

The seventy resolutions are mainly what we would expect in a
highly devoted, disciplined, and intensely religious person. What
is most interesting are those that do not quite fit these expecta-

tions, as, for example, Resolution 1: "That I will do whatsoever I think to be most to the glory of God *and my own good, profit and pleasure* [italics mine], in the whole of my duration." (*JE*, 38). We are not surprised by Resolution 38: "Never to utter any thing that is sportive, or matter of laughter, on a Lord's Day" (*JE*, 41); nor by Resolution 47: "To endeavor, to my utmost, to deny whatever is not most agreeable to a good and universally sweet and benevolent, quiet, peaceable, contented and easy, compassionate and generous, humble and meek, submissive and obliging, diligent and industrious, charitable and even, patient, moderate, forgiving and sincere, temper; and to do, at all times, what such a temper would lead me to; and to examine strictly, at the end of every week, whether I have so done" (*JE*, 42).

During his senior year, in 1722, he was licensed to preach and briefly served a Presbyterian congregation in New York City as a supply preacher. He returned to Yale to complete his studies, and was appointed as a tutor. In 1726 he fell ill and was bedridden for several months. During this time he became engaged in a profound soul struggle, being very knowledgeable in religious matters but by no means satisfied by the degree of inner religious experience which he had attained. Twenty years later he confided his reflections on this period to an essay which he called *Personal Narrative* (*JE*, 57–72). Some scholars think that it ranks with the *Confessions* of Augustine in its depth of understanding.

THE NORTHAMPTON PASTOR

In 1727 Jonathan Edwards was called to be assistant pastor at his grandfather's church in Northampton on the Connecticut River; a remote parish, but located in a prosperous area. Here, as was Congregational policy, he was ordained by the minister and congregation.[9] At the time of his settlement, he also married Sarah Pierpont, then seventeen, a very pretty young woman of great wisdom and ability. Theirs was a love match that resulted in a large family. As was the practice at that time, the minister was given land to cultivate, and paid not in cash, but in services and goods such as firewood, the erection of a barn, and supplies of foodstuffs, clothing, and tools. This was by no means an amicable arrangement in many New England parishes, and Northampton was no exception. In later years there was considerable dispute between Edwards and his parishioners over nonpayment of what he considered they owed him.

Beginning in 1679, Solomon Stoddard, the minister of North-ampton, had reaped five "harvests," as he called his revivals. These were occasions when his pulpit eloquence had brought about conversions among his parishioners. Northampton people were therefore prepared for what Edwards was to accomplish.

His duties as pastor included visiting the sick, bereaved, or distressed, which he performed faithfully, and parish calling, which he did not do, considering it to be a waste of time since such calls were usually social occasions. Instead, he frequently summoned certain parishioners to his study for counseling, reproof, or instruction, and on occasion met with small groups for the same purpose. These meetings were common among Puritans, and were much like the *collegia pietatis* of Jacob Spener and the Pietists in Germany. People at them prayed and discussed their religious experiences. Edwards also taught children from time to time.

Like other ministers of the time, Edwards conducted two services each Sunday as well as a weekday meeting at which he gave a lecture. The sermon was the centerpiece of the service, the chief means of mediating grace. Unlike Whitefield, Edwards did not indulge in extemporaneous preaching, but instead read his sermons from closely written notes. The content of his sermons was highly personal and subjective, not abstruse like that of many of his colleagues.[10] He had a thin, piping voice, and as he preached from the high pulpit he leaned on one elbow, and stared fixedly at the bell rope instead of making eye contact with his congregation. He preached in measured tones, seldom if ever raising his voice or underlining his words with gestures. He was anything but dramatic, and not at all charismatic.[11]

Why then was he so effective as a preacher? This remains an enigma, all the more so since his sermons (like Whitefield's) make dull reading. Yet Edwards is reputed to have held his congregations spellbound.

Edwards' grandfather Stoddard died in 1729 at the age of eighty-six, and Edwards became the sole pastor of the church. His services continued to be well attended, as did his weekday lectures, and many, on their own initiative, came to his study for counseling, and attended group meetings. Despite occasional quarrels over failures to supply promised goods and services, he seems to have enjoyed good relations with his parishioners. Some became disaffected, however, when he discontinued Stoddard's practice of inviting unregenerates to partake of the Lord's Supper. Indeed, this eventually became the chief issue that led to his dismissal by the congregation in 1750.

Edwards led a very disciplined, austere life. He was up at four in the morning during the summer, and at five during the winter. He was abstemious in diet, and in all respects led a very spartan existence. Sometimes he would take pen, ink, pins, and bits of foolscap with him on walks in the woods, or when he went riding for exercise; as thoughts occurred to him, he would write them down and pin them onto his coat. Sometimes he would come home covered with notes. He also cut up pieces of foolscap and sewed them into little books in which he constantly wrote ideas. These later became his sources for published books as well as sermons.

Edwards first became known in Boston after giving a lecture there in 1731, *God A Divine and Supernatural Light,* which impressed the clerical audience so deeply that it was published in 1734. In it, Edwards argued that God is antecedent to all experience, and that history is the full expression of divine grace. (The sovereignty of God was always his central theme.[12]) To fellow ministers, all of this was, of course, merely sound doctrine, but Edwards apparently had powers that made his message particularly impressive to his contemporaries. The published lecture was widely discussed both in the colonies and in Britain. From that time on, Edwards was widely known. In particular, he won the admiration of Benjamin Colman, the dean of the Boston clergy.

THE NORTHAMPTON REVIVAL OF 1733–35

In general, times were prosperous in the 1730s. Some merchants and large landowners were becoming wealthy, and others had hopes of becoming so. There was considerable preoccupation with worldly concerns and, with it, a decline in spirituality which disturbed Edwards very deeply. Many young people in the frontier communities along the Connecticut River were enjoying "tavern haunting" and "night walking" (keeping company) on the Sabbath, or at other times when he was conducting meetings. Edwards complained of these behaviors later in his *Narrative of the Surprising Works of God,* but it is difficult to be certain what was meant by them. There is an implication of drunkenness, and, possibly, sexual activity. His denunciations, however, may have reflected his own prudery:

It had been their manner of a Long Time, & for Ought I know, al-
waies, to make sabbath day nights & Lecture days, to be Especially
Times of diversion, & Company Keeping; I then Preach'd a sermon on
the Sabbath before the Lecture, to show them the unsuitableness, &
Inconvenience of the Practice, & to Perswade them to Reform it. (*JE*,
73)

Edwards "urged it on Heads of Families that It should be a
thing agreed among them to Govern their Families, & keep them
in at those times" (*JE*, 73). Apparently, the parents thought their
youngsters were doing nothing wrong, and paid no heed. However, Edwards was delighted to note increasing "Remarkable Religious Concern" as young people became preoccupied with the
state of their souls during 1733 and 1734.

The Northampton Revival began in 1734, with the emergence
of a "remarkable religious concern" at a little congregation called
Pascommuck, where a few families were settled three miles from
Northampton. In April of that year, a young man "in the very
Bloom of his youth, who was violently siezed with a Pleurisy &
taken Immediately out of his head . . . died in two days" (*JE*, 74).
Soon after, a young married woman died who had been in "Great
Distress in the Beginning of her Illness," but seemed to have satisfying evidence of God's mercy to her before her death; so that
"she died full of Comfort, and in a most Earnest & moving manner, warning & counselling others" (*JE*, 74). By the end of December and the beginning of January 1735, "All the Talk in all
companies, & upon occasions was upon the things of Religion,
and no other talk was anywhere Relished; & scarcely a single Person in the whole Town was Left unconcerned about the Great
things of the Eternal World" (*JE*, 75).

Even children were so preoccupied with their spiritual concerns that they talked of nothing else. Church attendance in
Northampton increased, and some in his normally sober congregation were so moved that they cried out, wept, or even fainted.
Edwards was convinced that the Holy Spirit was at work in his
parishioners. He believed that he had been the instrument by
which the Holy Spirit had roused people to an intense sense of
conviction, after which some, though by no means all, experienced conversion. To Edwards, God appeared to be a spiritual vol-
cano who showered his creatures with heavenly fire.

An elderly person died "which was attended with very unusual
Circumstances, which much affected many People." Moreover,
"about that Time began the Great noise that there was in this

Part of the Countrey about Arminianism, which seemed strangely to be overruled for the Promoting of Religion" (*JE*, 74). Although frequently railing against this doctrine, Edwards used the term both in its more precise theological sense and more loosely, to mean worldliness thinly disguised by superficial professions of piety.

People in Northampton became concerned with the state of their souls, manifesting all sorts of obsessive preoccupation with religious issues. This was at first regarded with amused condescension outside of Northampton: "The news of [the religious concerns] filled the neighboring Towns with Talk, & there were many in them that scoffed and made a Ridicule of the Religion that appeared in Northampton" (*JE*, 75), but the phenomenon soon spread to neighboring hamlets, villages, and towns along the Connecticut River, such as Green River, Longmeadow, Enfield, Coventry, and as far south as New Haven and Guilford. Those who had formerly questioned even a little the doctrines of their faith now became fearful of eternal punishment.

About this time Edwards went to New York (for his health) and heard more about the evangelical work of Frelinghuysen and the Tennents in the Jerseys, thus establishing a link between these revivals and his own in Northampton. After his return, Abigail Hutchison, a parishioner, told him of "the sense she . . . had from day to day of the glory of Christ, and of God, in his various attributes," so that Edwards thought she had "as immediate an intercourse with him, as a child with a father."[13]

Even more astounding was the case of a very young child, Phebe Bartlett, aged four. In May of 1735 she was "affected by the talk of her brother, who had been converted . . . at age eleven." She became more and more engrossed with religion and retreated to a closet five or six times a day "and was so engaged in it, that nothing would, at any time divert her from her stated closet exercises" (*JE*, 85). Then, one day (Thursday, 31 July), she crept into her favorite hiding place and prayed: "Pray, BLESSED LORD, give me salvation! I PRAY, BEG pardon all my sins!" Then she came out of the closet, sat by her mother and sobbed in anguish. "I am afraid I shall go to hell!" After some time, she suddenly quietened, smiled, and said, "Mother, the kingdom of heaven is come to me!" She then retired to her closet again. When her mother returned from a visit to a brother, Phebe said, "I can find God now! . . . I love God!" (*JE*, 86). Indeed, Edwards wrote, she now said she loved God more than she did her father and mother or her sister Rachel. She was asked if the fear of going to hell had made her cry, and she replied, "Yes I was [afraid], but now I shall not [be]!" She was asked the next day why God had made her. "Every body should serve God," she said, "and get an interest in Christ." She burst into tears again in concern for the state of soul of Abigail, her sister: "Poor Nabby!" She was afraid that her sisters Naomi and Eunice would go to hell, and could not be reassured.

Phebe became devoted to her church, going, she said, "to hear Mr. Edwards preach" (*JE*, 88). Passages of Scripture came to her mind: "Behold, I stand at the door and knock: If any man hear my voice, and open the door, I will come in, and sup with him and he with me."(Revelation 3:20). Phebe became a missionary among the children she encountered, including her sisters, and was said to exemplify the Christian virtue of compassion and love for all.

Edwards was particularly struck by the conversion of someone so young. He thought it could only be explained as the work of the Holy Spirit, unassisted by any human agency. Just as he had seen incontrovertible proof of the work of the divine in rainbows, the behavior of spiders, and the remarkable variety of colors when he was a boy, he now perceived that, in ways that could be explained only in supernaturalist terms, certain very unlikely persons underwent regeneration.

Revival fervor spread down the Connecticut River into the neighboring colony, and also affected the revivals already in progress in northern New Jersey. The revival in Northampton, however, had an abrupt and tragic end. Jonathan Edwards' Uncle Hawley committed suicide while depressed:

> [T]here has Happened a thing of a very awfull nature in the Town; My Uncle Hawley, the Last Sabbath day morning, Laid violent Hands on himself, & Put an End to his Life, by Cutting his own throat. He had been for a Considerable Time Greatly Concerned about the Condition of his soul; till, by the ordering of a sovereign Providence he was suffered to fall into deep melancholly, a distemper that the Family are very Prone to; he was much overpowered by it; the devil took the advantage & drove him into despairing thoughts: he was Kept very much awake at nights, so that he had but very Little sleep for two months. (*JE*, 83)

Obviously, Hawley suffered from what now would be diagnosed (and treated) as a clinical depression.

After the shock of Hawley's suicide, the religious excitement gradually died in Northampton. According to Edwards and most of his parishioners, the Holy Spirit would be present in a community only temporarily, and then move on. If a person did not undergo conviction and conversion at such a time, the opportunity was lost. Perhaps the Holy Spirit would return again some day, perhaps not. Those who missed the opportunity would have to live in dread of damnation until the next visitation.

When Benjamin Colman of Boston first heard of the Northampton revival, he wrote Edwards, asking for details. The latter replied with a lengthy narrative of the events above (*GW*, 73–91). Concerning Phebe, Abigail Hutchison, and others, he noted certain "distinguishing marks" which proved that their conversions were genuine experiences, not to be explained in any natural way. His "proofs" were that, after a time of inner anguish over their sins, passages of Scripture occurred to them, the impact of the minister's sermons deeply impressed them, and as they turned to Christ for help in humility and supplication, they experienced deep inner joy accompanied by concern for the souls of others.

Colman was duly impressed with Edwards' description of the revival, asked him to expand on it, and published it in 1736, and again, in expanded form, the next year. They called it *A Faithful Narrative of the Surprising Work of God in the Conversion of Many Hundred Souls in Northampton and the Neighboring Towns and Villages.*

This book had a great impact throughout the colonies, in Britain, and, in translation, on the Continent as well. Indeed, *A Faithful Narrative* became the model for later accounts of revival experiences. As such it became one of the primary vehicles for revival. By 1739 it had gone through three editions and twenty printings.[14] As Perry Miller notes: "Edwards made no secret of why he could maintain detachment from events in which he was deeply implicated: he had a technique for analysis, the Lockean psychology. He was as empirical as Boyle or Huygens, and wrote the Narrative as though for the Transactions of the Royal Society."[15]

THE NEW ENGLAND AWAKENING BEGINS

The Holy Spirit visited the communities along the Connecticut River again in 1740, the year that marks the beginning of the Great Awakening in New England. In this second series of revivals, Edwards emerged as one of the three central figures of the movement, the others being George Whitefield and Gilbert Tennent.

Unlike the other great revivalists, Edwards did not become an itinerant, but was nevertheless frequently invited by the incumbents to preach in neighboring churches. One such invitation brought him to the town of Enfield, just south of the Massachusetts line on the Connecticut River. The pastor there was disturbed by the complacency of his congregation, and asked Edwards to shock them into a proper concern. He did this with the most famous of his sermons, *Sinners in the Hand of an Angry God*. He warned the people that they were loathsome in God's sight, as loathsome as spiders, and that God was suspending them even at that moment above the pit of hell. Some men staggered to their feet in terror, fearful that the very floor would open beneath their feet. Women shrieked, and some fainted. Yet, as was his style, Edwards preached this frightening sermon in his usual calm and detached manner.

Later, he wrote the *Treatise on Religious Affections* (1746) in which he attempted to explain evangelical religious experience, drawing upon the events of these years. This, Edwards' major work, was to be used as a textbook in theological seminaries well up into the nineteenth century, and is still highly regarded. His pamphlet debate with Charles Chauncy, the leader among the Boston Opposers, which will be discussed in detail later, further establishes his reputation as a leading figure in the Great Awakening.

Edwards' own life proved hard and frustrating, despite his successes. Because he refused to serve the Lord's Supper to unregenerates, in addition to some other wrangles of a pedestrian nature, he was fired by his Northampton congregation in 1750 and took a charge in Stockbridge, a frontier settlement where he ministered to Native Americans. There he developed a theological system which was later called the "New Divinity." In this, Edwards emphasized the sovereignty of God, predestination, and election, Calvinist doctrines which he inspired with new life. He stressed religious experience (affects), the inner life of the soul rather than the legalistic features of Calvinism. Very few ministers embraced the New Divinity, perhaps because the intellectual complexity of Edwards' thought baffled them. In 1757, he accepted an appointment as President of New Jersey College, which in later years became Princeton University. No sooner had he arrived than he allowed himself to be innoculated with a primitive smallpox vaccine, contracted the disease as a result, and died. He was still a fairly obscure figure at this time, and it was only during the later years of the century that, thanks to Samuel Hopkins and other adherents of his New Divinity theology, Edwards became more generally known and admired, a man of towering stature and genius of whom many biographies have been written and published during the twentieth century.

5

George Whitefield in America

WHITEFIELD'S FIRST EVANGELICAL TOUR

As EARLY AS 18 SEPTEMBER 1737, WILLIAM SEWARD, WHITEFIELD'S traveling companion and press agent, paid for a front-page announcement in the London *Daily Advertiser* of 19 September stating that Whitefield was about to sail for Georgia. He did so the following year. Franklin somehow learned of it, and reprinted the story in the *Pennsylvania Gazette*. Thanks to London newspapers and the correspondence network, Whitefield and his evangelism in Britain had become well known throughout the American colonies. Franklin became one of his most active public relations men, not for religious, but for business reasons. The Philadelphia printer, influenced by the Enlightenment, was well on his way to becoming the most famous *philosophe* in colonial America.

In 1738, as mentioned earlier, Whitefield had visited Savannah, Georgia, with intentions of founding an orphanage in the newly established colony. At the time, however, Whitefield was not yet ordained. He returned to England, and was so on 14 January 1739. He continued his evangelical itineraries throughout Britain, stories of which were widely publicized in the American press, especially by Franklin's *Pennsylvania Gazette*.

For six months before Whitefield's arrival in Lewis Town, Franklin had been arousing public curiosity by his frequent stories about him, emphasizing the size of the crowds he had been attracting and the strange pulpits he spoke from, such as tree limbs and tombstones. By so doing he made Whitefield a celebrity. The constant flood of publicity roused great anticipation among Pennsylvanians by the time the *Gazette* announced Whitefield's second arrival. On 30 October 1739 Whitefield was eagerly greeted by a large throng when he landed at Lewis Town, Delaware, accompanied by William Seward, who continued to play the role of his press agent and promoter. Whitefield hoped to raise funds for the orphanage on this visit by making a preaching tour of the Middle Colonies. Seward preceded him, preparing the way, as Whitefield made his progress from Lewis Town to Philadelphia, preaching to large crowds, which, according to reports, were in the thousands in some cases. The numbers were no doubt exaggerated by Seward and by other publicists.

It is difficult to know the reasons for Whitefield's great success. There is no question but that he was outstanding as an orator. However, he was also cross-eyed and overweight.[1] In his *Journal* (which was intended for publication, therefore promotional in tone) he emphasized the evangelical message he preached, the size of the crowds, and the spiritual effects on his listeners. Nevertheless, his successes varied, with some of his meeting and outdoor audiences being fairly modest. He had his most outstanding success in Philadelphia.[2]

Benjamin Franklin was one of Whitefield's most active promoters, entirely for business reasons. As Lambert says, Whitefield was advertised in the same terms as goods that had just arrived from England. Readers heard about "one who came offering them a new religious experience, a choice in the marketplace of religion that . . . extended beyond parish borders."[3]

In Philadelphia, the *Gazette* reported:

> On Thursday last, the Rev. Mr. Whitefield began to preach from the Court-House-Gallery in this City, about six at Night, to near 6000 People before him in the Street who stood in awful silence to hear him: and this continued every Night till Sunday. . . . Before he returns to England he designs (God willing) to preach the Gospel in every Province in America, belonging to the English.[4]

After preaching in Philadelphia and surrounding towns, he started for New York, evangelizing and fund-raising for his orphanage in the hamlets and towns along the way. He paused at Neshaminy to meet William Tennent, Sr., "an old grey-headed Disciple and soldier of Jesus Christ" (*GW*, 344).[5] He was again greeted as a celebrity along his route: "The multitudes of all sects and denominations that attended his sermons were enormous," according to Franklin.[6] In New Brunswick he met Gilbert Tennent, who, according to Whitefield, "went to the Bottom indeed, and did not daub with untempered Mortar."[7]

His visit to New York City, accompanied by Tennent, was much less successful, however. The Anglican commissary denied him permission to preach in the church even before he asked for it.

Although the weather was wintry, Whitefield preached outdoors in the fields, but attracted only small crowds of listeners. Indeed, the province of New York remained throughout almost untouched by the Awakening. Why? For one thing, the many Dutch inhabitants of the city, western Long Island, and the Hudson River valley were staunch members of the Reformed Church, very orthodox and formalist, and highly resistant to the evangelicalism of Frelinghuysen. Those of English descent were predominantly Arminian Anglicans who opposed Whitefield and his Calvinism. Migrants from Connecticut mostly became Presbyterians. Some responded to Jonathan Dickinson's evangelical preaching, but his strength lay chiefly in New Jersey.

On 23 November, Whitefield "parted with Dear Mr. *Tennent*" in New Brunswick, paused briefly again in Philadelphia, and, accompanied by Seward and other traveling companions, made his way south on horseback toward Georgia. In the southern colonies he encountered large areas unserved by any church, and much evidence of irreligion. As Lambert states in *"Pedlar in Divinity": George Whitefield and the Transatlantic Revivals,* "the farther south [Whitefield] traveled, the more dismal prospects appeared for a spiritual awakening."[8] There were several reasons for this, in addition to the lack of churches in the region. Many of the great plantation owners, such as the Byrds of Virginia, had large libraries and were avid readers of philosophical and scientific literature. As Whitefield found, to his dismay, there were thus many deists among the southern patricians, while those who professed Anglicanism tended to be Latitudinarian. These people were not interested in Whitefield's message of the New Birth.

Another reason for "irreligion" was the perceived inadequacy of the Anglican clergy at this time. Not only did the priests include many alcoholics among them, but many of them shared the hedonistic lifestyle of the plantocracy. It is clear from Whitefield's journal that, while his southern hosts treated him hospitably and often attended his services, they found him priggish and overly rigid. He no doubt bored many of them, since, from what he himself says, he seems to have been willing to discuss nothing but religion.

His only successes among whites in the South appear to have been among the Presbyterians, such as the members of the congregation in Charleston, South Carolina, and among the Huguenots of that community, French refugees of the Reformed Church and therefore, like himself, Calvinist. He does not seem to have been very effective among the poor white farmers of the southern tidewater, and did not venture into the hilly backcountry which historians call "the Piedmont."

Though the poorer folk of the South were nominally Anglican, in most cases, they felt uncomfortable in a church dominated by wealthy families, and were therefore mostly unchurched. The few contacts Whitefield had with them suggest that most of them regarded him as a rather tyrannical prude who would not allow them even the most innocent of pleasures.

Whitefield's most interesting encounters were with African slaves. At the time, few ministers took any interest in blacks. They were generally regarded as being little better than beasts of burden, without souls, and almost no attempts were made to evangelize among them. The one Protestant group that *did* believe that blacks were worthy of notice were the Moravians of Georgia, whom Whitefield much admired. While in Pennsylvania he met a few freed blacks, and conceived the idea of a communal school for them in that province. This was the idea that later resulted in the building of the house in Nazareth, Pennsylvania, which is named for him. Whitefield intended that a school for freed blacks be located there. It still stands, and was the original nucleus of what was originally intended to be a community of Moravians and immigrant English Evangelicals.

With this project in mind, Whitefield made a point of visiting slave cabins in the plantations where he stayed. He found the blacks to be very responsive to his preaching, and this encouraged him in his project. Apparently his plantation hosts were not disturbed by his interest in their slaves. Perhaps they even encouraged it in order to ensure docility in their workers by emphasizing bliss in the life to come.

Though Whitefield had been fund-raising for his Georgia orphanage in Philadelphia and elsewhere in the Middle Colonies, he seems not to have done so as he made his progress through the southern colonies. Perhaps he knew in advance that the project was of little interest to the planters of the area, and so he and his companions simply made their way south, accepting hospitality, and preaching occasionally in those Anglican churches where the incumbent priest permitted it.

WHITEFIELD'S ACCOUNT OF HIS SOUTHERN JOURNEY

On initially leaving Pennsylvania Whitefield and his companions first arrived in the northeastern district of Maryland. "Little notice having been given, there were not above fifteen hundred people; but God was with us, and many were deeply affected" (*GW*, 364). After crossing the Susquehanna by ferry, Whitefield and his party stayed at the home of a "gentleman [who] told us he had been a little melancholy, and had therefore sent for some friends to help him to drive it away. The bottle and the bowl, I found, were the means employed." Later, after supper, "I went to bed pitying the miserable condition of those who live a life of luxury and self-indulgence. They are afraid to look into themselves and, if their consciences are at any time awakened, they must be lulled to sleep again by drinking and evil company" (*GW*, 365). Here we encounter examples of the hedonistic planter lifestyle that so disturbed Whitefield in the course of his southern journey.

At Joppa, Whitefield, given a rare opportunity by the priest, preached to around forty people in the Anglican Church, spent the next night in Newton, and then rode on to Annapolis (a little town, but the metropolis of Maryland), arriving at four in the afternoon. He was cordially received, "but the people seemed to be surprised when they heard us talk of God and Christ." After supper, he mused: "It grieves me in my soul to see poor sinners hanging as it were by a single hair, and dancing (insensible of their danger) over the flames of hell." Here, he and his friends were received by both the governor and a hospitable Anglican priest, who "offered me his pulpit, his house, or anything he could supply me with." Whitefield had "some useful conversation":

Our conversation ran chiefly on the new birth, and the folly and sinfulness of those amusements, whereby the polite part of the world are so fatally diverted from the pursuit of the one thing needful. Some of the company, I believe, thought I was too strict, and were very strenuous in defence of what they called *innocent* diversions; but when I told them everything was sinful which was not done with a single eye to God's glory, and that such entertainments not only discovered a levity of mind, but were contrary to the whole tenor of the Gospel of Christ, they seemed somewhat convinced. (*GW*, 366)

Later, he confided to his journal: "I trust it set them *doubting*, and I pray God they may *doubt* more and more, for cards, dancing, and such like, draw the soul from God, and lull it asleep as much as drunkenness and debauchery." (*GW*, 366) (Although he speaks of raising doubts in some and moving others, it is very possible that he was overly optimistic on that score, and that his listeners were simply being accommodating. One suspects that he roused mirth in some and irritated others, but that they were too polite to reveal either to him. Southern gentry and their ladies were noted for their courtesy and charm.)

He was not pleased by the Maryland gentry: "for women are as much enslaved to their fashionable diversions, as men are to their bottle and their houses. Self-pleasing, self-seeking is the *ruling principle* in both" (*GW*, 367).

In spite of his strictures, the Marylanders of Annapolis treated Whitefield and his companions well. The governor took time to come to morning service, and dine with him. He was not favorably impressed by the local Anglican priest despite his affability: "The minister seemed somewhat affected, and under convictions; but I fear a false politeness, and the pomps and vanities of the world, eat out the vitals of religion in this place" (*GW*, 368).

In Upper Marlborough, fifteen miles from Annapolis, Whitefield "supped with a gentleman who kindly entertained both me and my fellow-travellers. Our talk ran upon the fall of man. I fear Deism has spread much in these parts. I cannot say I have yet met with *many* here who seem truly to have the fear of God before their eyes" (*GW*, 368).

Some of his planter hosts were clearly annoyed with him. On Monday, 10 December, Whitefield's party reached the Potomac, six miles wide at that point. They were guests at the ferryman's home, and crossed the next day. They were wet and miserable by six in the evening, when they arrived at Seals Church twenty-nine miles south of the Potomac. Later, on the road to Williamsburgh, they stayed with a planter who not only had no food to spare for the party, but accused Whitefield of being a Quaker. Whitefield confided to his journal, "If I talk of the Spirit, I am a Quaker! If I say grace at breakfast, and behave seriously, I am a Presbyterian! Alas! what must I do to be accounted a member of the Church of England?" (*GW*, 370).

By the evening of 14 December, they were in Williamsburgh. Here Whitefield paid his respects to Commissary Samuel Blair of the Society for the Propagation of the Gospel, "by far the most worthy clergyman I have yet conversed with in all America." Blair was successfully proselytizing Anglicanism in the colonies, encouraging improved behavior on the part of priests, and attempting to reach unchurched people. Whitefield warmly praised Blair "in raising a beautiful college at Williamsburgh, in which is a foundation for about eight scholars, a president, two masters, and professors in the several sciences" (*GW*, 371). However,

Blair's religious orientation was Arminian and not Calvinist, and he was inclined to Latitudinarianism. Therefore, Whitefield's approbation was in some respects surprising.

Whitefield preached on Sunday morning, 16 December, and then the party continued on their southward way, reaching the young, sparsely populated colony of North Carolina on 19 December. "It is by far the longest stage, and the roads are the worst we have had since we began our journey" (GW, 375). There were few large plantations in North Carolina, and Whitefield and his companions seem to have been intent only on making their way south as quickly as possible.

He had a mixed reception in the communities where he preached. At Bath-Town, Whitefield preached to around a hundred in the Anglican church. "I felt the Divine Presence, and did not spare to tell my hearers that I thought God was angry with them, because He had sent a famine of the Word among them for a long while, and not given them a teaching priest. All seemed attentive to what was spoken" (GW, 376). Then, on Christmas Eve, they crossed the five-mile-wide Pimlico River and reached Newborn Town at dusk. On Christmas Day, Whitefield took Holy Eucharist in the courthouse, "but mourned much in spirit, to see in what an indifferent manner everything was carried on." He preached in the afternoon. "The people were uncommonly attentive, and most were melted into tears" (GW, 377). He was vexed with the minister of Newborn Town, "who I heard countenanced a dancing-master, by suffering his own son to be one of his learners. . . . It grieves me to find that in every little town there is a settled dancing-master, but scarcely anywhere a settled minister to be met with" (GW, 378).

A few days later, after crossing the Trent River, the party was given hospitality by a young man who had been one of his parishioners in Savannah. Whitefield wrote in his *Journal* that he "went, as my usual custom is, among the negroes belonging to the house. One man was sick in bed, and two of his children said their prayers after me very well. This more and more convinces me that negro children, if early brought up in the nurture and admonition of the Lord, would make as great proficiency as any white people's children" (GW, 379).

New Year's Day 1740 found the party in South Carolina. "Here I immediately perceived the people were more polite than those we generally met with; but I believe the people of the house wished I had not come to be their guest that night." A New Year's party had been planned and several of the neighbors were enjoying country dances. "I went in amongst them whilst a woman was dancing a jig. At my first entrance I endeavoured to shew the folly of such entertainments, and to convince her how well pleased the devil was at every step she took." The dancer "endeavoured to outbrave me" and

> neither the fiddler nor she desisted; but at last she gave over, and the musician laid aside his instrument. The rest of the company, one by one attacked me, and brought, as they thought, arguments to support their wantonness. . . . All were soon put to silence, and were, for some time, so overawed, that after I had discoursed with them on the nature of baptism, and the necessity of being born again, in order to enjoy the Kingdom of Heaven, I baptised, at their entreaty, one of their children, and prayed afterwards as I was enabled, and as the circumstances of the company required. (*GW*, 381–82)

Whitefield's triumph, however, was brief. After he went to bed he heard the music and dancing again. He scolded the revelers very early the next morning, "who were very attentive, and took it in good part."

They arrived in Charleston on 5 January. Here Whitefield received letters from New York, "informing me how mightily the Word of God grew and prevailed there." He must have been pleased, though, as mentioned, the effects of his evangelism in New York were considerably less satisfying than the comment might lead one to think. He did not preach in the Anglican church in Charleston "because the curate had not a commission to lend the pulpit, unless the Commissary (then out of town) were present." Still, "Most of the town, however, being eager to hear me, I preached, in the afternoon, in one of the Dissenting meeting houses, but was grieved to find so little concern in the congregation. The auditory was large, but very polite." What was worse, from his point of view, "I question whether the court-end of London could exceed them in affected finery, gaiety of dress, and a deportment ill-becoming persons who have had such Divine judgments lately sent amongst them. I reminded them of this in my sermon; but I seemed to them as one that mocked" (*GW*, 384). However, Charlestonians wanted to hear Whitefield again, and this time he preached in the French church, presumably Huguenot, "and blessed be God, I saw a glorious alteration in the audience, which was so great that many stood without the door. I felt much more freedom than I did yesterday. Many were melted into tears. One of the town, most remarkably gay, was observed to weep." He preached in the French church again, had supper, and then "had an opportunity, for nearly two hours, to converse of the things of God with a large company, and retired to my lodging, full of joy at the prospect of a good work having begun in that place" (*GW*, 384–85).

On 8 January, the Whitefield party set out for Georgia in an open canoe rowed by five African slaves, who "were very civil, diligent, and laborious." They reached Savannah before noon the next day, "where I had a joyful meeting with my dear friends" (*GW*, 385–86). It was 9 January 1740, journey's end.

Having reached Savannah once more, Whitefield turned his attention to the orphanage project. He built *Bethesda,* meaning "place of refuge," on his five hundred acres and began gathering orphans. Continued fund-raising for this orphanage became a major reason for his later preaching tours.

Whitefield reflected on his experiences and "put down some remarks which I have made on the state of religion in those provinces, which I have lately passed through."

> And here I cannot but give Pennsylvania the preference. To me it seems to be the garden of America. Their oxen are strong to labour, and there seems to be no complaining in their streets. What is best of all, I believe they have the Lord for their God. This, I infer, from their having so many faithful ministers sent forth amongst them; and, except Northampton in New England, the work of conversion has not been carried on with so much power in any part of America, that I can hear of, as under the ministry of Messrs. Tennent, Cross, and the other labourers before mentioned. The Constitution is far from being arbitrary; the soil is good, the land exceedingly fruitful, and there is a greater equality between the poor and rich than perhaps can be found in any other place of the known world. (*GW*, 386)

It is interesting, and to me refreshing, to note the intimations of social conscience here, after what I find to have been tedious, repetitious professions of piety coupled with priggishness over the most innocent of pleasures and pastimes. In some personalities, unfortunately, the one goes with the other. What follows in this 9 January entry in the journal is particularly intriguing:

> For my part, I like it [Pennsylvania] so well, that, God willing, I purpose taking up some land to erect a school for negroes, and settle some of my English friends, whose hearts God shall stir up, or whom the fury of their enemies shall oblige to depart from their native land. (*GW*, 386–87)

Acting on this resolve, as mentioned previously, Whitefield purchased a tract in eastern Pennsylvania to which he gave the name "Nazareth." His plan was to encourage hard-pressed Moravians in Georgia to move north to Pennsylvania to build a school for Africans. The project failed before it began, and Whitefield ultimately sold the land to the Moravians who had settled in nearby Bethlehem. Nevertheless, Whitefield was certainly among the first to recognize the humanity of the Africans, to credit them with having immortal souls worthy of salvation.

One of the positive aspects of Evangelicalism during the eighteenth century was the campaign against the slave trade launched by William Wilberforce (1759–1833), a reformer of the Evangelical faction of the Church of England. He launched the first social crusade in British history, which achieved complete success the year of his death when not only the slave trade but slavery itself was abolished throughout the British Empire. The seeds of this crusade were sown by Whitefield's work among the slaves of the southern colonies during 1739–40. He, in turn, probably became inspired to devote himself to the salvation of blacks because of the example set by the Moravians. His concern, moreover, was not only with the state of their souls, but with the conditions of their worldly lives. Whitefield deplored slavery, and was one of the first in public life to do so.

Stuart Henry asserts that Whitefield made little if any favorable impression in the South during this journey,[9] as do most other historians. I disagree. However, it is quite clear that he did not have the same impact on audiences in the southern provinces as in the north later that year. A few Anglican priests had lent him their pulpits, and there had been occasional preaching opportunities. In some, he had been effective; in others less so.

WHITEFIELD'S SECOND TOUR

Having launched his orphanage at Bethesda, Whitefield returned to Charleston in March, in company with Seward. Here they took ship for New Castle, Delaware, arriving at eight o'clock on the morning of Sunday, 13 April 1739, after a ten-day voyage from Savannah, Georgia ("in which God was pleased to exercise my body with sickness, and my soul with spiritual conflicts") (*GW*, 405).The Anglican priest ("who has been my advocate") was ill, and accepted Whitefield's offer to take the morning service. Whitefield preached twice that day. "People were surprised, but much rejoiced at the news of my arrival, which they expressed by flocking, as soon as they were apprised of my coming, to hear the afternoon sermon." The local Scotch-Irish Presbyterian minister also came, with a large part of his congregation. Whitefield then went on to Wilmington. "Preached to near three thousand people, at eleven in the morning," he recorded in his journal. After the service, he and his companions dined with a Quaker "who seemed to have the right spirit within him, and could speak as one experienced in the things of God" (*GW*, 406).

On Tuesday, 15 April, he arrived in Philadelphia. Here he met the governor of the province and also paid his respects to the commissary who was not home, "but afterwards, speaking to him in the street, he told me that he could lend me his church no more, because I had not treated the Bishop of London well, in my Answer to his late Pastoral Letter; and also, because I had misquoted and misrepresented Archbishop Tillotson," the latter being one of the leading Latitudinarians. Denied access to the Anglican Church, Whitefield preached outdoors on Society Hill. Here he once more denounced Tillotson, the Archbishop of Canterbury and therefore his superior, for his Latitudinarianism (*GW*, 406–7).

On Wednesday, 16 April, Whitefield preached to six thousand in the morning and eight thousand in the evening, or so he claimed in his journal (*GW*, 407). Ben Franklin heard him preach from the steps of the courthouse in Philadelphia. He later wrote in his autobiography:

> I happened . . . to attend one of his Sermons, in the Course of which I perceived he intended to finish with a Collection, and I silently resolved he should get nothing from me. I had in my pocket a handful of copper money, three or four silver dollars, and five pistoles in gold. As he proceeded I began to soften, and concluded to give the coppers. Another stroke of his oratory made me asham'd of that, and determin'd me to give the silver; and he finish'd so admirably, that I empty'd my pocket wholly into the collector's dish, gold and all.[10]

Franklin wrote that he was chiefly persuaded by Whitefield's appeal for funds to support his orphanage.

Notwithstanding their differences in religious outlook, Whitefield and Franklin had become friends. On one of Whitefield's visits to Philadelphia he wrote thanking Franklin for his offer of hospitality given "for Christ's sake." Franklin replied, "Don't let me be mistaken; it was not for Christ's sake, but for your sake."

Thus, Franklin had "contriv'd to fix [the credit] on earth."[11]
There is no suggestion that Whitefield made much effort to convert Franklin.

Whitefield then repeated his first tour through Pennsylvania
and New Jersey, attracting huge crowds wherever he preached.
As before, however, he made little impression on New Yorkers. As
Lambert shows, there is no question but that his successes were
largely because of newspaper publicity and the promoters, like
Seward, who preceded him, so that he was awaited everywhere
with great anticipation. One strongly suspects that what appealed most was not his evangelical message, but his dramatic
style as an actor, and that the crowds who flocked to his meetings
were less in search of salvation than entertainment.

On 16 May he again set sail for Savannah.

WHITEFIELD'S THIRD TOUR

Reports of Whitefield's remarkable triumphs in Britain had
been eagerly read by New England divines whose interest in experiential religion had been roused by Edwards' *A Faithful Narrative*. Three of these were Timothy Allen, Jonathan Barber, and
James Davenport, radical disciples of David Ferris who later became significant figures in the Awakening.

Benjamin Colman of the Brattle Street Church was among
those who had been excited by the news of Whitefield's triumphs
in England. As a result, Whitefield received an invitation from
Colman to preach in Boston soon after his arrival in Georgia (*GW*,
457).

The Anglican revivalist took ship and arrived at Newport,
Rhode Island, on Sunday, 14 September 1740. The local Anglican
vicar reluctantly allowed him to preach at morning and afternoon
services the next day, which he did to large interdenominational
audiences, something previously unheard of. It was the first time
in which Anglicans, Congregationalists, Baptists, and Quakers in
Newport had worshiped together.

Whitefield was very impressed with Jonathan Barber, who had
crossed over from Long Island to meet him in Newport. The latter
then accompanied the Grand Itinerant on his evangelical wanderings, which took them first to Boston. Whitefield sent promoters
ahead of him to advertise that he was coming. On Tuesday, the
young English evangelist preached to a still greater audience
than he had gathered in Newport. On Wednesday, accompanied

by Jonathan Barber and other admirers, he took the ferry to Bristol and rode to Boston the next morning. Barber, whom we will discuss at greater length later, was later appointed spiritual superintendant of the Bethesda Orphanage, just before Whitefield returned to England (*GW*, 500).

After attending prayers at King's Chapel (then Anglican and now Unitarian), Whitefield accepted an invitation from Benjamin Colman to preach at the Brattle Street Church. It was, as was now usual at Whitefield's meetings, packed with an interdenominational congregation. Most Boston ministers greeted Whitefield with considerable warmth and support, and during the course of the week he preached every day to huge congregations at various churches. Six thousand attended a morning service at the Reverend Checkley's New South Church, overflowing into the street to the alarm of conservative Boston citizens, since the crowd soon became unruly and boisterous. On another occasion, there was much excitement inside the meetinghouse before his arrival. When he arrived, "on a sudden, all the people were in an uproar, and so unaccountably surprised, that some threw themselves out of the windows, others threw themselves out of the gallery, and others trampled upon one another; so that five were actually killed, and others dangerously wounded" (*GW*, 461). A huge crowd also flocked to hear him at Joshua Gee's Second Church. During the week, the evangelist made his way to Cambridge, where he preached at Harvard College, secretly confiding in his journal: "Discipline is at a low ebb. Bad books are become fashionable" (*GW*, 462).

Continuing his fund-raising (and hell-raising), Whitefield then accepted an invitation from Thomas Foxcroft to give the Thursday lecture at First Church. That evening he dined with Governor Belcher, then on the following day took the ferry to Charlestown, where he preached to yet another huge congregation of hysterical people. The disturbances during Whitefield's visit to Boston led the *Boston Evening Post* of 29 September 1740 to express relief after he left "that the Town is in a hopeful way of being restor'd to its former State of Order, Peace and Industry." This negative comment was answered by a correspondent to the *Boston Weekly News-Letter* (2 October 1740), who praised Whitefield's "Plain, Powerful, and Awakening Preaching." Those who agreed with the latter became known as "Friends of Revival," or *New Lights*. Dissenters, at first few in number, were called "Opposers," or *Old Lights*. The rift between the two factions widened rapidly.

From Boston, Whitefield extended his tour to the nearby towns of Roxbury, Marblehead, Ipswich, Newbury, and Hampton, then rode to Portsmouth, New Hampshire, and from there northeast to York in Maine, that region being then a part of Massachusetts. He preached to large audiences of all Protestant persuasions wherever he went (*GW*, 463–67).

On his triumphal return to Boston (2 October), Whitefield preached at Thomas Prince's and Joseph Sewall's Old South Church, and on Sunday, 12 October, out-of-doors to a crowd estimated at thirty thousand. Each evening, he confided his thoughts to his journal. His comments were not always favorable to the ministers whose pulpits he had preached from on their invitation. He preached against unconverted ministers and said in his journal that he "would not lay hands on [ordain] an unconverted man for ten thousand worlds" (*GW*, 470).

Whitefield, accompanied by a party of ministers and laymen, then rode west toward Northampton, preaching each day in the meetinghouses of the villages and towns along the way: Concord, Marlborough, Worcester, Leicester, Brookfield, and Cold-Spring. He spent a very busy weekend in Northampton in company with Edwards, who was somewhat skeptical of him, though impressed enough to weep all through the service (*GW*, 477). Then, on 20 October, Whitefield began his southward journey back to New York by way of the Connecticut River valley and the coastal towns of the Connecticut colony, once again preaching to large hysterical crowds of villagers and farmers along the way: Springfield, Suffield, Hartford, New Haven (where he was secretly critical of the spiritual barrenness of the ministers, professors, and tutors); then, swiftly, through Milford, Stratford, Fairfield, Newark, and Stamford in Connecticut, Rye in New York Colony, and finally, on 30 October, New York City once more.

GILBERT TENNENT'S PREACHING TOUR THROUGH NEW ENGLAND

On his arrival in the New York area, Whitefield met Gilbert Tennent again on Staten Island, and the two rode down to New Brunswick together. Along the way, Whitefield persuaded Tennent to follow up on his (Whitefield's) successes with an evangelical tour of his own to consolidate the gains. Tennent was reluctant, but after the two men had argued and prayed together, Tennent became convinced and promptly set off for Boston while

Whitefield and his companions continued on their way to Philadelphia.

WHITEFIELD'S GOOD NEWS

By then, at age twenty-five, Whitefield had become the man he was to be for the next thirty years, preaching the same message he was to reiterate in every one of his eighteen thousand or more sermons. It was a simple message, very familiar to all who heard it, theologically the same gospel that was being preached from every Protestant pulpit in both the Old and New Worlds, except for his emphasis on the terrors of hellfire and damnation. His sermons do not make inspired reading, and in fact, when they were published, both his sermons and his journals roused much more hostility than he encountered on his preaching tours. He was often tactless and blunt, and on the printed page his uncharitable comments about colleagues in the ministry did his cause much harm.

Why, then, did Whitefield arouse such hysteria in his audiences? There was very little doctrinal content in Whitefield's sermons; almost nothing for the mind, in fact. Instead, the youthful orator had the popularity now reserved for rock stars, some members of the British royal family, and film celebrities. He was fair-skinned and reasonably handsome, though rather fat, with deep blue eyes (one of which was askew, allegedly because of childhood measles). He was also very youthful (as were all of the revivalist preachers); a man with a ready wit. He was a brilliant conversationalist with a rollicking sense of humor. Whitefield was particularly attractive to young people of both sexes, as well as to children.

Whitefield, if he had been a political figure, could easily have become a dictator. The emotional appeal of his preaching was intense; his expressions spontaneous. He did not speak from manuscript or notes, but always as he thought the Holy Spirit moved him. He was what today we would call a "crowd-pleaser," a demagogue able to manipulate vast numbers of people with the dramatic skills of the most talented of actors. We need only recall the effects Adolf Hitler had on the Nuremberg Rallies to appreciate what the charismatic Whitefield was able to achieve. Even the young Benjamin Franklin was thrilled by him, rationalist though he was. Franklin writes, "His delivery . . . was so improv'd by frequent repetitions that every accent, every emphasis, every modulation of voice, was so perfectly well turn'd and well plac'd, that without being interested in the subject, one could not help being pleas'd with the discourse."[12]

Whitefield had no interest in theology, philosophy, or abstract thought of any kind. He has been called a Calvinist, but he never read *The Institutes of the Christian Religion.* Instead, he insisted that he believed in predestination because he had been taught it *personally* by Jesus Christ in the Gospel. He was never a biblical scholar in the sense that he studied commentaries, or was an expert in exegesis. It was rather that the Bible was so deeply familiar to him that passages of Scripture constantly impressed themselves on his mind. He took these to be special revelations, and on that account, to his distress, he was sometimes accused of being an Antinomian. This he was not. He subscribed to all thirty-nine articles of the *Book of Common Prayer,* and accepted the disciplines of the Church of England. However, he considered himself on such intimate terms with the divine that he was constantly moved by the Holy Spirit. He was very Christocentric: he always felt that Christ was with him in everything he thought, felt, and did. "What think ye of the Christ? If Jesus Christ be not the very God of very God, I would never preach the gospel of Christ again."[13] The essence of his message was that "Jesus lives and reigns" and his goal was to be the instrument of the Holy Spirit whereby his unregenerate listeners were convicted of sin and born again.[14]

Tennent was no Whitefield. However, he was welcomed in December 1740, though with some reservations, by the Boston clergy and laity, Chauncy excepted. The latter regarded him as "an awkward Imitator of Mr. Whitefield, and too often turned off his Hearers with mere Stuff, which he uttered with Spirit more bitter and uncharitable than you easily imagine."[15]

Unlike Whitefield, Tennent shouted to his listeners that they were all *"Damned! Damned! Damned!"* His voice was harsh, and, in his case, spontaneous preaching was not accompanied by nice manners. To make matters worse, it was the worst winter in memory and those who came to hear Tennent's hellfire and brimstone threats had to struggle through mountains of snow to get there and hear his "beastly brayings."[16]

In consequence, those Bostonians who, like Chauncy, had been discreet about broadcasting their doubts concerning Whitefield felt no such inhibitions about denouncing Tennent. Timothy Cutler, an Anglican vicar, called him "a monster! Impudent and noisy!"[17] A letter in *The Boston Weekly Post-Boy* of 12 January

1741 wondered why he was there at all: "was not the Reason of your travelling so many hundred Miles to preach the Gospel in this Place, founded upon the Insufficiency of the Ministers here for their Office? Why travel so far in such a rigorous Season to preach the Gospel, if the Gospel was really preach'd by the Ministers here?"

More than a few critics in Boston took Tennent to task for deserting his own congregation. Most disapproved of itinerancy on principle. However, some liked him, but even then with reservations. Thomas Prince found him "free, gentle," but even he thought that the visitor from New Jersey "seemed to have no regard to please the eyes of his hearers with agreeable gesture, nor their ears with delivery, nor their fancy with language."[18]

Tennent followed Whitefield's route from Boston to Northampton, then down the Connecticut River valley, and from thence to New York once more, arriving in early March. Everywhere he left divided congregations in his wake. The controversies intensified when Whitefield's *Journal* was published in 1741, without his prior knowledge or permission. Ministers and laity who had welcomed him so warmly the year before discovered how uncharitably he had regarded them. For instance, in the entry for 29 October 1740, he was unkind enough to write, "I think the ministers preaching almost universally by note, is a mark that they have, in a great measure, lost the old spirit of preaching. . . . [I]t is a symptom of the decay of religion, when reading sermons becomes fashionable where *extempore* preaching did once almost universally prevail" (*GW*, 483). "As for the Universities, I believe it may be said their Light is become Darkness, Darkness that may be felt, and is complained of by the most godly Ministers."[19]

No doubt not a little of the resentment felt was because Whitefield had expressed none of this while he was in New England. The publication of the *Journal* was not a wise move for Whitefield's supporters, and did much to undo the effect he had achieved by his preaching. As Gaustad asserts, in the end, the printed word had more effect than the spoken. The faculty members of Harvard and Yale were, of course, incensed, as were the clergy when Whitefield had the temerity to remark that most "do not experimentally know Christ." Chauncy wrote a friend in Edinburgh, "What was the great Good this Gentleman was the instrument of?"[20]

The Anglican vicar Timothy Cutler of Boston, in a letter to a colleague in England, deplored the "confusion and disturbance occasioned by him: the divisions of families, neighborhoods, and towns; the contrariety of husbands and wives; the undutifulness of children and servants; the quarrels among the teachers; the disorders of the night; the intermission of labour and business; the neglect of husbandry and the gathering of the harvest."[21]

Whitefield returned to Savannah in December of 1740, and left for England on 18 January 1741, not to return until 1744. The Awakening was then left in the hands of the colonial itinerants, of which the most radical was James Davenport.

6

The Mad Enthusiast

Aᴌᴛʜᴏᴜɢʜ Wʜɪᴛᴇғɪᴇʟᴅ ᴀɴᴅ Tᴇɴɴᴇɴᴛ ꜱᴛɪʀʀᴇᴅ ᴍᴜᴄʜ ᴄᴏɴᴛʀᴏᴠᴇʀꜱʏ in New England and the Middle Colonies because of their attacks against unconverted ministers, they did not make the revival completely disreputable. Instead, they caused factionalism, pitting Friends of Revival against Opposers. James Davenport of Stamford, Connecticut, however, caused such acrimonious dispute in New England that the Friends of Revival (or New Lights) split into proponents of experiential religion who remained within the established churches, and those who separated and founded independent congregations. In Connecticut and eastern Long Island the latter formed what they called "strict congregational" churches after the Awakening, the term "strict" referring to their reversion to the predestinarianism of the Cambridge Platform. As the chief denouncer of the unconverted clergy and the founder (at least indirectly) of Strict Congregationalism, Davenport is consequently a very significant figure in the Great Awakening. This was fully acknowledged by Joseph Tracy, whose history of the revival was written on its centennial. He discussed Davenport in considerable detail. Contemporary historians such as Perry Miller, Leonard Trinterud, and Edwin Gaustad have devoted some space to him, but not nearly as much as he deserves. To his contemporaries, he was the villain who destroyed the Great Awakening and was therefore exceedingly important. Davenport, in turn, involves another figure, David Ferris. The latter was a divinity student who was older than most of his classmates at Yale, and had great impact on a group of whom Davenport was a member. Since Ferris became a Quaker, and had shown tendencies in that direction before going to Yale, the radical phase of the Great Awakening had its origins in a kind of informal Antinomianism which was akin to that of the more radical of the Quakers.

JAMES DAVENPORT: EARLY LIFE

James Davenport was born in Stamford, Connecticut, in 1717.[1] His great-grandfather was John Davenport, the founder of the New Haven Colony. James Davenport's grandfather and father, both named John, were Puritan pastors who were highly regarded for their strict observance of Puritan belief and customs. James Davenport's father was born in Boston in 1668, ordained in 1691, refused a call to be assistant pastor at Easthampton, Long Island (originally founded by migrants from New Haven Colony), taught for a year in a grammar school, and then accepted a call to the Puritan church in Stamford, Connecticut. This town was within what had been the old New Haven Colony.[2] John Davenport was very learned, especially in Greek and Hebrew, and occasionally read his Scripture lessons from the pulpit in the original tongues.[3] He was married twice. From his first marriage he had five daughters (Abigail, Sarah, Martha, Elizabeth, and Theodora) and two sons, John and Deodate. Little Theodora died in 1712 at the age of nine, but the other children all survived, very unusual for the time. All of the surviving daughters married pastors, most of whom became lifelong friends of his son from his second marriage, James. Sarah, for instance, married Eleazar Wheelock, the founder of Dartmouth College in New Hampshire, who in his younger years was a missionary to the Native Americans at a time when most Puritans regarded them as subhuman vermin, and rejoiced when they were decimated by disease or war. Abigail Davenport married a Reverend Stephen Williams of Long Meadow, Massachusetts, in 1718. He was a lifelong friend of James. Martha Davenport married a Puritan pastor in 1733, the Reverend Gaylord of Wilton, Connecticut. Both John and Deodate became farmers near Stamford.[4]

From John Davenport's second marriage came James and his full brother Abraham, who spent his life in Stamford. In later years, Abraham became a judge of great renown and, after the Revolution, a member of the state legislature.[5] Because the Davenport family was one of the most distinguished in Connecticut, James was treated more leniently than he might have been save for his family connections. As mentioned, contemporary critics blamed his radicalism on David Ferris, who they said corrupted a number of young divinity students, Davenport being one.

DAVID FERRIS

Ferris was born in a farm family near New Milford in 1707. During the revival of 1727 (following an earthquake), Ferris had a religious experience while following the plow in a melancholy mood of spiritual distress.

On a certain day, in this season of despair and in deep distress, I concluded to leave my native land and go into some foreign country, to spend the residue of my days; where I purposed to remain unknown and that none of my relations or acquaintances should know what was become of me. Being, in my own apprehension, a poor, lost reprobate creature, I was not willing to remain at home, to be a disgrace to my relations and country people. This was a day of deepest affliction and distress that I had known. Toward evening, as I followed the plough, my attention was arrested, as it were, by a still small voice saying, "The blood of Jesus Christ, his son, cleanseth from sin." But I put it by; saying in my heart, "It is too late; there has been a day wherein I might have been cleansed; but, alas! I have let it pass over my head forever." Some time after this, (perhaps half an hour) while I was musing on what land I should flee to, the same words passed through my mind again, with more authority than before, and commanded my attention rather more closely than they had done; but I again put them by, concluding that I had lost all right to apply them to myself. . . . In the meantime my sorrow and anxiety increased so that I was not able to support it, or go on with my business. But while I was still musing, the same words unsought for, and unexpectedly passed through my mind with greater power and authority than at any time before, "The blood of Jesus Christ, his son, cleanseth us from all sin." At the sound of them my soul leaped for joy. I felt that a door of hope was opened, and said in my heart "If all sin why not mine?" Then a living hope sprang in my soul. I saw the arms of mercy open to receive me and the way cleared before me as a road through the thicket. The Holy Spirit, that blessed teacher, with whom I had formerly been favored but had forsaken, was now restored to direct and instruct me in the way to peace and rest. . . . I do not know that there was one moment, whilst I was awake, for the space of nearly two years, in which I could not sing living praises to him who liveth forever and ever. No losses, crosses or disappointments did, in any degree disturb me; at least not perceptibly, either to myself or others; for my delight was in objects very different from anything this world can give, or take away. I dwelt as on the mount, out of my enemy's reach and, apparently out of danger from any evil. Here I hoped to remain all the days of my life, and that I never should be moved.[6]

After his religious experience, the world seemed to Ferris to be a "panorama of sham and vanity" spread at his feet. He made new like-minded friends, and they joined the church at New Milford.[7] Soon after, however, Ferris and his friends were tried for heresy by ministers from New Milford and the surrounding parishes. During the trial Ferris freely admitted that his beliefs were indeed like those of the Quakers, though he averred that he knew little about the sect.[8] The pastoral judges convicted him. According to Daniel Boardman, a classmate of Ferris, the latter was dismissed from membership in the New Milford church for calling the local minister and his congregation "jungle beasts."[9] As an anonymous correspondent wrote Chauncy at the time, Ferris professed to having attained both moral and spiritual perfection, and to having not sinned at all since his conversion. Particularly significant was his insistence that every random thought that occurred to him was a special revelation.[10]

According to Timothy Allen's letter to Chauncy:

> David Ferris, one of the New-Milford Quakers, came to New-Haven in the year 1729, and was admitted into College about June, or July, in that Year; pretending to have forsaken his quakerish and enthusiastick Tenets: But all was false, for though he at first did not think proper to own them, yet he endeavour'd to lay a Foundation to propagate them, and instil his Poison into all as far as he could; which he did by acting under a Shew of Zeal and Sanctity, whereby some were ensnared by him, who have since been the Propagators of his Doctrines and Tenets. . . . For when he found his Mind strongly engaged in any Thing, although inconsistent with Reason or Revelation, yet he would confidently affirm Those Impulses to be from the Spirit of GOD. . . . [Those] who having mixed something of Devotion with their mellancholly Tempers, became his Admirers. . . . They endeavor'd to imitate him in all Things as far as they could. Mr. Davenport, Whelock [sic], Pomroy [sic], and others, were those who liv'd with this Ferris most familiarly, and have since divulg'd his Errors, and fill'd Places where they have preach'd with the Superstitions and groundless Opinions, they learn'd from him, who was their Father and Dictator as to their Belief.[11]

Yale College Years

At Yale, therefore, Ferris, who was in his twenties, dominated a small circle of devout youths which included Timothy Allen (Chauncy's informant), James Davenport, Benjamin Pomeroy, and Jonathan Barber, all of whom later became radical New Lights. Pomeroy, on graduation, accepted a call to the church at Hebron and later joined Davenport as an itinerant preacher. Allen, who accepted a call to Westhaven, was later tried for Antinomianism, rejecting the authority of the Scriptures, and for his belief in inner illumination, all typical of the more ardent of the Quakers. He was also a close lifelong friend of Davenport, and later accepted appointment as head of the Shepherd's Tent, a school for revivalist preachers and exhorters which he and Davenport founded.[12] According to Allen, Ferris returned to his "Quaker friends" in New Milford in March, 1732.[13]

Eleazar Wheelock was not one of Davenport's friends at Yale,[14] but became so after his marriage to the latter's half-sister Sarah in 1734. Wheelock warmly encouraged experiential religion, and was a Friend of Revival during the Great Awakening, but he did not share the radicalism of Ferris and his disciples. He later devoted himself to missionary work among the Native Americans, and after years of service as pastor at Lebanon, moved north to New Hampshire, where, as we have said, he founded Dartmouth College. This was one of the earliest missions to First Nation peoples in New England.

After his graduation from Yale at the age of seventeen (the youngest on record), Davenport remained in New Haven to pursue his theological studies further under the tutelage of the rector. We have a published letter from this time which he wrote to Stephen Williams in 1734. In it he wrote in part: "I find continual supplies of grace and strength from above, that I maintain a close walk with God; divine wisdom and prudence to behave aright to and before others, so as to give no offence."[15]

At this time he suffered the onset of an affliction described as a "cancry humour" on his leg (cancer according to a 1934 source,[16] but more likely an incurable ulcer) and recurrent attacks of the fever which was to plague him at intervals for the rest of his life. For several months he stayed at the home of the Reverend Jared Eliot, who, like many Puritan divines, was a physician both of the soul and of the body, and the progress of the ailment was halted. Good Puritan that he was, Davenport regarded this as a special providence.[17]

After his recovery, Davenport returned to New Haven, finished his studies with the rector of Yale, and was licensed to preach. He was ordained in the New Haven church. He at first refused calls to Hopewell (now Pennington), Connecticut and Maidenhead (now Lawrenceville), New Jersey.[18] In October 1738 he accepted a call to the Puritan church in Southold, Long Island.[19] He was then twenty-one. Joshua Hempstead, the Justice of the Peace of New London, attended a service conducted by Davenport at Southold not long after the latter became minister there and made no adverse comments about him.[20]

Southold, located on Little Peconic Bay on the westernmost of two peninsulas at the end of eastern Long Island, was founded in 1638 as part of the New Haven Colony. It had a tiny population. Though politically part of New York, eastern Long Island had been settled by Connecticut Yankees and their closest ties were with the people of the Connecticut Colony across Long Island Sound. They had little contact with the predominantly Dutch settlements of western Long Island, and almost none with faraway New York.

The eastern Long Islanders were highly conservative people of little education who farmed, fished, and hunted whales. Near Southold, on the same peninsula, were hamlets such as Oyster Ponds and Old Man's and across Peconic Bay, on the eastern peninsula, were the villages of Easthampton, Bridgehampton, and Southampton. Only the most primitive roads linked the eastern Long Island communities with the chiefly Dutch communities of Nassau County in western Long Island.

JONATHAN BARBER AND JAMES DAVENPORT ON LONG ISLAND

When Davenport took up his charge, his former classmate Jonathan Barber was minister of the congregation at Oyster Ponds (now Orient) on the tip of the peninsula. Some time In March 1740 Barber became obsessed by a scriptural passage: "For the vision is yet for an appointed time, but at the end it shall speak, and not lie: though it tarry, wait for it; because it will surely come, it will not tarry" (Habakkuk 2:3). Barber took it to be a special revelation. He sat up most of Saturday night and the following morning, his mind wholly preoccupied by the passage, desperately trying to interpret its meaning in terms of his present situation. At random, he flipped through his Bible and pointed to a passage. It was the thirteenth verse of Psalm 102: "Thou shalt arise, and have mercy upon Zion: for the time to favour her, yea, the set time, is come." He then slipped into a trance and emerged from it barely in time to stagger to the meetinghouse and struggle through the service.[21]

During the next few days he made calls on his parishioners and told them of his experience, insisting that it had been like Ezekiel and Daniel fainting in the presence of God. He said that it was a sign that a great work of the Holy Spirit was about to begin in Oyster Ponds. Then, obeying the gospel command (Matthew 10:9–10), Barber set off on foot, taking no money with him or change of clothing. He walked to Southold where he preached in a highly excited way to Davenport's congregation about his experience.

As they talked together, the two young ministers convinced themselves that it was a time of crisis. The Day of Judgment was at hand, and there was urgent need to save sinners. The Holy Spirit was using Barber in his work; Davenport hoped that he would be called as well. Both became deeply engrossed as they searched for signs, shared spiritual confidences, and sought hidden meaning in the random religious thoughts and scriptural passages that came to mind.

Barber then apparently returned to Oyster Ponds, where he ranted to his congregation during divine service, uttering whatever came first to mind. Another scriptural passage became fixed in his consciousness: "The Lord hath been mindful of us: he will bless us; he will bless the house of Israel; he will bless the house of Aaron. He will bless them that fear the Lord both small and great." (Psalm 115:12–13). He interpreted this passage as a call to the elect to be ready for the Day of the Lord. After this, Barber returned again to Southold, where he preached, exhorted, and testified there, warning that the Day of Judgment was at hand.[22]

He then went on from village to village throughout the neighborhood, preaching in all of the local parish churches. Everywhere he went he declared that he had laid aside study and premeditation, and that when he spoke, it was not he but the Holy Spirit who was speaking through him. He declared that he did not know from one moment to the next what he would say, since he was continuously receiving messages from the Holy Spirit. Moreover, he said, God immediately revealed to him the spiritual state of anyone he met, so that with complete certainty he knew who was saved and who had been passed over. Preaching this message to every congregation in the neighborhood of Southold, and apparently to every individual and group whom he encountered, he wandered from hamlet to hamlet until he found himself in Old Man's, forty-five miles from Oyster Ponds. Here, according to a letter written to Charles Chauncy by an anonymous friend on Long Island, the Holy Spirit abandoned Barber.[23]

He loitered there for months, becoming "fat and ragged," probably accepting board and lodging from the locals, and refusing either to preach or to go back to Oyster Ponds. When some of his parishioners came and tried to bring him home, he insisted that the Holy Spirit had led him there and intended him to stay where he was until he received further instructions. Near the end of that summer, the Holy Spirit apparently finally gave him orders to return to Oyster Ponds. Hearing there that Whitefield was in the Carolinas, Barber had a special revelation which told him that the Evangelist actually was on his way to Newport, Rhode Island. Barber took ship and sailed there immediately, and had his prophecy fulfilled when Whitefield, indeed, arrived not long after.[24]

Whitefield was very impressed with Barber. The latter then accompanied the Grand Itinerant on his evangelical wanderings, which took them first to Boston. Later, as mentioned earlier, Whitefield appointed Barber religious superintendent of the orphanage he had founded in Bethesda, Georgia.

DAVENPORT SEES THE LIGHT

Soon after Barber's second visit to Southold, Davenport assembled his congregation, ranted at them for twenty-four hours, and then collapsed. No doubt his congregation was in a state of collapse as well. When he recovered, Davenport followed Tennent's example and made calls on all his parishioners in which he demanded religious confessions of them. He called those of whom he approved "brethren," and he called those of whom he did not approve "neighbors." In this, he of course attributed his decision to the Holy Spirit. There were many "neighbors," very probably a majority. The numbers of "brethren" may have increased somewhat after he predicted that a mentally ill woman who was "distracted and dumb" would "be delivered and recover her speech" on a day he named as a result of his fasting and praying over her. "On the very Day [predicted], the Woman died, without having spoken a Word, or discovering any Signs of being in her right Mind." Davenport maintained that his prediction was accurate in that "[s]he was delivered . . . by being received to Heaven."[25]

In November 1740, following his evangelizing in New England, George Whitefield arrived in Philadelphia and began revival work in the Middle Colonies. Even in the isolated hamlets of eastern Long Island there was much talk about Whitefield's triumphs both there and in New England. Abandoning his parish, Davenport rode off on horseback to meet the Grand Itinerant in New York with several of his "brethren." In his journal Whitefield wrote: "Several New York friends came hither to meet me. I talked with them on the way, of the things of God." (*GW*, 483).[26] They all had supper at the home of a Mr. Noble, one of Whitefield's admirers:

> After supper, the Lord filled my heart, and enabled me to wrestle with Him in prayer for New York inhabitants, and my own friends. To add

to my comfort, the Lord brought my dear brother Davenport from Long Island. (*GW*, 483–84)

In late 1740, therefore, the Evangelists, except for Jonathan Edwards, all came together for the first time, and the separate revivals flowed together in the high tide of the Great Awakening.

THE EVANGELISTS TRAVEL TOGETHER

The Evangelists and their traveling companions then made their way to Staten Island, where Whitefield, who had just returned from his New England tour, preached to a huge, fervently excited throng of farm folk. A young man in great distress rushed to him begging to be converted. An elderly man told him "how God had brought [him] from darkness to light." Whitefield later wrote in his journal that he "was much refreshed with the sight of Mr. Gilbert Tennent." The latter had been recently bereaved, his wife having just died. "Yet," according to Whitefield, "he was enabled with great calmness to preach her funeral sermon, whilst the corpse was lying before him." Her last illness and death did not deter his evangelical zeal. "Since his wife's decease," Whitefield wrote, "Mr. Tennent has been in the West Jerseys and Maryland, and told me how remarkably God had worked by his ministry in many places" (*GW*, 485–86).

While on Staten Island Whitefield preached to three or four hundred folk from a wagon. From there he and Tennent went to Newark, ten miles away, where Whitefield again preached; then to Baskinridge. Whitefield wrote in his journal:

> I found Mr. Davenport had been preaching to the congregation, according to appointment. It consisted of about three thousand people. I had not discoursed long when, in every part of the congregation, some one or other began to cry out, and almost all were melted into tears. A little boy, about eight years of age, wept as though his heart would break. Mr. Cross took him up into the waggon, which so affected me, that I broke from my discourse, and told the people that, since old professors were not concerned, God, out of an infant's mouth, was perfecting praise; and the little boy should preach to them. As I was going away, I asked the little boy what he cried for? He answered, his sins. I then asked what he wanted? He answered, Christ. (*GW*, 487)

From Baskinridge, Whitefield, Tennent, Davenport, and their companions rode south to New Brunswick. Whitefield preached

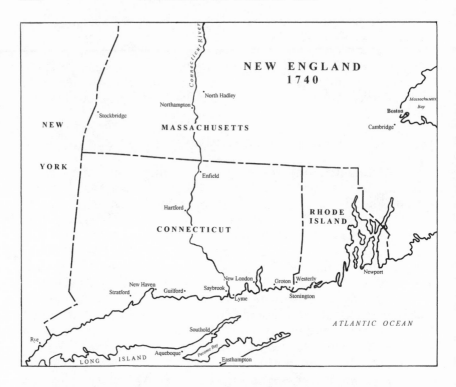

in Tennent's meetinghouse there with the usual enthusiastic response he evoked wherever he spoke that year.

Whitefield wanted to go to Freehold, the late John Tennent's parish, and also to nearby Shrewsbury. However, William Tennent, Jr., arrived whom Whitefield "wanted to consult about his brother Gilbert going to Boston. He [Gilbert Tennent] (diffident of himself) was at first unwilling, urging his inability for so great a work; but afterwards, being convinced it was the Divine Will, he said, 'The will of the Lord be done'"(*GW,* 488–89). The Harvard tutor Daniel Rogers, who had much to do with persuading Tennent to make the evangelical tour, was to accompany him.

> God has been pleased to work upon his heart by my ministry. I cannot but think he will be a burning and shining light. It being the last time we should be together for a long season, we thought it best to spend some time in prayer together. Mr. Gilbert was our mouth to God. Many were greatly affected. About eleven o'clock we parted in tears, but with a full assurance that we should see and hear great things before we met again. I then went on towards Trenton, in company with Mr. Davenport and some others. (*GW,* 489)

(Whitefield wrote nothing more about Tennent's personal loss, nor expressed concern about who was caring for his motherless children.) After parting company with Tennent, Whitefield, Davenport, and the others rode on to Trenton on Saturday, 8 November, where Whitefield preached in the morning "though not to a very large or much affected auditory" (*GW*, 489).

After dinner, Whitefield, Davenport, and their companions set off for Philadelphia. On the way, they had problems crossing two rain-swollen creeks: "In one of them two of my fellow travellers, in all probability, must have perished, had not a woman cried out, and bid us stop. A man who had been reached by my ministry, hearing my voice, came and swam our horses over the other creek, and conducted us safely over a very narrow bridge"(*GW*, 489). Around eight that evening they reached Philadelphia safely. Here, the next day, which was Sunday, Whitefield found that a tabernacle had been built for him in his absence: "It is a hundred feet long, and seventy feet broad. . . . Both in the morning and evening, God's glory filled the house. It was never preached in before. The roof is not yet up, but the people raised a convenient pulpit, and boarded the bottom. . . . Great was the joy of most of the hearers when they saw me; but some still mocked" (*GW*, 489–90). Young Benjamin Franklin was in the congregation, and wrote later, "The multitudes of all sects and denominations that attended his sermons were enormous."[27] Despite the implication in Whitefield's journal that the tabernacle was built solely for his use, Franklin makes it clear that "both house and ground were vested in trustees, expressly for the use of any preacher of any religious persuasion who might desire to say something to the people at Philadelphia. . . . [E]ven if the Mufti of Constantinople were to send a missionary to preach Mohammedanism to us, he would find a pulpit at his service."[28]

On Sunday, 15 November, Whitefield preached to a large throng in a snowfall. Whitefield and Davenport then separated. Whitefield rode south to Savannah; Davenport made his way to Stamford, Connecticut, where he encountered opposition when he preached in his home church. But "the Lord gave a poor vile worm wonderful supplies of grace, strength and courage."[29]

DAVENPORT'S ITINERANCY IN LONG ISLAND AND CONNECTICUT

Soon after returning to Southold one of Davenport's "brethren," a layman by the name of Daniel Tuthill, urged him to leave his parish once more and continue his evangelism. Tuthill became Davenport's assistant, the first of a group of laymen whom the latter recruited as exhorters. Tuthill accompanied Davenport on all of his subsequent evangelical tours.

Both Davenport and Barber had adopted the practice of flipping through the pages of their Bibles, pointing at a passage at random, and then applying it as a divine directive. This was called "sortilege," the casting of lots with the Bible to secure a specific divine direction. It was the form of divination that John Wesley resorted to when he decided to publish his sermon on "Free Grace." Whitefield said of sortilege: "I am no friend to casting lots; but I believe, on extraordinary occasion, when things can be determined no other way, GOD, if appealed to, and waited on by prayer and fasting, will answer by lot now as well as formerly." [30]

Many of Davenport's parishioners were disaffected with him because of his absence. However, not long after his return to Southold, Davenport flipped the pages of his Bible and pointed, by chance, to 1 Samuel 14:6–14, the story of Jonathan, the son of Saul and his armor-bearer, who attacked the Philistines and slew twenty of them.

The story meant to Davenport that he and Tuthill must go to Easthampton on the "yonder side" of Peconic Bay from Southold and convert exactly twenty unregenerates. The pair waded knee-deep through the snow a distance of fifty-three miles by land. When they reached Easthampton, Davenport stalked into the church, and pronounced the aged pastor, Nathaniel Huntting, unconverted, a blind guide who was leading his parishioners to perdition. Exactly twenty members of the congregation responded to Davenport's exhortations, left the church, and from then on held devotions of their own in private homes under lay leadership.[31]

Early in the summer of 1741 Davenport heard the Holy Spirit again. He rallied his "armour-bearer" and several other lay exhorters from Southold, and on 14 July set sail across Long Island Sound to the village of Stonington on the Connecticut shore.[32] He found the people there in a high state of religious excitement. Whitefield and Tennent had passed through Connecticut only a few months before, and there had been revivals in nearby Groton, Lyme, Norwich, New London, and Preston, as well as in Stonington. Local pastors such as Jonathan Parsons of Lyme, Benjamin Pomeroy of Hebron, Eleazar Wheelock of Lebanon, Joseph Bellamy of Bethlehem, and John Graham of Southbury had taken up the task of consolidating the gains made by the itinerants in their own parishes and in neighboring rural districts.

Davenport immediately pronounced the pastor of the Stonington church unconverted. He was warmly welcomed by some of the New Lights in the congregation. Many of them were impressed by his preaching. Other Friends of Revival were not. Davenport and his companions stayed a few days, and made about a hundred converts, eight of them Indians. After a brief side trip to Westerly, Rhode Island, he set off for New London, leaving the pastor with a badly divided congregation.[33]

In New London he preached three sermons which threw the whole town into a religious frenzy. His services were the most extravagant displays of histrionics the townspeople had ever seen. Joshua Hempstead reported:

> Divers women were terrified and cried out exceedingly. When Mr. Davenport had dismissed the congregation some went out and others stayed; he then went into the broad alley, which was much crowded and there screamed out, "Come to Christ! Come to Christ! Come Away! Come Away!" Then he went into the third pew on the women's side, and kept there, sometimes singing, sometimes praying; he and his companions all taking their turns; and the women fainting and in hysterics. This confusion continued until 10:00 at night and then he went off singing through the streets.[34]

He left a badly divided congregation and a hard-pressed minister, Eliphalet Adams. In order to quiet the furor, Old Light ministers came to his aid from surrounding parishes.[35]

From New London proper, Davenport and his band then went to the north parish, where he demanded that Pastor Jewett give him a full account of his religious experiences. When the latter refused, Davenport promptly pronounced him unconverted even though he was a New Light, and had caused a revival in the parish the year before with his own evangelical preaching.[36] As this example shows, Davenport attacked New Lights as fiercely as he did Old, making his impressions the basis of deciding whether or not anyone he met was a regenerate. Those who hesitated to give him a testimonial of their religious experiences were always branded "blind guides" and "wolves in Sheep's cloathing," who were leading their congregations straight to perdition.[37]

Charles Chauncy cites a description by a witness in Connecticut of a typical sermon of Davenport at this time:

> At lenth, he turn'd his Discourse to others, and with the *utmost Strength* of his Lungs addressed himself to the Congregation, under

these and such-like Expressions; viz. You poor unconverted Creatures, in the Seats, in the Pews, in the Galleries, I wonder you don't drop into Hell! It would not surprise me, I should not wonder at it, if I should see you drop down *now, this minute* into Hell. You Pharisees, Hypocrites, *now, now, now,* you are going right into the Bottom of Hell. . . . Then he came out of the Pulpit, and stripped off his upper Garments, and got into the Seats, and leapt up and down some time, and clapt his Hands, and *cried out* in those Words, the War goes on, the Fight goes on, the Devil goes down, the Devil goes down; and then betook himself to *stamping* and *screaming* most dreadfully.[38]

Davenport then made his way to Groton, where he met two sympathizers, Andrew Croswell and John Owen. They were among the few clergymen whom he accepted as converted during this crusade. At some of the outdoor meetings held in Groton, Davenport preached to as many as a thousand people. His service of 23 July went on from sundown until two in the morning. Some of his audience stayed all night under the trees, and others slept in the meetinghouse.[39] Croswell was later to become Davenport's sole defender.

On Sunday, 24 July 1741, Davenport and his companions were back in Stonington. Nathaniel Eels, the pastor of the west parish, refused him use of the pulpit. Davenport pronounced him unconverted, then preached under the trees near the meetinghouse, warning Eels' parishioners that their minister was a "carnal" man, an unconverted blind guide, and that their souls were in peril if they did not leave him and form a true church of the converted. He spent the remainder of July in the vicinity of Groton, and then went on to Lyme. There two pastors, George Griswold and Jonathan Parsons, Friends of Revival, received him with warm cordiality. Davenport accepted both as regenerates. On his arrival he seems to have preached with restraint, and to have behaved with discretion. At those times Griswold found it hard to reconcile the profound and scholarly sermons with the man's reputation for incoherent ranting. However, Davenport soon reverted to his more fervent style, causing Griswold to regret having invited him to preach from his pulpit. He was disturbed by his "strange methods to scare people into fits."[40] He was, however, pleased with Davenport's success among the neighboring Indians, twenty of whom became converts.

The other local minister, Jonathan Parsons, agreed with Davenport's objections to unconverted ministers, but did not think they should be denounced publicly. (Both ministers found it hard to reconcile his usually generous nature with his arrogant way of judging his colleagues.) Parsons also took exception to Davenport's encouragement of schisms and separatism in the congregations he visited.[41]

While In Lyme, the story of Joshua and the walls of Jericho (Joshua 6:1–17) occurred to Davenport as another special revelation. Drawing analogies from this biblical story, Davenport saw himself as Joshua, and his little band as the wandering Israelites on their way to the promised land. To him, the Connecticut River was the Jordan, and the town of Saybrook on the other side was Jericho; the unregenerates were the walls, and William Hart, the unconverted pastor, was the king. Like Joshua, Davenport sent spies ahead of him to prepare the way for his coming: in his case, two of his traveling companions. Once he was in Saybrook, he thought the walls would collapse when he blew his ram's horn of sound doctrine. As with Joshua, he was sure the Lord would do his wonderful work in seven days.

There was at first a great feeling of anticipation in Saybrook when Davenport and his band rode in. Even the children eagerly greeted him. Some became so excited that they fainted. Immediately on arrival he strode into the parsonage and demanded that the local pastor, William Hart, allow him to preach from his pulpit. When Hart questioned him on his beliefs and behavior, Davenport freely admitted that he "would have Men go ten or twenty Miles to hear a converted Minister, or even set up private Meetings among themselves, rather than attend Worship under their own Ministers, being unconverted; and that Parish-Bounds are nothing; and that himself would go ten Miles on Foot to hear a private Brother rather than an unconverted Minister." He then rose, smiled, and cried out, "Come, let us go forth without the Camp, after the Lord Jesus, bearing his Reproach. . . . O this is pleasant to suffer Reproach for the blessed Jesus! Sweet Jesus!"[42]

A delegation of ministers from neighboring towns went to Davenport's lodging the next day and demanded to speak with him. Davenport was upstairs at the time, and sent word that he would see them when he was ready. He came down a few minutes later and launched into a lengthy monologue, calling them "Wolves in Sheep's cloathing, blind Guides, enemies to GOD and his Cause in the World, and Persecutors of CHRIST in the Person of himself his Servant."[43] He then fell on his knees and prayed for their conversion. At the end of this display the bemused pastors told him that they had come to demand an explanation of his behavior. He responded that he had no more time to give them, as he was about to begin a meeting. However, if later on it would appear to be "for God's glory for him to spend Time that might be employed in discoursing on these Matters," he would speak to them, but, if not, he would spend the time praying for Hart's conversion.[44]

Up to now, Davenport had been drawing large crowds of enthusiastic supporters. In Saybrook, he did not. His outdoor meetings were poorly attended, and at the end of the week he had failed to bring the walls of Jericho thundering down. "[H]e had the Mortification to tarry his Days, and was obliged, at last, to leave the Walls standing more firmly than when he came to demolish them."[45] As elsewhere, he left a divided congregation and contentious bickering. However, most citizens had stood loyally by their own pastor and had not been swayed by the visitors.

Undaunted, Davenport and his band rode off for New Haven, stopping at villages along the way to preach and exhort, arriving there in early September. Joseph Noyes, the pastor, was an Old Light, an Opposer. New Haven was also the home of Yale, whose faculty repudiated the revivalists and discouraged students from attending their meetings. Noyes assembled the leading citizens of the town at a meeting to which Davenport was invited because of both his great-grandfather's reputation and his own reputation for piety. When Davenport arrived, he fell on his knees and prayed, to the embarrassment of those present, most of whom were paying him little attention in any case. According to Charles Chauncy's informants, who included the Rector of Yale, Thomas Clap: "some declar'd to Mr. DAVENPORT, that his praying in that Manner was a taking the Name of GOD in vain: And so the Assembly broke up in great Consternation."[46] Davenport promptly labeled Noyes unconverted. Noyes refused him his pulpit, and dismissed him with disgust. Nevertheless, Davenport preached to small groups in the town, with some success. He and his friends then returned to Southold to spend the winter.

The results of Davenport's first itinerancy were mixed. Old Lights consistently opposed him; New Lights, however, were divided in their reactions. To William Hart, an Old Light with probable Arminian leanings, Davenport was simply arrogant. In Hart's view, salvation is attained not through crisis, but by a gradual process whereby the person is enabled to understand Scripture and to adjust his or her life more fully to God's ways. Like Hart, all Old Lights were highly offended by Davenport's aggressive denunciations of them, and alarmed by his use of lay exhorters. They ridiculed his "impulses and impressions."

A class conflict was also involved. The clergy were among the ruling elite, and enjoyed the support of the wealthier merchants and farmers. Although, unlike Massachusetts, backward Connecticut had no gentry of either town or country to speak of, there were sharp class differences present based on wealth, and, in general, affluent folk tended to be either Old Lights or else New Lights distinguished by circumspect behavior. Davenport's popularity, and, indeed, his lasting significance, lay chiefly in his stirring up of the "lower orders," poorer farmers and artisans, especially in Windham and New London counties, in what had been the old and still the poorest part of the New Haven Colony. Those who lived west of the Connecticut River tended to be more affluent, and here Davenport encountered more resistance. Worried citizens of substance were alarmed by the rabble-rouser, and discussed ways of keeping him out of the colony.

Acting on the appeal of a number of ministers, the governing body of the Connecticut Colony, the General Court, when it met in October 1741, called for a general synod in Guilford. At this synod, the assembled ministers recommended that legislation be enacted forbidding any pastors to preach in parishes other than their own without the express permission of the incumbent. It was also recommended that those from outside the colony be forbidden to preach at all. These recommendations were enacted into law by the General Court in May 1742.[47]

No sooner had these regulations come into force when Davenport and his "armour-bearers" returned to Connecticut, and were joined by Benjamin Pomeroy, Davenport's former Yale classmate. The Sheriff of Hartford and his deputy were ordered to arrest Davenport and Pomeroy and to bring them for trial before the General Court, then in session. The two Evangelists were promptly taken to Hartford and lodged in the sheriff's home to await trial.

Coming before the assembly, Davenport adopted a bizarre pose. The correspondent to the *Boston Weekly News-Letter* remarked that "his air and posture there; that inflexibility of body, that affectatious oblique reclining of the head, that elevation, or rather inversion of the eyes, that forced negligence and retirement of soul, and that uncouth shew, that motly mixture of pride and gravity wrought up to sulleness, is not easily to be described."[48] The delegates to the General Court were particularly perturbed by Davenport's terrifying apocalyptic warnings. "By pretending some extraordinary discovery and assurance of the very near approach of the end of the world; and that tho' he didn't assign the very day, yet that he then lately had it clearly open'd to him, and strongly imprest upon his mind, that in a very short time all these things will be involv'd in devouring flames." They were even more disturbed "by an indecent and affected imitation of the agony and passion of our blessed SAVIOUR; and also, by voice and gesture, of the surprize, horror and amazement of persons suppos'd to be sentenc'd to eternal misery." They were shocked by his "vehemently crying out, That he saw hell-flames slashing in their faces; and that they were now! now! dropping down to hell; and also added, Lord! Thou knowest that there are many in that gallery and in these seats, that are now dropping down to Hell! etc."[49]

He stood like a statue "till the adjournment and withdrawing of the assembly that evening; when, amid the thronging multitude (on that occasion very numerous) remov'd and moving out of the meeting house, he and Mr Pomroy took their stand upon the assent to the front door, and there exhibited a lively specimen of their flaming zeal." When the sheriff tried to take his prisoner from the courthouse, Davenport yelled, "Lord! thou knowest somebody's got hold of my sleeve, strike them! Lord, strike them—" while Pomeroy, who was also hysterical, cried out at the sheriff and his deputies, "Take heed how you do that heaven daring action! 'Tis heaven-daring presumption, to take him away! And the God of Heaven will assuredly avenge it on you! strike them, Lord, strike them!"

A mob swirled around the sheriff and his prisoners, sighing, groaning, and beating their breasts. Some rushed to attack the sheriff and his deputies, who shouted for help but got none. Still others screamed that the sheriff was in league with the devil. "The tumult rose even to an uproar." The sheriff and his men hung on to their prisoners with great difficulty and dragged them away, trailed by an excited crowd. Davenport continued to exhort, sing, and pray.[50]

On the next morning, the delegates to the General Court dismissed the charges against Pomeroy for insufficient evidence, but decided that Davenport must be mad. The *Boston Weekly News-Letter* reporter goes on to say, "Yet it further appears to this assembly that the said Davenport is under the influences of enthusiastical impressions and impulses, and thereby disturb'd in the rational faculties of his mind, and therefore to be pittied and compassionated, and not to be treated as otherwise he might be." It was decided to deport him.

Noisy mobs roamed the streets of the town that night, and it was near dawn before the commotion died down. Next morning, the local militia was called out, and, around four in the afternoon,

Davenport was marched down to the riverside under the military escort of forty musketeers, and put aboard a small vessel belonging to a Mr. Whitmore, who was under orders by the General Court to treat Davenport "with all proper care, tenderness and humanity." [51] Presumably, although they are not mentioned, his "armour-bearers" were deported as well. The ship took them back to Southold, Long Island.

THE EFFECTS OF DAVENPORT'S ITINERANCY IN CONNECTICUT

On eastern Long Island and eastern Connecticut across the Sound, Davenport had attracted large crowds of villagers and farmers, most of them uneducated rustics. In Stonington, Groton, and Lyme, for instance, there had been many who thoroughly enjoyed his vituperative attacks against the unregenerate ministers. On the other hand, Davenport's attacks against the clergy in Stonington and in Saybrook attracted few followers and aroused little interest. Since the seminary, which was later moved to New Haven and given the name of Yale College, was then in Saybrook, it is possible that there were more educated folk there than in the villages and hamlets on the other shore of the Connecticut River. There were considerable differences, moreover, between people of New London and Windham Counties, and those residing in the other coastal districts of Connecticut. These differences were of long standing, since London and Windham Counties had made up the old colony of New Haven founded by John Davenport early in the seventeenth century. The Davenport family continued to have much prestige there, and being a member of it, James was treated with considerable respect whether or not he personally inspired it.

Therefore, what appears to be chiefly important in determining which communities responded positively to the Evangelists was the level of education of the people. The rustic folk of Connecticut included few who were well read. They were much less so on average than were the people of Northampton, Massachusetts, as we have seen, which, despite its being a frontier settlement, had a fairly significant elite of educated gentry who dominated the church and local government. In the economically depressed parts of Connecticut and eastern Long Island where most people were simple folk living by subsistence agriculture or fishing, Davenport won significant followings. No doubt there were many who took delight in his attacks against unconverted ministers and church members when the latter were of the gentry.

There were few printing presses in Connecticut, and no local newspapers. The comparatively few educated people were chiefly Yale tutors and scholars, such as William Hart. In New Haven there was also an Anglican church, the members of which had been hostile to revivalism from the start. Even among the New Lights in New Haven, many were offended by Davenport's vicious message, so much so as to rouse doubts about the revival.

The educated minority of Connecticut and eastern Long Island included a few who corresponded with the editors of the *Boston Weekly News-Letter* and *Boston Weekly Post-Boy*, supplying them with detailed accounts about Davenport. After Davenport's visit to Boston, Charles Chauncy solicited accounts from ministers on Long Island and in Connecticut about him. In 1743 he published them in *Seasonable Thoughts on the State of Religion in New England,* the most complete source of documents concerning the Southold itinerant.

From these accounts it is apparent that Davenport thoroughly alarmed many people both in Connecticut and on Long Island; that they regarded him as a madman. It is also evident that Davenport was a hero to many people of the humble classes, and that he had a considerable following among them. The effect of his itinerancy on Long Island and in Connecticut was to split New Lights into two factions. One party warmly embraced revivalism but opposed attacks against unregenerate ministers, Davenport's encouragement of lay exhorters, and his fostering of separations from the established churches. The other faction delighted in Davenport's anticlericalism, preferred lay exhorters to most ministers, and withdrew from the churches to form separate congregations, which met at first in private homes.

The Old Lights had their reservations about Whitefield, were offended by Tennent, and outraged by Davenport. After Davenport's departure, opposition to the revival mounted wherever he had gone in Connecticut and on Long Island. To increasing numbers, the Awakening now seemed to be madness.

After Davenport was forcibly transported back to Southold, the excitement he had roused soon abated in Saybrook, Hartford, and New Haven, while opposition to revivalism grew. Revivalist enthusiasm continued, however, in New London, Stonington, Groton, Lyme, and the other communities of what had once been the New Haven Colony, as also in eastern Long Island, where congregations were badly divided. His own congregation of Southold, which he had split between "friends" and "neighbors," was exasperated with him, his opponents including many who were New Lights.

7

A Radical Evangelical

THE SHEPHERD'S TENT

BACK IN SOUTHOLD, AFTER HIS DEPORTATION FROM HARTFORD, DAVEN-port found, not surprisingly, that many members of his much ne-glected parish had wearied of a pastor who deserted them so often and for such long periods of time. In his absence, the congrega-tion had asked advice of neighboring ministers, and, as a result, an advisory board made up of local clergymen met with the gov-erning council of the congregation. It was decided that Davenport be put on probation and dismissed if he persisted in his itineran-cies, a remarkably lenient decision.[1] Davenport, however, was completely unrepentant. He regarded himself as the founder of a new Evangelical movement, distinct from the New Lights as well as from the Old. The center of this movement was to be the Shep-herd's Tent, a seminary for the training of lay exhorters and lay preachers.

Ministers were jealous of their status, and even the most ar-dent of New Lights, such as Whitefield and Tennent, regarded the ministry as a sacred calling, set apart, and only for those who were knowledgeable concerning theological doctrine, and prop-erly educated in Hebrew, Greek, Latin, and Theology, so as to be able to read the Scriptures in the original tongues. They were particularly insistent on candidates for the ministry being subject to the discipline of traditional preparation by properly qualified authorities. The nearest approach to less formal preparation for ministers was that of William Tennent, Sr.'s, Log College in Nes-haminy, Pennsylvania, which, indeed, was not regarded as being an adequate training school by Old Side Presbyterian ministers in the Middle Colonies. However, Tennent was actually a very learned tutor, and, as mentioned, subjected ministerial students to a rigorous course of study in the ancient languages and in the-ology so that their education was probably the equivalent of those trained at Edinburgh and other universities.

133

Davenport and Timothy Allen had conceived of a very different kind of school for a very different ministry. It is not clear when the idea came to them, or which one was the actual originator (though Allen is probably the founder), but they appear to have thought of it during the spring of 1742. The name, a biblical allusion, presumably came from the shelters where Israelite shepherds gathered to exchange views with one another, tell stories, and above all, pray together. After such meetings, they would disperse singly or in pairs to tend their sheep. Davenport and Allen wanted a seminary of sorts open to all, in which there would be prayer and exhortation, hymn-singing, and other revivalist exercises. It would be spontaneous in character, and what critics called "impulses and impressions" would be encouraged as direct experiences of the Holy Spirit. This idea was essentially anticlerical, being based on the radical Protestant concept of the priesthood of all believers held by the Anabaptists during Reformation times, and by the Antinomians, Familists, Levellers, Ranters, and Quakers during the Commonwealth era in England. Of these sects, only the Quakers had survived in the colony. At their meetings, which were held in simple houses in which there were no symbols or decorations of any kind, those moved by the Holy Spirit rose to speak, pray, or exhort. Unlike their predecessors of the mid-seventeenth century, the Friends, as they called themselves, no longer evangelized, and were distinguished for puritanical sobriety in behavior. In their midst, however, there were radicals of the older type, of whom David Ferris was one when he joined. The Shepherd's Tent may have been inspired by Ferris's Quakerism.

Richard Warch discusses the Shepherd's Tent in an article in *American Quarterly*.[2] He maintains that the proposed school arose because of profound dissatisfaction with ministerial training at Yale and Harvard. Whitefield, it will be recalled, condemned both institutions for their "darkness," as did Edwards. Warch traces the origins of the Shepherd's Tent to a remark in passing by Isaac Backus in his history of the New England Baptists: "It was impressed upon sundry minds, that they must go their way forth, and erect a *shepherd's tent* at New London to educate persons in for the ministry."[3] Warch then mentions, but makes no comment on, what is, to me, one of the most fascinating aspects of the scheme: that the school was to welcome as students not only men but "good women." At a time when, following Paul's preaching, women were supposed to keep silence in church, it was shocking enough for women to cry out during church services. It was far more astonishing that some of them intended to become itinerant lay ministers, and even more so that Allen and presumably Davenport were happy to receive them in the Shepherd's Tent.

According to Croswell, another strong supporter of the seminary idea, the program required

> that extraordinary means should be used . . . for training up the students in vital religion and experimental and practical godliness, so that they should be holy societies; the very place should be as it were sacred; they should be, in the midst of the land, fountains of piety and holiness.[4]

Warch stresses the motivation of the three who had most to do with the original conception of the Shepherd's Tent: Davenport, Allen, and Wheelock. Davenport, as we have seen, had been declared *non compos mentis* by the assembly at Hartford and deported; Allen had been dismissed from the ministry by the Consociation of New Haven, as we shall see, and Wheelock had been refused an opportunity to preach at Yale.[5] Therefore, all had come to the conclusion that their aim, revitalizing religion, could not be met within the Establishment.

Timothy Allen, late of the Westhaven church, was to be superintendent of Shepherd's Tent. Allen was another of the circle of Yale students influenced by David Ferris, and had remained a close friend of Davenport. According to Samuel Whittelsey in a letter to Chauncy:

> This Timothy Allen was, for a while, the Pastor of the Church at West-Haven; but his old spirit, reviving and operating in the late Times, in a Manner too extravagant to be born with, his People enter'd their Complaints against him, and he was, after a fair Hearing of the Case, dismist from them according to the Method of Discipline, in the CONNECTICUT Churches. Among the many Articles exhibited against him, I shall single out one; and this I chuse to mention rather than any other, because it is so clearly descriptive of the dangerous Length, this giving Heed to Impulses, and the Notion of the Spirit's immediate extraordinary Guidance will carry Men. It is in these Words of a Letter from a Friend, "Sir, at your Desire I have look'd into the Papers on File, relating to Mr. T. A. late Minister of West-Haven; and find that one of the Articles charged and prov'd against him was, that he had publickly said, that the Word of GOD, as contained in the old and new Testament, is but as an old Almanack: For which, and various other Crimes prov'd against him, he continuing obstinate, was depos'd by the Consociation."[6]

(The charge against Allen, that he compared the Bible to an "Almanack," was not true: he had actually said that reading the Bible without the inspiration of the Holy Spirit would serve no better to convert a sinner than reading an almanac.)

By the summer of 1742, the Shepherd's Tent was in existence. Its sessions were held in the upper rooms of a private home in New London, and probably included villagers and country people who had been drawn to Davenport's preaching during his itinerancy among them. According to Joshua Hempstead, the exercises consisted of testimonies, noisy prayers, singing, and lengthy exhortations.[7] From this description, it seems to have been less a school (though it was called that) than a church or conventicle. In Connecticut, as has been stressed, there was at that time a Standing Order. Only Anglicans, Quakers, and Baptists were exempt from attendance at the services of the established Congregational churches, which, in turn, were strictly supervised by the semi-Presbyterian consociations. It was expressly forbidden for any except the three denominations officially exempt from support of the established church to found independent congregations without obtaining special permission.

The Shepherd's Tent was considered seditious by members of the General Assembly in their session in Hartford in October 1742. With the Shepherd's Tent apparently in mind, the assembly adopted a law requiring that persons intending to found schools obtain a license. Violators were to be subject to heavy fines.[8] This law as far as is known was never enforced; but the Shepherd's Tent in any case avoided the law by combining with a Separate church which *did* receive permission under the Standing Order.

DAVENPORT GOES TO BOSTON

During the spring of 1742, Davenport sailed to Newport, Rhode Island, the way that eastern Long Islanders usually went to eastern Massachusetts. From Newport, where he seems to have done no public preaching, he made his way on horseback to Boston.

His reputation had preceded him, and when he arrived two pastors immediately took him across the Charles River to Charlestown, where he was arraigned before the ministerial association there. Davenport responded to his critics that he had been called to preach the word wherever he went, and that God spoke through him. He then launched into a testimonial that went on until eleven at night. At the end of this, the exhausted pastors issued a declaration in which they charitably acknowledged that Davenport was very pious, but that he was a "Gentleman [who] acted much by sudden Impulses, upon such Applications of the Holy Scriptures to himself." They also told him how much they disapproved of his attacks against fellow ministers as well as his demands that they give him testimonials, and that he had not "acted prudently, but to the Disservice of Religion," especially when he went through the streets with his friends singing hymns. In addition, they very much disapproved of his private meetings with laymen, "a Practice which we . . . [find] big with Errors, Irregularities and Mischiefs."[9]

Davenport's accusers among the pastors included both Old and New Lights. Pastors such as Nathaniel Eels, Benjamin Colman, and Rev. Gee, who had welcomed the revival when Whitefield and Tennent had appeared in New England, were among Davenport's harshest critics. When he heard what Davenport was doing, Tennent, then in New Jersey, also revised his original opinion, and censured Davenport for the intemperate tone of his attacks against unconverted ministers. Tennent himself had preached a vigorous sermon entitled "The Danger of an Unconverted Ministry" in Nottingham, Pennsylvania, and had been much criticized for it; however, Davenport's ranting was too much even for him. Colman complained about Davenport to Whitefield, and he, too, expressed his dismay.

A few Boston ministers were friendly to Davenport: Nathaniel Rogers of Second Church, for example, who was taken to task for this in a published pamphlet by the Reverend Mr. Pickering, a prominent Opposer.[10] The rest refused him access to their pulpits in no uncertain terms. His most outspoken supporter was Andrew Croswell, who came to his defense in a tract called *Reply to the Declaration of the Associated Pastors of Boston* (1742). Croswell sharply criticized the Boston clergy who had taken Davenport to Charlestown, and there attacked him for leaving his parish and embarking on an evangelical tour. Davenport's accusers were guilty of inconsistency, he said, since they had invited Whitefield to come to Boston, had welcomed him to their pulpits, and had raised no objections when Tennent had appeared soon after. Had Davenport not been doing the same as Whitefield and Tennent? Had not Whitefield and Tennent also denounced unconverted ministers?[11]

It is true, as we have seen, that both Tennent and Whitefield did indeed attack unconverted ministers. But neither did so publicly on an *individual* basis, as Davenport did. Whitefield confided personal attacks to his *Journal*, and preached only in general terms about the dangers of an unconverted clergy. (When his *Journal* was published, it did, however, as we have seen, arouse much anger in those he attacked.) Tennent similarly confined his attacks to unconverted ministers as a class. Davenport, by openly labeling most ministers as unconverted, and villifying them, attempted to "silence the voice of established authority" and thus placed himself as an enemy of the recognized leaders of society.[12]

Croswell also accused Davenport's critics of "Arminianism," the current term for religious liberalism. He accused both the New and Old Lights of putting too much reliance on works. "For Ministers to lessen the Burden of Sinners," he wrote, "is, in Truth, only to stop them from coming to Christ."[13] At the time, as we have said, few had yet openly professed to Arminianism. Congregational and Presbyterian pastors continued to hold to orthodox Calvinism and the Federal Theology, and to emphasize the doctrines of predestination and election.

Even Croswell, however, had his reservations. He disapproved of Davenport's practice of declaring a person unconverted on first meeting, and he also deplored the latter's encouragement of lay exhorters. Since both of these were essential parts of Davenport's ministry, he was therefore isolated from almost all of his colleagues, both Friends of Revival and Opposers. Indeed, Croswell feared that Davenport was also uncomfortably close in his views and forms of expression to the Quakers.[14]

Therefore, after his meeting with the Boston Ministerial Association, Davenport found nearly all churches in the area closed to him. He took instead to the streets, the Commons, and Copps Hill. Night after night, Davenport held open-air meetings until ten or eleven. A correspondent to the *Boston Evening Post* described one of these mass meetings thus:

> He has preached every Day . . . upon the Commons to pretty large Assemblies, but the greatest part very far from admiring him, or being willing to give him any Countenance—when he first ascends the Rostrum, he appears with a remarkably settled composed Countenance, but soon gets into the most extravagant Gesture and Behaviour both in Prayer and Preaching—His expressions in Prayer are often indecently familiar; he frequently appeals to God, that such and such Impressions are immediately from his holy Spirit, but especially his Sermons are full of his Impressions and Impulses, from God. He does not seem to be a Man of any Parts, Sprightliness or Wit. His Sermons are dull and heavy, abounding with little low Similtudes. He

has no knack at raising the Passions, but by a violent straining of his Lungs, and the most extravagant wreathing of his Body, which at the same time that it creates Laughter and Indignation in the most, occasions great meltings, screaming, crying, swooning and Fits in some others. People in Fits, tho' often almost suffocated for want of Air, are not suffered to be removed into more open Air, lest the Spirit should be disturbed in its Operations. He boldly asserts, that a Man cannot be convicted and doubt about it, any more than have the Air blow upon him and not feel it. He exhorts the people to meet together in private Assemblies, and in despite of all Family Order and Government, to spend whole Nights till Day-break in Prayer. . . . Some think he is crazy, others that he is not, but that he is a rank Enthusiast, which last Opinion I am most inclined to. Though were you to see him in his most violent Agitations, you would be apt to think, that he was a Madman just broke from his Chaines: But especially had you seen him returning from the Commons after his first preaching, with a large Mob at his heels, singing all the Way thro' the streets, he with his Hands extended, his Head thrown back, and his Eyes staring up to Heaven, attended with so much Disorder that they look'd more like a company of Bacchanalians after a mad Frolick than sober Christians who had been worshipping God. He has got a Creature with him as a Companion, whom some call an Armour-Bearer, who assists him in praying and Exhortations at private Houses. He always stands with him upon the same Eminence when he is Preaching: for my part, when I see them together, I cannot for my Life help thinking of Don Quixote and Sancho-Pancha.[15]

When not preaching in the open air on the Commons or Copps Hill, Davenport held meetings in the homes of his admirers. This correspondent estimated that as many as a hundred may have crowded into a private house on one such occasion.

He continued with the themes begun in Connecticut and on Long Island. He warned people against their ministers, most of whom he branded unconverted. In his meetings, he writhed in simulated agony, imitating Christ on the cross, with a host of shouting men and wailing women in hysterics all around the joiner's stool on which he stood. Pointing an accusing finger, he warned his congregations that they were already damned, and that at the very moment he was preaching, he could see "Hell-fire flashing before their Eyes" with them "falling into the infernal Abyss." His exhorters were scattered about, stirring up the people, helping to turn them into a howling mob. At one meeting in July, according to a *Boston Evening Post* correspondent, no fewer than ten people were preaching or exhorting at the same time. The meetings, he said, were devoid of all form. Davenport and his disciples constantly went from preaching and prayer to singing and exhortation, then back to singing again. In this way the meetings would go on for hours in a high pitch of excitement.[16]

More than any other Evangelist during the Awakening, Davenport made singing in the streets at all hours of the day or night a basic part of his mission. He composed hymns himself, two stanzas from *A Song of Praise* being an example:

> My Soul doth magnify the Lord,
> My Spirit doth rejoice
> In God my Saviour, and my God;
> I hear his joyful Voice.
> I need not go abroad for Joy,
> Who have a Feast at home;
> My Sighs are turned into Songs,
> The Comforter is come.
>
> Such Joys as are unspeakable,
> And full of Glory too;
> Such hidden *Manna,* hidden Pearls,
> As Worldlings do not know.
> Eye hath not seen, nor Ear hath heard,
> From Fancy 'tis conceal'd,
> What thou Lord, hast laid up for thine,
> And hast to me reveal'd.[17]

Although psalms had been traditionally sung in churches, the type of hymns introduced by Davenport were emotional, Christocentric, and extrabiblical, and expressed the importance of "impulses and impressions." They "betrayed . . . something of the Antinomian ecstasy."[18]

Charles Wesley and Isaac Watts were also hymnologists, and hymn-singing played a great role in the Evangelical Revival in England as well. In both America and Britain the effect on the singers of these hymns was not unlike that of *Yankee Doodle* or *La Marseillaise* during the American and French Revolutions, respectively, though in a religious context. Modern evangelical music can trace its roots to the English and American revivalists of the eighteenth century.

Fund-raising for charities or institutions in the colonies was a new phenomenon which had begun with Whitefield. It was much resented by Old Lights, and bewildered many New Lights who, for the most part, were penniless and contributed clothing and other items rather than actual funds. Nevertheless, raising funds for Shepherd's Tent, his new school, now became Davenport's chief project.

Boston was noted for its many printers, and in addition to many broadsheets and pamphlets, newspapers such as the prestigious *Boston News-Letter,* the *Boston Evening Post,* and the new *Boston Weekly Post-Boy* carried lengthy stories about Davenport's antics in every issue. For instance, one article entitled "A Gentleman in Boston to a Minister in the Country" describes Davenport's preaching in considerable detail:

> As to his [Davenport's] Preaching in this Town, it has, I think been generally levell'd against Opposers and unconverted Ministers; often signifying to the People, that a time of great Persecution is speedily to be expected. His Gestures in preaching are Theatrical, his Voice Tumultuous, his whole speech and Behaviour discovering the Freaks of Madness, and Wilds of Enthusiasm.
>
> His Audience at first was not great, and has, I think, been decreasing ever since, and is now chiefly made up of idle or ignorant Persons, and those of the lowest Rank, except some few who go out of meer Curiosity, to hear something new. On Wednesday the 28th, he had a collection in the Common . . . to carry on the building of a Seminary call'd by him the Shepherd's Tent, wherein none are to be admitted but converted Children. What the Collection amounted to, I cannot yet learn, but I believe no great sum. However, 'tis past Doubt some credulous Folks were eas'd of their Pence, which they could very ill spare, and 'tis certain one good Woman put in two pair of Stockings; the wiser and better sort of People, will, I think, scarce be wheedled a Second Time into Collections for building Castles or Colleges in the Air.
>
> When the Exercise of the Common is over, the Rabble follow their leader to his Lodgings, (sometimes singing Hymns as they pass) where praying, singing, exhorting, and consequent thereon, falling down, screaming out, . . . and faintings are the Nocturnal Entertainment; the Night being best calculated to celebrate such dark and mysterious Juggles.
>
> Sometimes these meetings in the Fields have been attended with very great Disorders; several Jangles and Quarrels have happened among the Multitude; the Ferment has rose high, and not ended without Blows: and I verily fear that if these Meetings continue, such Quarrels will proceed to more dangerous Lengths, unless the Civil Magistrates . . . interpose their Authority to prevent them. For so far as a Judgement can be formed from the Behaviour and menacing Speeches of some of Mr. D—pt's Adherents, their zeal is so red hot, that I verily believe they would make nothing to kill Opposers, and in so doing, think they did God Service.[19]

Observers noticed that most of Davenport's followers were very young, many of them children. His audiences appeared to be made up mostly of people of the lower orders, according to contemporary newspaper accounts, but not even they were always thrilled by him.[20] Many, indeed, came to laugh and jeer. However, all clearly enjoyed his aggressive attacks against the clergy. His "armour-bearers," meantime, collected funds for the Shepherd's Tent. This was all quite alarming to the Establishment because he was obviously starting some kind of popular movement which threatened their prestige and status.

No better picture of Davenport in Boston exists than that offered by an anonymous bard. A few selected lines from his "Curious New Sonnet Dedicated to the Street Musicians" are as follows:

> Boston rejoice, lift up your voice
>   For D—pt is come.
> He loves you all both great and small
>   as Indians love strong rum.
>
> With him two men of might are come
>   They're armour bearers call'd by some
> Whose business is to carry on
>   The work this pretty man's begun.
>
> To hold his hat when he does preach
>   Sometimes to exhort and sometimes preach
> For sure one man is not enough
>   In noisy mob to ding and huff.
>
> One hand he waves and sets to stayes
>   From him not David's metre
> For doubtless he takes him to be
>   an unconverted creature.
>
> With mind perplexed he looks a text
>   And seems most dreadful glad,
> And on he'll run as sure as gun
>   And talk like any mad.
>
> Now look around the holy ground
>   Some gape, some cry, some laugh,
> It looks like, too, the ancient crew
>   That worship senseless calf.
>
> O Boston kind! Still hold of mind
>   to lend him your wide common,
> No place too fit for him to get
>   A little of your mammon.

For if you grutch or think too much
    To part with ready cash,
He'll take old shoes or dirty hose
    Or any other trash.

But if your heart is loath to part
    With worldly things so dear,
He'll scold and prate at such a rate,
    Good people all stand clear![21]

There were, to be sure, some in Boston among the propertied classes who admired him: the unknown "female admirer," for instance, who wrote:

The sacred Man is to his Shade convey'd
On Cammomile his aking Temples laid;
Here roses, Honey-Suckles, Jessamine
In beauteous Arches o'er the Champion twine.[22]

Davenport caused much dissension in Boston. In one of the comparatively few scholarly articles concerning him, "Religion, Finance, and Democracy in Massachusetts" (1933),[23] John Miller suggested that under Davenport's leadership, the Great Awakening became a popular protest against the upper classes. Miller asserted that Davenport's preaching whipped the public in Boston into a fit of intense excitement, and that the popular support he enjoyed was chiefly because of general animosity against the established clergy, most of whom were identified with the gentry. Davenport, he contends, caused class conflict in a community already divided over economic issues. While Davenport translated popular discontent into religious terms, it is clear from the expressions of alarm on the part of both the clergy and gentry that they were much disturbed by the mobs Davenport and his "armour-bearers" were encouraging.

By the autumn of 1742 reports about Davenport had reached England. They aroused just as much alarm there as in New England and the Middle Colonies, and for the same reasons. Davenport threatened the prestige of the clergy; he was a rabble-rouser; he was also discrediting the Evangelical Revival.[24]

ARREST, TRIAL, AND DEPORTATION

Toward the end of the summer of 1742 feelings against Davenport reached a climax. The clergy prevailed upon the magistrates to have Davenport arrested and charged with slander. He was taken into custody on 19 August. Two "gentlemen" offered to pay his bail at the time of his arrest, suggesting that not all members of the gentry were opposed to him.[25] He refused bail, and was incarcerated in comfortable quarters, probably because of his distinguished family connections. He was arraigned before a grand jury on 24 August. The presentment drawn up against him charged him with

> Praying, Preaching and Exhorting in Divers Places and Times in the Towns of Dorchester and Boston, and at Divers Times in July last and August current [and because he did] maliciously Publish and with a loud Voice utter and declare many Slanderous and Reviling Speeches against the Godly and Faithful Ministers of this Province [and] advising his Hearers to withdraw from the said Ministers and not hear them Preach.[26]

At the time of his arrest, some of Davenport's followers insisted that he was being persecuted, and that the jury was biased.[27] However, ministers and magistrates alike proved to be remarkably patient with him. The ministerial association was disposed to clemency, and sent a note recommending leniency, though their gentleness toward him may have reflected a fear of mob violence if he was ill treated.

Once more, Davenport stood trial. Completely unrepentant, he again denounced the unconverted ministers and warned people away from their services of worship, not failing, once more, to utter his prophecies about the state of their souls.[28]

The jury of twenty-three handed in a verdict of guilty by a majority of twenty-one to two. The two dissenters were a lay exhorter and a Quaker. The latter disapproved of Davenport, but held that his arrest violated religious freedom. One juror, probably the lay exhorter, insisted that the charge against Davenport that he accused the ministers of "knowing nothing of Jesus Christ" had not been proven. During the last days of September, the court pronounced Davenport *non compos mentis,* and he returned to Southold after a short stay in Concord, raising money for the Shepherd's Tent.[29]

After his departure, a female friend published the following:

> Go dear lov'd C—w—l rest on D—p—t's Bed
> To ease the pains that seize your lab'ring Head,
> There let your tuneful Soul with Angels join
> There let your Sentiments and Stiles reside.[30]

The Opposers

The departure of Davenport was followed by an acrimonious debate among the clergy of Boston. His excesses raised serious doubts about the Awakening among all but a few of the ministers, and convinced them that it was a dangerous affair. Was the revival the work of the Holy Spirit? Or was it an example of demagoguery?

The argument took the form of debates in newspapers and in published sermons. Boston's five newspapers were chiefly read by members of the educated classes, and the articles tended to be less newsworthy than discursive. The Boston printers also published large numbers of pamphlets, sermons, and tracts. Bostonians of the upper classes were very class conscious, more so than the rustic folk of Connecticut, and far more articulate in their expressions of opinion. Consequently, through Davenport had certainly roused much controversy in the latter colony, there had been much less general discussion. His itineraries there, as well as his trial and deportation, were chiefly known locally.

Davenport was the chief cause of the rise of the antirevivalists in Boston who, at the time, were called "Opposers" both by themselves and by their critics. These must be distinguished from Old Lights in general, since the latter were mainly conservatives who preferred the traditional Puritanism of their forefathers, whereas the Opposers were Old Lights who later became Arminians.[31]

Most members of the gentry in class-conscious Boston were highly offended by Davenport; not only the clergy, who were the butts of his attacks, but the majority of the lay gentry as well. Though belief in the devil and Hell was declining among the educated on both sides of the Atlantic, there had been quiet approval of the new hellfire and damnation preaching of Whitefield and Tennent because of the salutary effect it had on the "rabble." But though Davenport also preached the "terrors of the law" (hellfire and damnation), he coupled that with assaults against the ministers. The gentry rallied to their defense, and were thoroughly alarmed by his open-air mass meetings on Copps Hill and the Common.

In Boston, the gradual transition from the Puritanism of the Federal Theology to Arminianism had gone further than elsewhere in the colonies. Thus, whereas doctrine remained formally orthodox, informally, attitudes had changed. Timothy Cutler, formerly a Connecticut Congregationalist and now rector of King's Chapel, had become both Anglican and Arminian.[32] He had refused his pulpit to Whitefield, and had been very hostile to Tennent. Davenport was, to him, utterly outrageous.

During the autumn of 1742, Colman expressed his alarm concerning Davenport and Croswell to the English evangelical hymn-writer Isaac Watts. The latter replied, "Such warm spirits as Davenport and Croswell are not fit for managing so important a work as God has begun and carrys on amongst you."[33]

At Harvard, rationalism prevailed and emotional religion was suspect. Harvard was theologically orthodox, but there was an Arminian emphasis there on morality and works.[34] According to Conrad Wright in *The Beginnings of Unitarianism in America,* Harvard-educated ministers predominated among the Congregational ministers in Boston and the coastal districts of Massachusetts by 1740. Charles Chauncy, a Harvard graduate, detested emotionalism, and was utterly appalled by Davenport. Not long after Davenport's departure from Massachusetts, Chauncy began a campaign against him, chiefly in the form of published sermons and pamphlets.[35]

By this time the early excitement of the Great Awakening had abated, leaving much squabbling among ministers, and contentious debates concerning the nature of the conversion experience. Whitefield's charisma had become so diminished that he had but little effect when he returned to America on an evangelical tour. In March of 1743 Jonathan Edwards had published *Some Thoughts Concerning the Present Revival of Religion in New England.* This had been answered in September of the same year by Charles Chauncy's *Seasonable Thoughts on the State of Religion in New England.* Much of the debate that then ensued between Edwards and Chauncy centered around Davenport, with Edwards arguing that the revival had been a genuine Work of God, and Chauncy seriously doubting this because of the excesses of Davenport in particular. Much of Chauncy's book consists of correspondence he solicited from Connecticut and Long Island concerning Davenport. One of these informants gave him information concerning David Ferris and the effects the latter had on a small coterie of unstable Yale students. Chauncy was also informed about Jonathan Barber's doings on Long Island, and of the bizarre behavior both Davenport and Barber had exhibited soon after they accepted calls to their respective parishes on eastern Long Island. Chauncy blamed Ferris for the excesses, and then drew parallels with other examples of what he called *enthusiasm:* the French Prophets, a group of Huguenot Antinomians, and various Commonwealth era sects such as the Famil-

ists, with which Anne Hutcheson had been associated. All were
guilty of religious anarchism resulting in social disorder.[36]

DAVENPORT'S NEW LONDON ORGY

By February of 1743 schisms seem to have divided the members of the Separate Church and the Shepherd's Tent, although
the sources do not tell us why. According to Chauncy's informant,
a delegation sailed from New London to Southold to "invite the
grand Enthusiast D—t over to Organize their Church (as they
term'd it)."[37] However, according to Joshua Hempstead's *Diary,*
Davenport went to New London on instructions from God during
a service in Southold "Concerning the Shepherd's Tent & other
Such things."[38]

Davenport and Daniel Tuthill sailed to New London immediately, ignoring the decision of the Long Island council which had
put him on probation, as well as a law passed by the Connecticut
General Assembly the previous year imposing heavy fines on returning deportees.[39] Davenport was ailing. He had for years suffered from a "cancry humour" in one leg, and could only walk
with Tuthill's support. He was also suffering at this time from a
high fever, and was occasionally delirious.

When Davenport arrived in New London "he published the
Messages which he said, he received from the Spirit in Dreams
and otherwise, importing the great Necessity of Mortification and
Contempt of the World." He preached to his followers in New
London in an "impetuous, exclamatory sermon" in which he told
his disciples that the Holy Spirit had told him of the need for
"casting away all idols."[40] For the sake of their immortal souls,
they must throw away any worldly possessions to which they
were attached. Davenport focused with particular vehemence on
the books of certain divines such as John Flavel, Increase Mather,
William Beveridge, Samuel Russell, William Hart, Benjamin Colman, Charles Chauncy, and Eliphalet Adams, all presumably unconverted. This was not surprising: they were either Puritans of
the older generation or Opposers. What is *more* interesting is that
he also included as pernicious books and pamphlets by Jonathan
Parsons, a supporter of the revival (though concerned about its
excesses), and Solomon Williams of Lebanon, a New Light and
former classmate at Yale, whom he had formerly regarded very
highly. Those who had such books must cast them on the flames.
They must also cast away wigs, jewels, fine clothing, indeed any-

thing that made them guilty of the "heinous sin of idolatry."[41] After this harangue, Davenport collapsed and was taken to the home of one of his disciples where he was confined to bed with a high fever.[42] There are conflicting reports on what happened next.

Davenport's inflammatory sermon was followed by either one or two bonfires, most authorities agreeing that there were two, on two successive days. Chauncy's informant describes only one.[43] The *Boston Weekly Post-Boy* describes two, the first on March 6 of books, and the second, on the following day, of books and other possessions.[44] According to the *Post-Boy,* Davenport's excited followers rushed home after his sermon, and returned laden with books which they deposited in a pile on Christopher's Wharf and ignited. In great excitement, they danced and howled around the fire, tossing the books on the flames. They caused so much commotion that several citizens thought a murder was being committed and came running.

The congregation was just then emerging from the regular church service in the town meetinghouse. By then, Davenport's followers were in a high state of hysteria. Some were shouting "Hallelujah!" and others were singing *The Gloria Patria.* As they danced around the flames, they continued to toss in the books. "Thus the Souls of the Authors of those Books, those of them that are dead, are roasting in the Flames of Hell; and that the Fate of those surviving, would be the same, unless speedy Repentence prevented."[45]

On the next day, "having given this fatal stroke to *heresy,* they made ready to attack *idolatry.*" Davenport sent them home to gather up their apparel, especially that meant primarily as ornament, and bring it to the wharf.

Some of them in the heighth of their Zeal, conferred not with Flesh and Blood, but fell to stripping and cast their Cloaths down at their Apostle's Feet; one or two hesitated about the Matter, and were so bold as to tell him they had nothing on which they idoliz'd: He re-ply'd, that such and such a Thing was an Offense to him; and they must down with them: One of these being a Gentleman of Learning and Parts ventur'd to tell Mr. D—p—t, that he could scarce see how his disliking the Night-Gown that he had on his Back, should render him, guilty of Idolatry. However, This carnal Reasoning avail'd noth-ing; strip he must, and strip he did: By this Time the Pile had grown to a large Bulk, and almost ripe for Sacrifice; and that they might be clear and well-warranted in the Enterprize, Mr. D—p—t order'd one of his Armour-Bearers to pray for a full Discovery of the Mind—in the Affair . . . but had no answer. . . . Next Mr. D—p—t pray'd himself;

and now the Oracle spake clear to the Point, without Ambiguity, and utter'd that *the Things must be burnt;* and to confirm the Truth of the Revelation, took his wearing Breeches, and hove them with Violence into the Pile, saying, *Go you with the Rest.* A young Sister, whose Modesty could not bear to see the Mixture of Cloaks, Petty Coats and Breeches, snatch'd up his Breeches, and sent them at him, with as much Indignation, as tho' they had been the Hire of a Wh— or the Price of a Dog.[46]

According to Dr. Alexander Hamilton of Edinburgh, a spectator (Deacon Green's son) later described one of the bonfires to him, probably the second:

[T]he women [then] made up a lofty pile of hoop petticoats, silk gowns, short cloaks, cambrick caps, red heeld shoes, fans, necklaces, gloves, and other such aparrell, and what was merry enough, Davenport's own idol with which he topped the pile, was a pair of old, wore out, plush breaches. But this bonefire was happily prevented by one more moderate than the rest, who found means to perswade them that making such a sacrifice was not necessary for their salvation, and so every one carried of[f] their idols again, which was lucky for Davenport who, had fire been put to the pile, would have been obliged to strutt about bare-arsed, for the devil another pair of breeches had he but these same old plush ones which were going to be offered up as an expiatory sacrifise.[47]

While the books were apparently allowed to burn, their owners had second thoughts about their other possessions, and, according to Hempstead, who was a witness, "each bird went home with its own feathers."[48]

According to the correspondent of the *Boston Weekly Post-Boy:*

At this Juncture came in a Brother from a neighboring Town; a Man of more Sense than most of them have; and apply'd warmly to Mr. D—-p—t, told him, *He was making a Calf,* and that he thot', *the D—l was in him*: Mr. D—p—t said, *He tho't so too;* and added, That he *was under the Influence of an* evil Spirit, *and that God had left Him.*[49]

Even his "armour-bearer" was disillusioned with Davenport. He later wrote:

That *altho' he had for three Years past* believ'd (and why not *known*) *himself to be a Child of God,* he now tho't *he was a Child of the D—l and a* Judas; *and tho't he should be hang'd between Heaven and Earth, and have his Bowels gush out.*[50]

No one has satisfactorily explained the book-burning incident at New London. What is most puzzling is why people who were accounted to be among the most unlearned and least intellectual members of the community had these learned theological tomes in their possession. Perhaps they were pilfered from the libraries of others. Many of the wealthy colonial families had extensive libraries, and more than a few of the young radicals, such as Curtis Hempstead, came from distinguished families. Perhaps the books were not their own, but belonged to their parents. However, none of the witnesses cast any light on this.

Hamilton's account of the bonfire implies that at least a few gentlemen "of Parts" took part, at least in the second of the two. Descriptions of what was thrown on the second fire include jewels and fine garments. This would suggest that the hysteria afflicted members of the more prosperous classes, and not just the idle and poor, and that both men and women were affected.

The community was remarkably lenient with those book-burners who remained in New London. True, they were arraigned and tried, but the charge was no more serious than Sabbath-breaking, and the penalties were small fines. The citizenry did not seem disposed to take vengeance on them, again suggesting that they were citizens of some status.

On March 30, 1743, a ministerial council of New Lights was convened in New London to consider the recent episode and its consequences. The council included several who had been well-known itinerants themselves: Solomon Williams, Benjamin Pomeroy, and Samuel Buell, for example. Jonathan Edwards presided. The books that had been burned were ritually restored; the New Lights publicly disassociated themselves from Davenport's excesses "to save the revival."[51]

> The drama of Davenport and the Separates had played itself out. No estates were confiscated; no lives were lost; no dangerous radicals were incarcerated in prisons.[52]

The New London incident could be considered either the end of the Great Awakening, or an aftershock of it. There is continued debate as to when the revival ended with some historians, such as Conrad Wright, suggesting 1745 as the terminal date.[53] In my view, it ended in 1742 with the general ebbing of revivalist excitement, with the New London episode only a delayed manifestation.

CONFESSION AND RETRACTIONS

Soon after the New London incident, Davenport apparently left town, as did Timothy Allen. The departure of the latter spelled the end of the Shepherd's Tent, and the Separate church with which it was associated disintegrated as well. We have one indication of his later movements in a letter by Sarah Peirpoint to Eleazar Wheelock, dated 30 May: "Mr. Davenport is very much alone in the world. His friends foresake him. He rides from town to town without any attendants."[54]

He was deeply disturbed by the episode of the New London bonfire(s). Had he been guided by the Holy Spirit, or had it been Satan? Reflecting on his earlier activities and the commotions he had aroused, he began to have doubts about these as well, and became deeply depressed.

He still believed, however, in his "impulses and impressions." He was as certain as ever that the Holy Spirit expressed himself in inner illuminations, but he did have profound doubts about some of his interpretations. Satan had surely misled him in his arrogance, in following his own thoughts and opinions, mistaking them for special revelations, when he should have, in all humility, listened only to the inwardly revealed Word of God. He wrote his friend Jonathan Barber about his doubts, and also warned him to profit by his example. "Take no part of the Glory to yourself," he wrote. "Neither lean on your own understanding. Oh! Be not wise above that which is written, nor leave the sacred unerring Oracle of Truth."[55] These words, written on 30 November, 1743, not long after the New London episode, are particularly interesting.

He also confided his doubts to two old Yale friends, Eleazar Wheelock and Solomon Williams. It will be recalled that he had caused the latter's pamphlets and books to be burned in New London along with the works of undoubted Opposers of the Revival. Both had been among the young men who had been entranced by Ferris, but never to the degree that Davenport, Barber, Allen, and Pomeroy had. In particular, Davenport wanted their opinion of his attacks against the allegedly unconverted ministers, and of the schisms in congregations which he had caused.

Both were delighted to respond. Wheelock and Williams each wrote Davenport a long letter. Both were published a year later. In them, they took Davenport to task for his attacks against fellow ministers, his encouragement of lay exhorters, and the schisms he had caused in so many of the congregations to which he had preached.[56] Wheelock reminded Davenport that every apostle had had a divine commission, and that every minister does as well. This commission sets the minister apart, and dedicates him to fulfill his appointed tasks. "Christ has set a sacred hedge about his work," he wrote, "and all those who are trying to pull down this hedge, are acting against the Kingdom of Christ."[57] He then asserted that the lay exhorters whom Davenport had been encouraging lacked proper Christian credentials and would inevitably lead people into errors. Therefore they should not be allowed to preach as if they were ordained ministers.

Williams wrote Davenport that while he agreed there was good reason to fear the effects on their congregations of unconverted ministers, he questioned how one could be certain of the state of the soul of another person. Because a minister is ordained to administer the sacraments and to preach the gospel, his own spiritual state is *not* a matter of importance. He also questioned the validity of any other test of regeneracy than what had been revealed in the Scriptures. Williams warned Davenport that his reliance in this matter on his own impressions that this or that person was unregenerate was too close to the antinomianism of the Anabaptists of Reformation times. He expressed the fear that this subjectivity too easily led to error.[58]

Owing to his illness, Davenport was undoubtedly vulnerable, and his ministerial counselors took full advantage of it. He was in a repentent mood, and they urged him to try to undo the harm he had done by publishing a full confession of his errors, and a retraction. They hoped that if he did so, some of his deluded followers who had separated from the established churches would see the error of their ways and return to the fold. Since Williams was one of those ministers who was a physician of the body as well as of the soul, Davenport was taken to Connecticut as soon as he was well enough to travel, and was cared for by Williams in his own home. There Williams and Wheelock were able to exert much pressure on him.

By the late spring of 1744 Davenport was well enough to travel. Either on his own initiative or, as is most likely, because of the pressure put on him by Williams and Wheelock, the remorseful Davenport made a penitential journey to the various towns and villages in Connecticut that had been the scenes of his most outrageous episodes. He was apologetic and contrite wherever he went. The Reverend Fish of Stonington, for one, gladly forgave him in Christian charity. He wrote: "He [Davenport] came with such a meek, pleasant and humble spirit, broken and contrite, as I have scarce ever saw excelled or equalled."[59]

June found him back in eastern Long Island, where he resigned his pulpit at Southold. However, the congregation prevailed on him to stay on as supply preacher until his successor was appointed. Significantly, the congregation stipulated that the latter must restore the Half-Way Covenant, suggesting how little lasting effect his radical evangelism had had in his own parish. There is no indication that the Southold church suffered serious schism, or that, as elsewhere in eastern Long Island, New Light dissidents separated and formed an independent congregation. Nothing further is known concerning Daniel Tuthill, his former "armour-bearer."

By 28 July 1744 he had finished and signed a remarkable document entitled *The Confession and Retractions of James Davenport.* Williams sent this manuscript on to Thomas Prince of Boston who was then collecting accounts of the revival for his series, *Christian History.*[60] It was published by Prince later in 1744, printed in the *Boston Weekly Post-Boy,* and soon appeared in pamphlet form as well.

It is very probable that Davenport's *Confession and Retractions* was more the work of Williams and Wheelock than of Davenport himself, but the point cannot be proved. The text is as follows:

ALTHO' I don't question at all, but there is great Reason to bless God for a *glorious and wonderful Work of his Power and Grace* in the *Edification* of his Children, and the *Conviction* and *Conversion* of Numbers in *New-England,* in the *neighbouring Governments* and *several other Parts,* within a few Years past; and believe that the Lord hath favoured me, tho' most unworthy, with several others of his Servants, in granting special Assistance and Success; the Glory of all which be given to JEHOVAH, to whom alone it belongs:

Yet after frequent Meditation and Desires that I might be enabled to apprehend Things justly, and, I hope I may say, mature Consideration; I am now fully convinced and persuaded that *several Appendages to this glorious Work* are no essential Parts thereof, but of a *different* and *contrary* Nature and Tendency; *which Appendages* I have been in the Time of the Work very industrious in and instrumental of promoting, by a misguided Zeal: being further much influenced in the Affair by the *false Spirit;* which, unobserved by me, did (as I have been brought to see since) prompt me to *unjust Apprehensions* and *Misconduct* in *several Articles;* which have been great Blemishes to the Work of God, very grievous to some of God's Children, no less ensnaring and corrupting to others of them, a sad Means of many Persons questioning the Work of God, concluding and appearing against it, and of the hardening of Multitudes in their Sins, and an awful Occasion of the Enemies blaspheming the right Ways of the Lord; and withall very offensive to that God, before whom I would lie in the Dust, prostrate in deep Humility and Repentance on this Account, imploring Pardon for the Mediator's Sake, and thankfully accepting the Tokens thereof.

The *Articles* which I especially refer to, and would in the most public Manner *retract,* and *warn others against*, are these which follow, *viz.*

I. The Method I us'd for a considerable Time, with Respect to some, yea many *Ministers* in several Parts, in openly *exposing such as I fear'd or thought unconverted, in public Prayer or otherwise*: herein making my private Judgement, (in which also I much suspect I was mistaken in several Instances, and I believe also that my Judgement concerning several, was formed rashly and upon very slender Grounds.) I say making my private Judgment, the Ground of public Actions or Conduct; offending, as I apprehend (altho' in the Time of it ignorantly) against the *ninth Commandment*, and such other Passages of Scripture, as are similar; yea, I may say, offending against the Laws both of Justice and Charity: Which Laws were further broken,

II. By my *advising and urging to such Separations* from *those Ministers,* whom I treated as above, as I believe may justly be called rash, unwarrantable, and of sad and awful Tendency and Consequence. And here I would ask Forgiveness of those Ministers, whom I have injured in both these Articles.

III. I confess I have been much led astray by *following Impulses* or Impressions as a Rule of Conduct, whether they came with or without a Text of Scripture; and my neglecting also duly to observe the Analogy of Scripture: I am persuaded this was a great Means of corrupting my Experiences and carrying me off from the Word of God, and a great Handle, which the *false Spirit* has made use of with Respect to a Number, and me especially.

IV. I believe further that I have done much Hurt to Religion by *encouraging private Persons to a ministerial and authoritative Kind or Method of exhorting*; which is particularly observable in many such being much puft up and *falling into the Snare of the Devil*, while many others are thus directly prejudic'd against the Work.

V. I have Reason to be deeply humbled that I have not been duly care-ful to endeavour to remove or prevent Prejudice, (where I now believe I might then have done it consistently with Duty) which appear'd re-markable in the Method I practic'd, of *singing with others in the Streets* in societies frequently.

I would also penitently confess and bewail my *great Stiffness* in re-taining these *aforesaid Errors* a great while, and Unwillingness to ex-amine into them with any Jealousy of their being Errors, notwithstanding the friendly Counsels and Cautions of real Friends, especially in the Ministry. . . .

And now may the holy wise and good God, be pleas'd to guard and secure me against *such Errors* for the future, and stop Progress of those, whether ministers or People who have been corrupted by my Words or Example in any of the abovementioned Particulars; and if it be his holy Will, *bless this public recantation* to this Purpose. And Oh! may he grant withall, that such as by Reason of the aforesaid *Errors and Misconduct* have entertained unhappy prejudices against Chris-tianity in general, or the late glorious Work of God in particular, may this Account learn to distinguish the *Appendage* from the *Substance* or *Essence* that which is *Vile* and *Odious* from that which is *precious, glorious,* and *divine,* and thus be entirely and happily freed from all those Prejudices referr'd to, and this in infinite Mercy through Jesus Christ; and to these requests may all God's children, whether Minis-ters or others say, *Amen.*[61]

The reaction of the New England clergy to Davenport's *Confes-sion and Retractions* was mixed. Most were relieved to accept his self-repudiation, although few wanted to have anything further to do with him. Benjamin Colman did not think that his *Confes-sion and Retractions* went far enough, considering the great dam-age he had done the cause of religion in New England; he expressed the hope that "the several ministers here and there misled by him [Davenport] . . . awake at length out of their dreams, or rather delirium, and despise their own image!"[62]

Davenport had been ill when he wrote his confession, and had remained so for some months thereafter. During his recovery he wrote his friend Jonathan Barber a lengthy confessional letter which he was persuaded to have published. In it he confessed with great contrition that he now was experiencing an inner peace such as he had never known before. He felt that God at last in truth was in his soul. It now seemed to him that he had only just now experienced conversion, and that all that had happened before had been the work of the Devil.[63] Since there is no record of

Davenport having experienced the traditional Puritan conviction and conversion crisis prior to his accepting the call to Southold, it would seem that he himself had been an unregenerate by his own standards! In retrospect, it now seemed to him (or, at least, he was persuaded to think thus) that he had been possessed by Satan, and that, unwittingly, his itinerancies in eastern Long Island, Connecticut, and Boston had been because the powers of darkness were using him. The more he made such confessions, the happier were his former victims, since the attacks against them could now be easily turned aside.[64]

Having alienated most of his colleagues in New England and disgraced himself with the gentry, Davenport had prudently accepted a call to supply the Presbyterian Church of Plainfield, New Jersey, shortly after resigning from his Long Island church. He appears to have married while still in Southold, although there is no mention of his wife's name and how they met. The move to the Middle Colonies had been a natural step for Davenport to make. The Congregational churches of Connecticut were semi-Presbyterian, and many Presbyterian candidates for the ministry, such as Gilbert Tennent, were educated at Yale. Davenport had made an evangelical tour of New York, New Jersey, and Pennsylvania in 1740, as one of the young evangelists in Whitefield's entourage, and knew the Tennents. On 26 September 1746 he affiliated with the New Brunswick Presbytery, dominated by the Tennents, and still aggressively New Side.[65]

Davenport remained in Plainfield as a supply preacher until April, 1745. Later that same year, or during the next, he accepted a call to the Connecticut Farms Presbyterian Church near Elizabeth Town. Joshua Hempstead visited him there in July 1749.[66] We have a glimpse of him in a letter dated 1750 that he wrote to Wheelock in the latter's collection in the archives at Dartmouth University:

> I give fond vent to that my love which I feel working and glowing in my breast and ended to that degree that I find it sensibly hard to keep from writing almost entirely on the beloved subject. [I hope that] false religion might come to an end and true religion survive and flourish.[67]

In that year he suffered more health problems, and was obliged to refuse a call to supply a pulpit in Virginia, offered him by the Synod of Maidenhead (Lawrenceville), New Jersey. At the time,

New Sides Presbyterian evangelists were preaching to the un-churched in Hanover County, Virginia. This marks the beginning of the Southern Awakening, the last phase of the revival.[68] How-ever, when his health improved the next year, Davenport gladly accepted a second call, and made a long trip on horseback south-ward through maritime Pennsylvania and Maryland to the Pied-mont districts of Virginia, as far south as the Roanoke River, almost on the border of North Carolina. As he traveled from par-ish to parish, once more the itinerant preacher, Davenport found his physical and spiritual strength returning. It was a rigorous journey which seems to have benefited him, and he returned stronger in health than when he had left.[69] He was thus among those New Sides Presbyterians who initiated the Southern Awak-ening.

He continued to serve the Connecticut Farms parish for four more years after his return. The congregation was very small, scarcely large enough to support a parsonage family, and Daven-port now had two sons, John and James.[70] The records of the New Brunswick Presbytery indicate that he accepted a call to the Pres-byterian Church in Philipps, New Jersey, in 1752.[71] In September he wrote Williams, complaining of the poverty of the parish and expressing doubts that the family could stay there.[72] Soon after he was called to the Hopewell (Pennington) Presbyterian Church, also in New Jersey. Whitefield was back once more in America, and Davenport wrote Williams that "many of God's people, espe-cially of his ministers, found their hearts not diminished."[73] In 1756, when the Seven Years' War broke out, Davenport issued a public prophecy that the war was an apocalyptic omen. A daugh-ter, Elizabeth, was born in 1757.[74] It is the last we hear of him. He died on 10 November 1757 at the age of forty or forty-one, and was buried in a little cemetery one mile west of what is now called Pennington, New Jersey.[75] His epitaph ignored his earlier contro-versial career:

O Davenport, a seraph once in clay
a brighter seraph now in heavenly day,
How glowed thy heart with sacred love and zeal.
How like to that the kindred angels feel.
Cloth'd in humility thy virtues shone.
In every eye illustrious but thine own.
How like thy master on whose friendly breast
thou oft has leaned and shall forever rest.[76]

The Significance of James Davenport
in the Great Awakening

Davenport had his most lasting effect in eastern Long Island, especially in the three Hamptons, Baiting Hollow, and a few other hamlets—but not in Southold, his own parish, as we have seen. Elsewhere, his personal impact was more ephemeral. In Connecticut he had had his greatest successes in New London. He had been very popular in Stonington, where the settled minister was not well liked, but had failed to gain much following in Saybrook, where Jericho's walls failed to fall. He had encountered fierce opposition in New Haven, though also enjoying some success among dissidents. He had attracted large crowds in the villages of Lyme and Groton, where there were many New Lights, including the incumbent ministers. He had had a mixed reception in Boston, attracting large crowds of enthusiasts and curiosity-seekers, but, from the reports, arousing as much mirth as inspiring convictions and conversions.

Nevertheless, James Davenport had a more lasting importance than would have been expected from the above. Despite his *Confession and Retractions*, some of his followers continued on the radical path he pioneered. He is thus an important founder of the Evangelical movement, an American form of Protestantism which flourishes today. Davenport, his associates, and followers reverted to forms of radicalism that paralleled those of the original Quakers of a century before his time. He was acting on the same principles as had the original Anabaptists in continental Europe, as well as the Ranters, Familists, Quakers, and other radical sects of the Commonwealth. All of them took the Protestant doctrine of the priesthood of all believers to its logical extreme. His "Great Fire of New London," as Alexander Hamilton called it,[77] was something the Anabaptists and the early Quakers might well have done, and for some of the same reasons.

However, the form that Davenport's revivalism took was as inimical to the New Lights as to the Old. In their article, Stout and Onuf argue that the radicals were not revivalists at all because their aim was not to fill the churches but to empty them. Whereas Whitefield and Tennent had been welcomed by the local ministers because they attracted people to their churches, increasing their membership, Davenport came bellowing "Come away! Come away!,"[78] and warned that it was better to "drink bowls of poison" than to listen to unconverted ministers who were "Wolves in Sheep's cloathing."[79] This was a radical threat to the religious establishment itself, and, by implication, the political order. It was also a challenge to the very *idea* of a church. Davenport and his enthusiasts exemplified the ongoing and insoluble conflict between religious spontaneity and institutional survival; between the priesthood of all believers and organized religion.

Davenport enjoyed the distinction of being a first-century Christian in the eighteenth century. To a very remarkable extent his practices and convictions resembled those of Paul. He was, indeed, more like Paul than any of his contemporaries. Paul probably would have approved of Davenport's "impulses and impressions." He would have found much to delight him in Davenport's conception of grace and the power of the Holy Spirit. Ernest F. Scott, commenting on Paul, remarks:

> Christianity is for Paul a religion of liberty. "Christ has made you free"; this ideal is ever and again repeated in different words, and may almost be taken as the central motive in Paul's message. He thinks of the Christian as released from all earthly bonds; to his own Master he stands or falls; he judges all things but is himself judged by no man.[80]

This could be a description of Davenport prior to his *Confession and Retractions*.

Davenport's defiance of both ecclesiastical and secular authority was based on no revolutionary zeal but on his sheer confidence that the Holy Spirit supported his stance. No tradition, no law, no passage of Scripture, and no creed bound him, only the Christ within. Like Paul, Davenport claimed "for every Christian a complete autonomy, and it was recognized that under such conditions there could be no settled creed or ethic."[81] Paul, being of infinitely greater wisdom than Davenport, realized the necessity of making practical concessions even though he never abandoned his ideal in principle. Paul finally came to realize that consideration for others, prudence, and common sense required at least a minimum submission to custom and law. It was a concession he made with great reluctance, but he made it.[82] Davenport, until the time he wrote his *Confession and Retractions*, made no concessions at all.

Stout and Onuf do not concur with John C. Miller's oft-quoted "Religion, Finance, and Democracy in Massachusetts,"[83] nor with the arguments of Heimert, Cowing, and others of what I have called the "Revolution school" which discuss the Great Awakening as a prelude to the struggles that culminated in Lexington and Concord. My own opinion is that though the Awakening, particularly in its most extreme manifestations, involved class conflict, and attempted to set up a sort of meritocracy of the spirit, this was confined to the religious sphere. Davenport never attempted to lead a revolt against political authority; he ignored it. Therefore, any relation of the Awakening to the causes of the American Revolution is tenuous.

Davenport's contribution to the legacy of the Great Awakening was therefore sixfold. First, his behavior brought the revival into disrepute, and may have hastened its end. Second, Davenport and his fellow radicals helped shatter the Puritan consensus. The result was a proliferation of sects and movements. Third, he left behind a legacy of a charismatic and democratic ministry in which experiential factors were more important than formal education, reason was hated, and class played no part. Fourth, he was among the founders of American itinerant revivalism and the Evangelical movement. Fifth, he pioneered in America the extrabiblical, Christocentric, emotional, and charismatic hymn-singing still found in churches today, particularly Evangelical and Pentacostal ones. Sixth, he illustrated in his own rise and fall the dangers of reliance on special revelation: impulses and impressions.

Davenport is consequently a very significant figure in the Great Awakening. This was fully acknowledged by Joseph Tracy, whose history of the revival was written on its centennial. Historians such as Perry Miller, Leonard Trinterud, and Edwin Gaustad have devoted some space to him, but not nearly as much as he deserves. To his contemporaries, he was the villain who destroyed the Great Awakening, therefore exceedingly important.

8

The Legacy

A Treatise Concerning Religious Affections

EDWARDS WAS THE LEADING APOLOGIST FOR THE GREAT AWAKENING. In his *A Treatise Concerning Religious Affections,* written after the Great Awakening, he expounded on issues that had preoccupied him during that time. He again attempted to distinguish between enthusiasm on the one hand and conversion and sanctification on the other. As mentioned in an earlier chapter, the heart of his argument lay in the concept of "the fruits of the spirit" as defined by Paul. The convert may indeed undergo bizarre behavior during conviction: deep melancholy or depression accompanied by weeping, twitching, crying out, and fainting. Conversion might well be accompanied by shouting in an explosion of joy, or other manifestations of ecstasy. All of this, he argued, happened because of the particular temperament of the person involved.

The proof of conversion, however, was considered to be a profound change in the quality of life as indicated by the "fruits of the spirit": an inner change reflected in outward behavior called "sanctification." The Protestant saint was said to be distinguished by moral behavior, piety, and circumspection. If *all* of the saints actually had exhibited the fruits of the spirit, even the most critically minded Old Lights would have been given pause. There were, to be sure, some very decent, circumspect, loving converts, but were their lives in every case really changed? Had some not been so before? Did the changes last? People who never do have what Edwards and other New Lights called a conversion experience could also change; could also lead pious, moral lives. There is almost nothing that reliably distinguishes the regenerate from the unregenerate. No one, including Paul, Augustine, Calvin, and Edwards, has solved this problem, even though many theologians and philosophers have tried.

Edwards' thoughts were far too abstruse for the people of his time. In the colonies there were very few capable of understanding him, and Cowing reckons that only five percent of ministers embraced his New Divinity.[1]

FREEDOM OF THE WILL

In later years Edwards continued to ponder the issues engendered by the Great Awakening, especially soteriology. In *Freedom of the Will,* Edwards returned to a theme that had preoccupied him when he was a student at Yale, and wrote an essay which he called "Notes on the Mind." In it he defended Calvinism against the attacks leveled against it by Latitudinarian Anglicans such as Daniel Whitby, a Cambridge Platonist; Samuel Taylor, the liberally minded Archbishop of Canterbury; and the deist Thomas Chubb. All three attacked the doctrines of predestination and election. Edwards, like Calvinists before him, argued that the omnipotence and sovereignty of God logically demanded divine foreknowledge of all that was to come, and that everything therefore was foreordained.[2]

He argued that to understand ourselves we must first understand God, and not the reverse. He rejected the Arminian contention that humanity is endowed with free will. He maintained that in a Newtonian cosmos of cause and effect, the individual cannot be self-determining. God is not capricious, but does everything for purposes we cannot comprehend with our limited minds. There are only two alternatives, he suggested: either God is not sovereign, in which case He is not God, or humanity is not free.[3]

Like Calvin, and before him Augustine, Edwards was wrestling with the fundamental illogicality of the doctrine of predestination. Like them, he had no success in reconciling free will with it. Like them, he posited false alternatives which were based on assumptions; for instance, in insisting that a sovereign God could not be limited in His powers. Edwards' central problem was that he was trying to apply logical analysis to doctrines that were essentially irrational, matters of faith. However, he may himself have come to realize this. Note the following comment on the Great Awakening: "True virtue or holiness has its seat chiefly in the heart, rather than the head." According to Richard Warch, "it therefore followed that true religion consisted principally of raised affections or passions."[4]

Based on Calvin, Edwards asserted that freedom is the power

to pursue an inclination. In following their inclinations human beings are accountable even though they have no choice in the matter, a point that is obviously illogical. To answer that charge, Edwards distinguished between natural and moral necessity. By nature, humanity is predetermined; however, not knowing the outcome of choices made, human beings must still act morally to God's greater glory.[5]

Edwards rejected the Federal, or covenant theology, and reverted instead to the full-blown Calvinism and Augustinianism of the Reformation. In doing so, he did for the generation of the Great Awakening what Karl Barth, Emil Brunner, and Reinhold Niebuhr did with the doctrine of Neo-Orthodoxy for the post–World War I generation. Rejecting infralapsarianism, Edwards argued that Adam did not have free will before the Fall. Instead he was predestined to disobey from the moment of his creation, and the damnation of humanity in a fallen world necessarily followed.

Edwards dwelt on humanity's deep alienation from God. He stated that it is an illusion to suppose that a person can save himself. God alone saves by working the transformation of human nature through the Holy Spirit. He saw no conflict between divine determinism and the latest scientific and philosophical theories. Instead, he thought that Newtonian physics and Lockean epistemology confirmed his theology.

CHARLES CHAUNCY

The Opposers included several scholarly ministers who collected and published testimonials from people who had experienced the Awakening. Chief among these scholars were Thomas Prince and Charles Chauncy. Prince, a moderate supporter of revivalism, collected documents and accounts of incidents during the Great Awakening, which he published serially in his journal *Christian History* (1744). Chauncy, as we have seen, collected correspondence about Davenport and other radicals as sources for his major work on the Awakening, *Seasonable Thoughts on the State of Religion in New England*, which appeared in 1743.

In *The New Creature* (1742), Chauncy had preached a sermon that was not very different in doctrinal content from Edwards' *Sinners in the Hands of an Angry God.* Was Chauncy a minister afraid to challenge his congregation and public opinion until it was a safe option, or was he simply slow to make up his mind

Charles Chauncy (1705–1787). Courtesy of the Harvard University Portrait Collection.

about the Awakening? We do not know. However, it is highly probable that Chauncy preached hellfire and damnation less from conviction than from expediency. At the height of the Awakening in Boston, it was prudent to follow the tide. Chauncy behaved as have so many religious liberal ministers since, especially those who, like Chauncy, were pastors of wealthy congregations. Edwards challenged his congregation in Northampton, and was dismissed for it in 1750. In contrast, Chauncy enjoyed a very long, comfortable pastorate, probably by keeping his unpopular notions to himself, not expressing them until public opinion had become liberal enough for him to speak freely without retaliation.

Therefore, while the revival was in full tide, Chauncy preached evangelical sermons. He carefully avoided any overt criticism of the universally popular Whitefield when the latter appeared in Boston in the autumn of 1740. However, when the unkempt and rough-hewn Gilbert Tennent appeared, and some of the gentry in Boston were offended, Chauncy joined in their disapproval, but still with discretion. But when the outrageous Davenport came in 1742, Chauncy probably felt increasingly free to express his real opinions with great vigor. Davenport's activities inspired him to preach and publish a sermon entitled *Enthusiasm Described and Caution'd Against* (1743). It was Chauncy's first public protest against the "religious Phrenzy." This was followed in the same year by a letter he published anonymously (though it appeared to be generally known that he was the author) entitled *Letter from a Gentleman in Boston, To Mr. George Wishart, One of the Ministers in Edinburgh, Concerning the State of Religion in New England.* In this letter Chauncy asserted that the Awakening was nothing but "the Effect of enthusiastic Heat" and a "Commotion in the Passions."[6] These two publications placed Chauncy in the leadership of the Opposers as their most outspoken advocate.

THE GREAT DEBATE

In March 1743, Jonathan Edwards of Northampton defended the revival as a genuine work of the Holy Spirit in *Some Thoughts on the Revival of Religion in New England.* He tried to explain away the weeping, shouting, and fainting which in his own experience often occurred during evangelical services, arguing that in some temperaments the effects of conviction and conversion were highly emotional. This, however, was irrelevant; a weakness of the flesh. The convictions and conversions in these individuals were no less the work of the Holy Spirit than were those in those whose experiences were attended by emotional self-control.

Edwards had strong views concerning the villification of the ministry. He was no less concerned about unconverted ministers than were Whitefield, Tennent, and Davenport. Ministers must themselves have been confronted by the Holy Spirit and have undergone conversion.[7] However, he objected in the strongest terms to the public denunciation of those who were deficient in spiritual qualifications. Such deficiencies should be dealt with in private by fellow ministers in strict confidence. The laity must not presume to judge the state of the soul of their pastors, and should not desert one for another, and most certainly should not be encouraged to attack the clergy in general.[8] He feared that the whole profession would fall into disrepute. His alarm in this regard had been raised by the critical comments published in Whitefield's *Journal,* and by Gilbert Tennent's much discussed published sermon which he had preached at Nottingham, Pennsylvania: *The Danger of an Unconverted Ministry*.[9] (Tennent was, however, also later shocked by Davenport. He attacked him, urging the devout to "rise up and labour to crush the enthusiastical Cockatrice in the Egg."[10])

Edwards' reservations concerning public attacks against the ministers did not go far enough for Chauncy. He was convinced that the Awakening itself had not been a work of the Holy Spirit, and that the disorders and commotions that had rocked New England during the past two years were because of unstable elements roused by fanatics such as Davenport. To answer Edwards, Chauncy traveled about Massachusetts and Connecticut interviewing ministers and collecting documents. He also engaged in correspondence with ministers in eastern Long Island and Connecticut concerning Davenport in particular, and in that way discovered that the extremes to which the Awakening had gone had a history that began with Ferris at Yale.

Seasonable Thoughts on the State of Religion in New England, published in September 1743, contained the results of his research. He dealt in detail with the radical Evangelists, comparing them to the Camisards, or French Prophets. The latter were Huguenots, who after the revocation of the Edict of Nantes in 1685 had undergone persecution in the France of Louis XIV. During this time some of them had experienced visions and what people of that era called "high transports," or episodes of hysteria. A Camisard family had settled in the Carolinas and caused considerable commotion there because of their wild, irrational religious behavior.

In *Seasonable Thoughts*, Chauncy maintained that most of what the Friends of Revival called convictions and conversions were better explained as exhibitions of enthusiasm. (According to *Merriam Webster's Collegiate Dictionary*, 10th ed. [1995], the latter term is derived from the Greek *enthousiasmos*, meaning to be infused with or possessed by the divine, and was first used in English in 1603. At that time, and up through the eighteenth century, it specifically meant "belief in special revelations of the Holy Spirit." Our modern meaning of the term is, of course, quite different: ardent involvement in any cause or interest, or something inspirational.) Both Chauncy and Edwards agreed that enthusiasm was undesirable: what they disagreed on was the degree to which it was involved in the Great Awakening.[11]

Chauncy's sources, which he quoted verbatim at great length, described what witnesses saw and heard in minute detail, giving evidence in very precise terms, usually without editorial comments of their own, or at least not confusing the two. He invited others, Edwards included, to evaluate his conclusions.

According to Gaustad, "Edwards was further from Davenport and Croswell than from . . . Chauncy, and closest to Dickenson, Colman, and Prince. Croswell was unable to discriminate [between false and genuine experiences in the Awakening]; Chauncy, after 1743, unwilling; while Edwards for over a decade and a half labored to distinguish meticulously the good from the bad."[12]

The intelligentsia on both sides of the Atlantic read both Chauncy and Edwards, and the more liberally minded concluded in the former's favor. Edwards could not make a convincing case for a benevolent creator and ruler of the universe. Liberals argued that Edwards' God of wrath was a monster. Edwards' arguments about the *fruits of the spirit* satisfied few as well.

In later years Chauncy's quiet defense of what Edwards called "Arminianism" enhanced his prestige. After the American Revolution, when he had privately come to the universalist conclusion that God in His benevolence saves all, and that there is no hell, Chauncy again kept his opinions to himself, save for his oblique comments to close friends. To disguise what he was really talking about, he called his doctrine of divine benevolence "the pudding." It was not until 1784 that he published, but still anonymously, a manuscript on a subject which he had been holding back for over twenty years: *The Mystery Hid from Ages and Generations, Made Manifest by the Gospel-Revelation; or, the Salvation of All Men the Grand Thing Aimed at in the Scheme of God.*[13]

THE AWAKENING ENDS

By 1743, and Davenport's New London episode, revival fervor had already cooled throughout most of New England. Indeed, it began to wane in Boston soon after Tennent's departure, but excitement continued for a time in the Connecticut River valley. By 1744 pastors were speaking of the Awakening in retrospect, so when Whitefield arrived that year he had very little success in rousing religious fervor, but instead was greeted with considerable hostility. In New Jersey, by 1746, Gilbert Tennent was speaking of the *late* revival of religion. The Great Awakening was over.

As a legacy, it left divided congregations, a small increase in church attendance, some expressions of personal concern on the part of people seeking spiritual guidance from their pastors, and little else. Butler and Lambert hold that it had little lasting social impact, and did not significantly enhance either individualism or democracy, as is, they claim, particularly evident from the studies made of the histories of towns in New England. They also maintain that it had no impact on the American Revolution. Furthermore, they argue that the Great Awakening did not result in the formation of any new denominations.[14]

In my opinion, Lambert and Butler overstate their case. The Awakening was more closely related to the growth of individualism and egalitarianism than they maintain; for example, in the decrease in deference to authority brought on by the religious fervor.

Also, it had another temporary, but important effect: the persistence of some of the two hundred or so separate churches founded in New England and Long Island during the height of the Awakening. For instance, radical evangelical dissenters withdrew from the Bridgehampton church as a direct result of Davenport's influence in 1741, and founded the first Separate church on Long Island. A building was erected in 1748, and Elisha Payne, a Separate minister from Connecticut, accepted a call to be the first pastor of the new congregation.[15]

The Radical Evangelical Tradition

Doctrinally speaking, the Separates combined traditional New England Puritanism with Whitefield evangelism in Connecticut, western Massachusetts, and New Hampshire. Their Congregationalism was apparent in their strict adherence to the Cambridge Platform of 1648, which institutionalized Calvinism. However, as mentioned previously, they did not adhere to the covenant theology, and they totally rejected the Half-Way Covenant. Though this was not necessarily their conscious intent, the effect was to restore the zealous Puritanism of the original founders of Plymouth and the Massachusetts Bay Colony. However, they differed sharply from the founders in that their ideal was not Winthrop's "Citty on a Hill" or Holy Commonwealth (which was collectivist), but the radical individualism of the New Birth. By emphasizing allegiance to the Cambridge Platform, they legitimized themselves, but the Puritanism to which they had returned was already a mythical ideal. Those among them who were reflective and articulate enough to express themselves in a theoretical way (and they were very few) claimed that the gathered church of born-again saints restored what had been lost by the formalism of the Puritan Church of the late seventeenth and early eighteenth century. Having testified to conversion, these new saints, like those of the Massachusetts Bay Colony when it was founded, entered into fellowship with one another promising, by the grace of God, to obey the Gospel and to walk "as becomes the followers of the Lamb of God."[16] They revived the old practice of demanding public testimonies of religious experience before the whole congregation as a condition of membership, and also the trials of miscreants in public by whole congregations serving as juries. In their intensity, we have the typical features of a sect as contrasted with a denomination, in Weber's terms.

Separate churches appointed "tested" members to the offices of deacon and minister, and ordained their own elders and clergy. The basis of such appointments was entirely experiential, unaccompanied by any educational requirements. Consequently, most Separate ministers and deacons were farmers or craftsmen endowed with the natural ability to preach and exhort, and they were "tested" by the congregations in these terms. Separate ministers adopted from Whitefield a peculiar form of preaching later called the "holy whine."[17]

As Marini asserts, the crucial thing about the Separates during the late 1740s and 1750s was their collective discernment of revealed truth in everything to do with eligibility for membership in the church and church discipline. Marini quotes Ebenezer Frothingham, a Separate preacher, who in 1750 declared, "A saint of God, having Divine light, shining into the Understanding and Love of God ruling in the soul, is also to know certainly that such and such persons are true converts or the saints of God."[18] Frothingham also described Separate meetings: "Crying out, falling down, twitching and convulsive motions, foamings and frothings, trances, visions, and revelations."[19]

A few of the early Separate churches survived and organized themselves into a sect called "Strict Congregationalism." The name implied a return to what the members believed to be the original Puritanism of the founding fathers. Strict Congregationalism flourished in Windham and New London Counties in Connecticut, and also in eastern Long Island.

THE LONG ISLAND STRICT CONGREGATIONALISTS

Because of Davenport, a schism occurred in the church of Upper Aqueboque, near Southold. Sixteen members became New Lights, and the resultant intrachurch bickering lasted eight years.[20] The New Lights complained to the New York presbytery of their minister, charging him with heterodoxy. The charge was dismissed after investigation proved it groundless. The arguments in the church continued, however, and, in 1750, the New Lights walked out of the church in a body during a Sabbath service, crossed the street to a private home, and founded a Separate church of their own. In 1758, this congregation became the first Strict Congregationalist church on Long Island, under the leadership of the above-mentioned Elisha Payne.[21]

The members of this Separate church adopted the Cambridge Platform as their creed, asserting that they professed the original Calvinism of their forefathers. Doctrinally speaking, they emphasized predestination and election, and that the saints know one another. As mentioned earlier, they repudiated the Half-Way Covenant and Stoddardeanism, limited church membership to saints, and revived the Puritan practice of demanding that candidates for membership give public testimonials of their religious experiences before the whole congregation.[22]

Because of the perceived vulnerability to disorder within their congregations caused by the Great Awakening, the majority of the remaining Long Island churches, both Old Lights and New Lights who opposed Separatism, decided to abandon independency and affiliate with the New York Presbytery. The churches of Southold, Bridgehampton, and Easthampton, Long Island, all became Presbyterian during the late 1740s. Other eastern Long Island independent churches formed the habit of asking the presbytery for advice, and in due course they affiliated as well.[23]

During the last half of the eighteenth century and the opening decades of the nineteenth, there were a dozen Strict Congregationalist churches in eastern Long Island. They considered themselves as the only churches worthy of the name. They all owed their origin to the Separate church of Upper Aqueboque, which, in turn, owed its origin to the evangelism of Davenport.

Strict Congregationalists in both eastern Long Island and Connecticut were uneducated farmers who demanded that their ministers be distinguished only by their spiritual gifts. They were highly suspicious of the educated clergy. A good example of a Long Island Strict Congregationalist minister was Daniel Youngs, who was called to the Aqueboque church in 1781. Youngs was a farmer whose highly emotional preaching produced no fewer than seven revivals. On one occasion, while he was in New York, he was told that his daughter had died in his absence, and that, at the same time, a youth in his parish who had been distinguished for his piety had left the church. Youngs remarked, "My heart was more deeply wounded with the latter intelligence than with the former."[24]

In eastern Long Island villages such as Baiting Hollow and Wading River, the Strict Congregationalist church was the center of the community. In Baiting Hollow, the people of the hamlet and surrounding farms met each Saturday to discuss any differences among them. These were settled with reference to the Scriptures.[25] In Wading River, the church was custodian of the village scales, and all business transactions in the community were conducted under the supervision of the minister.[26]

Strict Congregationalists also evangelized among the rapidly dwindling Montauk Indians of eastern Long Island. One Native preacher, Peter John, had been earlier converted by Davenport himself. John organized native Indian congregations at Islip, Poosepetauket, and Morchies. His grandson, Paul Cuffee, underwent conversion in 1776, was ordained a minister, and later became one of the founding members of the Strict Congregationalist Convention of Long Island in 1791. He spent a long pastoral career among the Montauks of eastern Long Island, and organized the Strict Congregationalist church at Shinnecock.[27]

The Long Island Strict Congregationalist Convention, formed in 1791, persisted until 1820.[28] By that time, however, the New Light characteristics of the Separates had moderated. They then affiliated with the Congregationalist denomination, which by then had become conservative and mainstream.

STRICT CONGREGATIONALISM IN CONNECTICUT

As had happened in eastern Long Island, some radical Evangelicals in Connecticut separated from the established churches and formed independent congregations. The first to do so was Canterbury, in January 1743. In doing this, they were theoretically subject to arrest, because they were required by Connecticut law to attend services in the churches of the Standing Order.[29] They formed a denomination called the Strict Congregational Convention of Connecticut in 1781. As on Long Island, the Strict Congregationalists of Connecticut considered themselves to be Separatists after the fashion of the Pilgrims who founded Plymouth. They asserted that the Saybrook Platform was a violation of Congregational principles, and insisted that there should be *no* connection between church and state. They strongly opposed tax-supported churches and the use of civil force to compel church attendance.[30] Like the Separates on Long Island, they rejected the Half-Way Covenant and opposed both Stoddardeanism and Arminianism. They opposed an educated clergy as well. Separatists in Connecticut, as on Long Island, were mainly industrious farmers of little or no education. They disliked the erudite sermons of the regularly licensed and ordained ministers, and preferred the emotional exhortations of people more like themselves.

Lay preachers were anathema to most people in Connecticut, including the vast majority of New Lights. Most also deplored Separatism. To discourage both, the General Court in 1742 had added an amendment to the 1741 act forbidding itinerants to preach in the colony. Under provisions of the amended act, lay exhorters were subject to arrest and imprisonment.[31] Separatists who refused to pay taxes for the support of the established churches, or who refused to attend the established church or the permitted alternatives, were also subject to imprisonment, as well as confiscation of property.[32]

An "act to relieve sober consciences" had been adopted early in the eighteenth century which exempted members of the Anglican, Baptist, and Quaker communions from support of the established (Congregational) church. However, the new Separate churches were not exempted by the General Court, though their existence was at best tolerated.

None of these measures discouraged the Separatists. In the face of disapprobation, they grew stronger, and many who were fighting for freedom of conscience joined their ranks. No fewer than thirty Separate congregations were founded despite the law.[33] Most of these new churches were in the poorest counties in the colony, New London and Windham Counties in eastern Connecticut.

It is not clear whether the more draconian provisions of the act were ever enforced. In 1769, however, the Separates threatened to petition the king for relief. The General Court moderated its course lest they be accused of depriving loyal subjects of their rights as Britons and so endanger the cherished charter.[34] As a result, persecution ceased, but the imposition of taxes to support the Establishment continued. Shortly before and during the Revolution, the Separates received further concessions. After the Revolution, Quakers and Anglicans (always called "Episcopalians" in the colonies) also took up the struggle for complete separation of church and state.

THE CONNECTICUT BAPTISTS

During the 1750s a number of individual members of Strict Congregationalist congregations, and around fifteen of their churches, shifted to the Warren Association and became Baptist. The Warren Association, modeled on the Philadelphia Baptist Association of 1707, was formed in 1757 as a radical evangelical organization. The Philadelphia Association was the original Calvinist Baptist organization in America, its theology based on the Savoy Confession of 1688, a restatement of the Westminster Confession with minor changes.

Prior to the Great Awakening, there had been but five Baptist churches in New England, nearly all of them in Rhode Island. By 1767 they numbered over a hundred. Only a minority of the Baptist congregations in Connecticut belonged to the Warren Association. Most were still independent on the eve of the Revolution. Still others belonged to small, highly localized and short-lived conventions, such as the Stonington Baptist Association of 1772 and the Groton Union Conference of 1783.[35]

The Baptists strongly supported lay exhorters at first, and insisted on a charismatic ministry, but by the 1750s the original fervor had abated, and efforts were made to upgrade the ministry. James Manning founded Rhode Island College at Providence, Rhode Island, to train ministers in a program that attempted to combine emotional fervor with scriptural and theological learning. However, candidates for the Baptist ministry were still required to prove regeneration.

The Warren Association provided New England Baptists with a new confessional and ecclesiastical structure which appealed to the Strict Congregationalists, not least because as Baptists they could avoid paying for the support of the Standing Order. Quite

174   A WONDERFUL WORK OF GOD

logically, since Separatism was founded on the Whitefieldian doctrine of the New Birth, it followed that pedobaptism was a meaningless vestige from Catholic tradition, and that baptism should
follow the conversion of adults. Many Strict Congregationalist
congregations had practiced adult baptism anyway. As early as
1753 there were attempts to establish bonds between Baptists
and the remaining Separates. In that year there was a convention
in Exeter, Rhode Island, attended by delegates from both groups.
However, a dispute between Isaac Backus and Solomon Paine, a
Strict Congregational preacher, shattered the alliance before it
had begun. Backus insisted on adult baptism, whereas Paine and
his followers remained attached to pedobaptism. A second convention the next year, this time at Stonington, Connecticut,
failed because the breach widened over the same issue, and the
ecumenical experiment was temporarily abandoned.[36]

During the years preceding the Revolution, Separates and Baptists in Connecticut led a struggle for separation of church and
state, as mentioned earlier. When the Revolution broke out, Baptists and Separates (like most other Americans at the time) ago-
nized as to which side to join, if any. A few became Loyalists and
eventually moved to Nova Scotia, where they were among the
New Lights who, under the leadership of Henry Alline, fostered
the Nova Scotia Awakening. Others took the same pacifist stance
as the Quakers, and remained neutral. Most, however, supported
the Revolution.

After the absorption of the Strict Congregationalists into the
Baptist sects, Connecticut Baptist evangelists Shuball Stearns
and Daniel Marshall introduced the Baptist message to Hanover
County, Virginia, in 1755. By so doing they initiated the Southern
Awakening, an aftereffect of the Great Awakening.[37] During
these same years, Whitefield made return visits to America and
also evangelized in the South. His converts, however, later became Methodists because of the revivalism of Francis Ashbury.
The Methodist and Baptist churches became the dominant ones
in the South during the nineteenth century. Hitherto, most people of the Piedmont, and many in the tidewater districts of the
South, had been unchurched. Anglicanism had long since lost its
hold on all but a small minority of southerners, chiefly the
wealthier planters.

Because of the evangelism of Marshall and Stearns, there is
continuity between the Strict Congregationalists of Connecticut
and the Baptists of the South, just as the Methodists in the South

owe their origins to Wesley, Whitefield, and Ashbury. Both denominations are the inheritors of the transatlantic revivals.

SUMMING UP

Very profound issues are involved in the Great Awakening, an
American colonial religious phenomenon which encapsulates
many of the issues one encounters in the history of world religions. One finds many religious alternatives within any one
religion: Quakers, French Prophets, Pietists, New Light Congregationalists, and New Sides Presbyterians have parallels in the
shamans of Central Asia and Siberia, the Dionysians and Eleusin-
ians of ancient Greece, the initiates in the Mystery Religions of
the Hellenistic Near East, the Jewish Hassidim, the Islamic Sufis,
the Hindu adherents of Tantra, and the Buddhists of the Amidist
sects.

The Great Awakening defined American Protestantism. One of
its effects was the furtherance of Americanization. The Presbyterians, for instance, abandoned their Old World connections with
the passing of the original Scotch-Irish pastors and the emergence of ministers who were either born in America or came
when very young, and who were prepared for the ministry in local
schools, of which the "Log College," founded by William Tennent, Sr., was the first. Dutch Reformed people in New Jersey and
New York gradually relinquished their ties with the mother
churches in Holland. New England Puritans were mainly of the
second or third generation, and their ministers were products of
Harvard and Yale. The Great Awakening emphasized their New
England origins even though many pastors regularly corresponded with British colleagues. Whitefield, alienated from his
Anglican connections, joined forces with colonial Presbyterian
and Congregational pastors in his evangelism, identified with
them, and was more affected by them than they were by his English ways. He returned to America on five more evangelical tours
after the Great Awakening, none of them successful. He died in
Philadelphia in 1770, by then as much American as English.

To a limited degree, the Awakening encouraged ecumenity.
This was most apparent in New England and the Middle Colonies
between Congregationalists and Presbyterians, whose differences, in any case, were mainly in church polity. However, the
Awakening also sharpened the clash between Congregationalists
and Anglicans in New England, though it had little or no effect

on the Baptists of Rhode Island and almost none on relations between the Congregationalists and Presbyterians on the one hand
and Quakers on the other. While Fredrick Frelinghuysen and Gilbert Tennent became friends, there were few ties between the
Dutch Reformed of the Raritan valley and the Scotch-Irish and
transplanted New England Presbyterians there. Whitefield initially admired and befriended the Moravians when he helped
found Nazareth, but he soon broke with them over theological differences. He had little contact with German Pietists in Pennsylvania, almost none with Quakers, and was strongly opposed by
the Anglican clergy and laity throughout the colonies. On the
other hand, the effects of itinerant preaching and the circulation
of printed pamphlets and sermons during the revival did much to
spread Evangelicalism itself, and, by so doing, had powerful effects that transcended sectarianism.

Whereas radical revivalists such as Davenport and Allen had
their greatest appeal among people of the lower orders, their hostility to the upper classes was chiefly confined to evangelical anticlericalism, attacks against the allegedly unconverted ministry.
Since many Opposers in New England were members of the mercantile and professional elite, there could be some implications
drawn here that a class struggle was involved in the Awakening.
However, this struggle was not political. The Friends of Revival
also included many who were of the gentry, so the class conflict
aspect of revivalism was further diluted.

The Baptists of Virginia were deeply offended by the cockfights,
horse races, dances, finery, and mansions of the Anglican gentry;
to them, as poor folk, an affront.[38] The issue was not class struggle so much as revulsion on the part of the Baptists against the
snobbery and self-indulgence of the gentry; they acted as though
they thought themselves too good to damn. This, I believe, was
an underlyling issue of the Great Awakening, so that whether or
not it actually had lasting effects, the revival itself raised issues
that are perennially relevant.[39]

Recent studies show that the Great Awakening had very little
impact on the political and social forces that contributed to the
Revolution in the north. However, as we have seen, some implications of class conflict in the South were present in Baptist evangelicalism on the eve of the Revolution.

While Lambert and some other revisionists insist that the
Great Awakening was an invention on the part of its promoters,
Lambert's own studies of Whitefield and the Awakening confirm
that there was much religious excitement in New England and

the Middle Colonies during 1740–42. He certainly does not deny that Whitefield, Edwards, the Tennents, and other itinerants drew large crowds at some of their meetings, if not all of them, and that there was much discussion of religious issues in the press. Why does this not deserve the title, "The Great Awakening"? However, the revisionists, beginning with Jon Butler, have increased our understanding of the revival by offering new insights while questioning some older ones. The discussions of the Awakening presented by Trinterud, Miller, and Gaustad are still valid in my opinion. What they chiefly lack is an understanding of the important role that promotionism played, discussed by Lambert.

The revisionists have *not* dealt with the theological issues that emerged from the Awakening, especially in New England. These have been discussed very thoroughly by Miller, Gaustad, and Wright, as well as in many journal articles. In my view, the principal outcome of the Awakening was doctrinal. The emphasis on sudden conversion on the part of the Evangelicals forced both the Friends of Revival and Opposers to rethink such issues as original sin, religious affects, and regeneration. These debates were followed by others of an even deeper theological nature: the sovereignty of God, predestination, grace, and the benevolence of the Deity. As Wright showed in *The Beginnings of Unitarianism,* the debates that followed the Awakening had profound effects on New England Congregationalism and ultimately resulted in its split into orthodox Congregationalism and Unitarianism.

Many historians apply the terms "Calvinism" and "Puritanism" to the Congregational and Presbyterian doctrines of the eighteenth and early nineteenth centuries. Both terms are inappropriate. *Calvinism* should refer only to the teachings of John Calvin himself in such texts as *Institutes of the Christian Religion.* Calvinism, though one of the movements of the Protestant Reformation, was already undergoing much diversification by the end of the sixteenth century. *Puritanism* only applies to the English and colonial American movement embraced by dissenters during the early seventeenth century. By the late seventeenth and early eighteenth centuries, both Calvinism and Puritanism had undergone much development as exemplified by Federal Theology, Arminianism, the New Divinity of Jonathan Edwards, and the Evangelicalism of the New Lights and New Sides in both New England and the Middle Colonies. We have here the evolution of a religious movement which began with the Reformation and which became increasingly complex and diversified during the

course of the seventeenth and eighteenth centuries. The Great
Awakening was one of several episodes that added to that complexity and diversity.

While neither the Friends of Revival nor the Opposers explicitly dealt with the issue of predestination, it underlay their debates. In general, the Evangelicals emphasized dependence on
divine grace manifest in the crisis of conversion, whereas the Opposers (whom they accused of Arminianism) stressed the gradual
infusion of divine grace over the course of the person's lifetime.
In later years the latter abandoned predestinarianism chiefly by
ignoring it. It was not explicitly and formally rejected until the
early nineteenth century, when Unitarianism emerged, and even
then, very cautiously, and chiefly by evasion. Neither the Friends
of Revival nor the Opposers denied divine sovereignty, but, instead, focused their attention on the signs of redemption in people who had undergone religious experiences. In that respect, in
modern terminology, the chief issues of the Great Awakening and
later were in the realm of the psychology of religious experience,
in those days called "religious affects."

Old Lights, such as Chauncy, were able to show that the "enthusiasts" were proud and arrogant, as well as boisterous and ex-
cessively fervent. The twice-born felt superior to those who had
not "seen the light." This, I think, is as true today as during the
Great Awakening, and is the thrust in the Old Light argument
against enthusiasm. Chauncy, Mayhew, and the other Opposers
were not very impressed by the character and behavior of Whitefield, Tennent, and Davenport; did not find exemplifications of
Christian love in them, but, to the contrary, much evidence of
pride and hate. Even at this distance in time, one easily detects
Whitefield's vanity in his *Journals.* He constantly boasts about
the size of the crowds he gathers, and about his impact on them.
Whitefield's hypocrisy in attacking leading New England ministers in his journal after being on apparently good terms with
them disgusted many ministers who had been friends of the revival. Davenport's and Tennent's vituperous attacks against the
"unconverted clergy" angered many. It was for this reason that
Edwards, Dickinson, and Chauncy argued so fiercely with the
New Lights about the "marks of a Work of God." They were concerned with the "fruits of the spirit," the changed attitudes and
behavior that regeneration was supposed to effect.

But the weakness in the "twice-born" message is that regenerates seldom behave any better than those who are unregenerate
and unconverted. The eighteenth-century revivalists, such as Ed-

wards in his *Faithful Narrative,* stridently asserted that the converts abandoned their drunkenness and/or sexual promiscuity, and that the disorders of the young ceased. But Edwards also admitted that the effects were short-lived, and that most of his parishioners reverted to their old ways. Such evidence as we have, and it is very limited, shows that the moral effects of the revivals were temporary. This, indeed, was the chief topic in the "paper war" which followed the Boston revivals in the wake of Whitefield and Tennent.

The eighteenth-century revivals shaped the history of American Protestantism. Beginning with William Ellery Channing's famous Baltimore sermon in 1819, after two decades of acrimonious dispute among Congregationalists of the still surviving Standing Order, the Arminians finally evolved into Unitarians. In 1825 they founded the American Unitarian Association which comprised 125 of the churches of Massachusetts.

The heritage endures and the issues persist. Today the visitor to Peterborough, Massachusetts, for example, will find two identical churches with tall steeples on the commons, both of them gleaming white and imposing. One church is called "First Congregational Church (Trinitarian)" and the other, "First Congregational Church (Unitarian)." They are relics of the Great Awakening.

But the spiritual descendants of the New Lights abound in the many Pentacostal churches which attract huge numbers of Americans today. The most recent revival of Evangelicalism and the New Birth has been during the 1970s and 1980s, testimony that the religious issues raised during the Great Awakening are far from exhausted.

Appendix I: Evangelicalism

THE GREAT AWAKENING AND RELIGIOUS EXPERIENCE

TO UNDERSTAND THE DEEPER ISSUES RAISED BY THE GREAT AWAKENing, it is necessary to discuss the Christian concept of conversion, or being twice born. In colonial America this phenomenon was interpreted in the context of Puritanism, which in turn stemmed from the teachings of the Reformer John Calvin, who revived and expounded upon Augustine's *Confession*. Augustine had a religious experience much like that encountered in the New Testament Book of Acts, the story of Saul's confrontation by Christ while on the Damascus highway. In Pauline teachings, experience is paramount, and this is reiterated in his letters, especially in his Epistle to the Romans.

EARLY CHRISTIAN ANTECEDENTS

Theologically speaking, the origins of Puritanism were in the teachings of Paul, Augustine, and Calvin. Paul emphasized the apocalyptic message of John the Baptist and Jesus, the good news that a new age was about to begin, the long heralded "Day of the Lord" of Isaiah and other Hebrew prophets. Paul expected the end-time to occur in his own day. His was therefore a crisis theology, a teaching for the last days. The central emphasis in the soteriologies of Paul, Augustine, and Calvin was the New Birth. According to all three, all human beings are born in a state of sin because of the disobedience of Adam and Eve. Christian theologians refer to this episode in Genesis 2:46—3 as the "Fall." Humanity was not only alienated from God, but from the natural world as well, and the natural world from God. Thus fallen man lives in a fallen world.[1]

Paul, and later Augustine and Calvin, held that God has predestined all human beings either for damnation or redemption. The latter is offered through reception of the saving grace of the

Holy Spirit, who alone works the transformation of the sinner into the saint. By *saint*, Paul meant one who underwent New Birth, or conversion, and, in consequence, becomes a child of God. Saints have been given an inner *habitus* which enables them to obey the will of God both in their inner life and their outer behavior. Only those who have been born again are of the elect, and only the elect are predestined for eternal bliss in the life to come.[2]

Paul

In C.E. 34 Saul of Tarsus was on the road to Damascus from Jerusalem when he was suddenly struck by a blinding light and heard the voice of Christ calling to him: "Saul, Saul, why persecutist thou me?" (Acts 9:4).[3] He fainted, was taken to Damascus, and there recovered from his blindness, a changed person. He had experienced what the Puritans call "New Birth," and to mark this momentous occasion he changed his name to Paul. Thereafter, he embarked on missionary journeys in which he preached the gospel of Christ in Asia Minor, Greece, and finally Rome, where he was put to death on the Appian Way in C.E. 64.

What little we know about Paul is from his letters and from the New Testament Book of Acts, which is a continuation of Luke. According to tradition, Acts was written by Paul's personal physician who accompanied him on his evangelical travels. Of the letters, at least nine probably were his. There is less certainty about the others. Some letters, such as 2 Corinthians, were edited a generation after his time and are thought by scholars to have been molded to fit the purposes of conservatives who were then consolidating and structuring the Church. Other letters, such as 1 and 2 Timothy and Titus, were composed by others, and attributed to him. Several interpolations, including 1 Corinthians 14:34–35 and Romans 16:17–18, are believed to have been added to emphasize sexually chauvinistic and authoritarian ideas. The letters that scholars agree were essentially Paul's are Romans, 1 and 2 Corinthians, Galatians, Philippians, Philemon, 1 Thessalonians, and, with less certainty, 2 Thessalonians. There is therefore considerable dispute among scholars concerning Paul's writings.[4] They are, however, what the Christian Church canonized, and are what Puritans, like other Christians, accepted without question as the revealed Word of God.

Since Pauline thought had enormous impact on early Christian theology, he has been regarded by many as a systematic theologian. This he was not. His letters were highly situational replies to particular issues put to him by troubled congregations. He was not concerned with doctrinal issues as a whole, and certainly did not present a *summa*.

What is most important to Puritanism in general and to the Great Awakening in particular is Paul's soteriology, or concept of salvation. His viewpoint was not individualistic, but cosmic and apocalyptic. He believed that he was living in the end-time, and that the Day of Judgment was at hand. The passages that have most preoccupied Evangelicals deal with the conversion experience, spiritual enthusiasm in the Greek sense of the term (*enthousiasmos*—to be possessed by a god or spirit), and the hope of future vindication.[5]

Paul believed that a new age had begun, that Christ was the first to be risen from the dead, and that others soon would be resurrected as well. His was therefore a crisis theology. Salvation was offered to all regardless of ethnic origin, to both Jews and Greeks (Romans 10:12–13). Because he took Christianity out of the synagogue and preached the "gospel of Christ" to gentiles as well as to Jews, it was with him that Christianity first became a world religion.

Much in his letters centers on contemporary issues such as "idolatry": not just the worship of graven images as such, but the deeper symbolic significance involved. God the Father, in Paul's teachings, is the wrathful supreme being of Judaism, but the apostle was radical in his rejection of Jewish law: probably, but not certainly, Torah. Particularly relevant to Puritanism and to the Great Awakening was his emphasis on divine wrath, which, as set forth in Galatians, Romans, and elsewhere, can only be escaped through faith in the Gospel, not through works. Faith is a disposition to accept and obey given by God as an act of grace, therefore unmerited. Law and works, to Paul, mean human efforts, and imply a person's ability to save himself, which Paul rejected completely. Instead, salvation from divine wrath is accomplished only through the *charisma* (or gift of God) paid for by Christ's sacrifice on the cross (Galatians 3:1–5). Faith confers a new relationship to God through baptism, in which the person dies to the old Adam, that is to say, the old self, and is born again in the new self (Galatians 3:26–29). Later Christians referred to this as *New Birth*. This was the central issue of the Great Awakening.

Paul referred to his own conversion on the Damascus road around C. E. 34 in two passages in his letters: 1 Corinthians 15:8 and Galatians 1:15–17. His confrontation by Jesus in that theophanic experience proved to him that Jesus was the *Messiah* or "anointed one"; in the Greek of the New Testament, *Christos*. This experience established his mystical relationship with Christ (Philippians 3:3–4). Paul refers to this as being *called* (Galatians 1:15–16) rather than being *converted,* which was the Calvinist term used by the Puritans. This is because his encounter with the risen Christ was a *call* for him to become an evangelist, or missionary, to the gentiles, or non-Jews. His former zeal for the law suddenly gave way to a commitment to bring about the inclusion of the gentiles into the community of those who were *in Christ, without* imposing the burden of the law (Romans 3:29–31). In this Paul differed sharply from the other apostles (such as James and Peter) who, in various degrees, insisted that converts to Christianity must conform to Jewish law. In this connection Paul stressed such features as flesh versus spirit, slavery versus freedom, and law versus promise.

These comments were always directed to immediate issues which were being disputed in the churches. In his brilliant letter to the Christian congregation in Rome, Paul presented a well-organized treatise on the righteousness of God revealed through faith (Romans 1:16–17). According to Paul, since all human beings are saved by faith rather than by works of self-justification, baptism inaugurates a new life in which slavery to sin is broken (Romans 6:3–5). God gives his creatures free will to work out their own salvation, but, being omniscient, God has foreknowledge of all that is to come. Those who are in Christ are *saints,* who alone will escape divine wrath.

Repeatedly, Paul stresses the contention that the law tempts people into aggressive self-righteousness, into pride. This, he warns, is the way that leads to death and destruction (Romans 3:20–24). Of particular concern to both the Puritans of the early seventeenth century and their descendants among the Evangelicals of the eighteenth century was Paul's teaching that true righteousness is a *gift* of God through faith. The New Age has begun. It occurs within the fallen world of sin and decay in which there is the eschatological hope for the triumph of righteousness. It will happen soon, accomplished by the love of God which triumphs even over death.

Paul's teachings were of prime importance to all Christians, but especially to Augustine, and later, to the Protestants. Whereas Catholicism is Petrine, the papacy being founded on Christ's words, "[T]hou art Peter, and upon this rock I will build my church" (Matthew 16:18), Protestants have emphasized the

Pauline doctrine of New Birth. As well as New Birth, Paul emphasized predestination (Romans 8:29–30) and covenant theology. All three were essential features of Puritanism. *Priorizein,* or "to mark out before" in Paul's letters, refers to a view of history that attributes the cause of all events to a previously decreed plan or decision of God.

His epistles, or letters, gave practical advice to young, struggling Christian congregations, and in them, as we have said before, he dealt with specific issues. Theologians later made isolated chapters and verses the basis of extended discussions. The ideas of theologians, including the Church Fathers, Augustine, Thomas Aquinas, and the Protestant Reformers, are their own. To give them authority they based them on scriptural passages, usually taken out of context. Biblical texts are always subject to all-too-human interpretation. In the case of terms such as *priorizein,* in Paul's letters, it is by no means certain that he necessarily attributed the cause of historical events to the so-called divine decrees. As the Arminian critics such as Daniel Whitby, a Cambridge Platonist, showed, those scriptural passages that Calvin and his followers interpreted as "decrees," and on which their doctrines of predestination and election were based, were subject to more than one interpretation.[6]

The Puritans spoke often of the "decrees." This biblical concept is a necessary corollary of divine control over nature and history. To the Puritans, the omnipotence of God, which is emphasized in both the Old and New Testament, implied predestination. There are many passages in both testaments cited by Augustine, Calvin, and the Puritan divines as scriptural warrant this belief. Second Isaiah's proclamation of future events is the means by which they are known, and also establishes that they are predestined:

> I have declared the former things from the beginning; and they went forth out of my mouth, and I shewed them; I did them suddenly, and they came to pass. Because I knew that thou art obstinate, and thy neck is an iron sinew, and thy brow brass; I have even from the beginning declared it to thee; before it came to pass I shewed it thee: lest thou shouldest say, Mine idol hath done them, and my graven image, and my molten image, hath commanded them. . . . I have shewed thee new things from this time, even hidden things, and thou didst not know them. (Isaiah 48:3–6).

In Isaiah 41:26: "Who hath declared from the beginning, that we may know? and beforetime, that we may say, He is righteous?

yea, there is none that sheweth, yea, there is none that declareth, yea, there is none that heareth your words." In the New Testament, Paul in Galatians 3:16 writes: "Now to Abraham and his seed were the promises made"; in 1 Peter 1: 20: "Who verily was foreordained before the foundation of the world, but was manifest in these last times for you." In Acts 2:23: "Him, being delivered by the determinate council and foreknowledge of God, ye have taken, and by wicked hands have crucified and slain." According to Paul:

> For whom he did foreknow, he also did predestinate to be conformed to the image of his Son, that he might be the firstborn among many brethren. Moreover whom he did predestinate, them he also called: and whom he called, them he also justified: and whom he justified, them he also glorified. (Romans 8:29–30)

Closely related to predestination is the doctrine of covenants, which was also essential to both Calvinism and Puritanism. Protestants of the Reformed faith read their Bibles in terms of a series of covenants beginning with the one that God makes with Noah. In Genesis 9:12–16:

> This is the token of the covenant which I make between me and you and every living creature that is with you, for perpetual generations: I do set my bow in the cloud, and it shall be for a token of the covenant between me and the earth. . . . . [W]hen I bring a cloud over the earth, that the bow shall be seen in the cloud: and I will remember my covenant, which is between me and you and every living creature of all flesh; and the waters shall no more become a flood to destroy all flesh.

The covenant with Noah is followed by many others, among them the covenant with Abraham which institutes the practice of circumcision as the mark of the chosen people (Genesis 17: 9–14), and the one with Moses on Sinai when he receives the tablets of the law (Exodus 20). God finally makes a covenant of grace with humanity through the resurrection of Christ with its promise of deliverance in the life to come (1 Corinthians 15:20–21, among many). Indeed, the terms New and Old Testaments *mean* new and old covenants.

The Patristic Writings

Christian theology was forged by the patristic writers, or Church Fathers.[7] These were theologians of Greek and Roman origin such as Ignatius, Origen, Tertullian, and Irenaeus, and mystics such as Dionysius the Areopagite. All were deeply learned in Greco-Roman philosophy and were influenced by the Greco-Roman religious traditions into which they were born. They interpreted Christian doctrine in terms of Greek philosophy. This is particularly true of the *Logos,* or Word, which, in Neo-Platonic and Stoic thought, referred to the link between the divine which is transcendent and perfect and the highly imperfect fallen world. In Christian thought, beginning with John 1:1–3, it is taught, "In the beginning was the Word [the *Logos*], and the Word was with God, and the Word was God. The same was in the beginning with God. All things were made by him; and without him was not any thing made that was made." Jesus Christ was the *Logos.* This teaching, which lends itself to possible Gnostic origins, was much expanded upon by the Catholic Church Fathers who emphasized both the full humanity and the divinity of Jesus the Messiah, or Christ.

The culminating work of the Church Fathers was the doctrine of the trinity, which was forged by Bishop Athanasius and adopted over the opposition of the Arians at the Council of Nicaea in C.E. 329. At that council, and also the subsequent Council of Chalcedon, the basic creed of orthodox Christianity was formulated and authorized by the Emperor Constantine. His support may have had something to do with its acceptance over the alternative offered by Arius, who, on the basis of equally sound scriptural exegesis, argued that Christ the Son, as the *Logos,* was the *first* creation of the Father, and not a person of the Trinity.[8]

According to the Nicene Creed, the Father, Son, and the Holy Spirit are entirely distinct persons of the Godhead. This is a familiar doctrine in the history of religions in which the divine as pure being is conceived to have modalities. In Zoroastrianism, for example, there are seven persons in the Godhead Ahura Mazda, one of which is Ahriman the Evil One. In Hinduism, Brahm-Atman, transcendent world soul, is manifest in ninety thousand modalities or persons which are not separate gods but *avatars* of the supreme being.

Before, during, and after the Great Awakening, the Nicene Creed was challenged by dissidents who espoused Arianism,[9] as well as later by Unitarians who, finding no scriptural warrant for the Trinity, asserted the unity of the Godhead and the simple humanity of Jesus as the Messiah whom God chose, and whom God resurrected from the dead to prove the reality of eternal life. Gnosticism was revived by the Antinomians, heretics who asserted in effect that the divine is manifest in impulses and impressions, special revelations to individual persons; that God does not reveal Himself in Scripture nor does He act through the medium of priests and ministers. Both the Antinomians and the Quakers, or Friends, argued that God reveals Himself to everyone in an Inner Light which supersedes Scripture. They also believed in the priesthood of all believers, and that sacraments are meaningless rituals.

All of these alternatives, and others, flourished in early Christianity. However, after the conversion of Constantine, the ruling classes in the Roman Empire embraced trinitarian orthodoxy. At that time, for political reasons as well as religious, one set of doctrinal standards or creeds were made mandatory, and all alternatives were ruthlessly suppressed. As the Western Roman Empire declined, and civilization was increasingly threatened by barbaric forces such as those of the German invaders and Attila the Hun, the Latin Church became increasingly authoritarian.

Augustine, C.E. 354–430

The greatest of the early Christian theologians was Augustine of Hippo (North Africa), who flourished during the last century of the Western Roman Empire, at a time when the classical civilizations of Greece and Rome were in decay, and when the young religion, Christianity, had become the state religion of the Empire.[10] Calvin's teachings were essentially a restatement of those of Augustine, and Puritanism was inherently Augustinian.

Augustine, like many in his time, undertook a religious quest. In the course of his spiritual journey he was befriended by Ambrose (339–97), the Bishop of Milan. In his *Confessions*, Augustine recorded his conversion experience. It happened one day while he was in a garden: "I was . . . weeping in the most bitter contrition of my heart, when, lo, I heard the voice of a boy or girl . . . chanting, and oft repeating, 'Take up and read; take up and read.'" Augustine took up his scroll of Romans at random, and read 13:13–14: "Not in rioting and drunkeness, not in chambering and wantoness, not in strife and envying. But put ye on the Lord Jesus Christ, and make not provision for the flesh, to fulfill the lusts thereof." At that moment, Augustine underwent a profound religious experience, a dramatic, life-transforming crisis wherein his sexual, willful, and spiritual conflicts were suddenly resolved in complete surrender to God.[11] Thus, in Augustine's case, as with Paul, his Christian life began with New Birth. His example was often cited during the Great Awakening.

Immediately after his conversion experience, Augustine was baptized in Milan by Ambrose (Easter time in C.E. 387). Thereafter, he became a prolific writer of Christian literature, his works including *De Immortalitate Animae* (On the Immortality of Souls) and *De Quantitate Animae* (On the Greatness of the Soul) which incorporated his new biblical theology enlivened by religious experience. Because of his emphasis on the latter, Augustine, among the early Christian writers, was of prime importance to Protestants. The above works were followed by his *Confessions* which he began at the age of forty-three. In 397, he was appointed as a bishop and had become an authority figure among Western Christians. He was by then located in Hippo in North Africa, where he spent the remainder of his days.[12]

The *Confessions* is not only a testimonial, but an essay on the doctrines of the incarnation and the Trinity. Here, based on his exegesis of Romans 9 and 11, Augustine denied that God actively predestined the nonelect for eternal damnation. Instead, God allowed them to receive the *just consequences* of their disobedience and alienation from Him. In part at least on the basis of his own conversion experience, he emphasized the central importance of a dramatic religious crisis, after which the believer assumes that he or she is one of the elect, or chosen, of God.

The Calvinist doctrine of predestination and election was essentially based on Augustine's writings, especially *De Libero Arbitrio* (On Free Will), one of his earlier writings.[13] In Platonic fashion, this presented a dialogue between himself and a fictional adversary whom he called Evodius. The topic is the apparent contradiction between evil and the goodness of the omnipotent deity. Evodius asks, "Tell me, pray, whether God be not the author of evil."[14] Augustine's reply is that God has endowed humanity with free will, which necessarily means that Adam and Eve were created in a blameless state, but had the power to choose between good and evil. Without this potentiality, they would have been automatons, no different from the animals, and certainly not creatures made in the image of God. They were endowed with reason and understanding, by use of which powers they could make moral choices. They chose to disobey God and therefore sinned; sin, by definition, being defiance of God's will. "Properly speaking," wrote Augustine, "human nature means the blameless nature with which man was originally created. But we also use it in speaking of the nature with which we are born mortal, ignorant and subject to the flesh, which is really the penalty of sin."[15] Augustine quotes Paul in Ephesians 2:3: "And were by nature the children of wrath, even as others." Augustine continues:

> As we are born from the first pair to a mortal life of ignorance and toil because they sinned and fell into a state of error, misery and death, so it most justly pleased the most high God, Governor of all things, to manifest from the beginning, from man's origin, his justice in exacting punishment.

Augustine added:

> When the first man was condemned, happiness was not so completely taken from him that he lost also his fecundity. Though his offspring was carnal and mortal, yet in its own way it could contribute some glory and ornament to the earth. . . . But if any of Adam's race should be willing to turn to God, and so overcome the punishment which had been merited by the original turning away from God, it was fitting not only that he should not be hindered but that he should also receive divine aid. In this way also the Creator showed how easily man might have retained, if he had so willed, the nature with which he was created, because his offspring had power to transcend that in which he was born.[16]

Augustine therefore wrestled with the problem of evil in a world ruled by an omnipotent God of love by saying that evil was the result of God's gift of free will. God gave man the potentiality for doing right or wrong. From the time of Adam's sin, however, all of his progeny inherited the inclination to do evil, and, though not wholly depraved, are impaired. This impairment can only be overcome by God's grace, hence the incarnation of God in Christ to pay man's debt and to enable those who are of the elect, or chosen of God, to be liberated from the burden of sin. God gives His grace knowing that many will refuse it. The entirely just consequence of this refusal, however, is damnation, which God does not will, but lets happen.

Augustine draws a distinct difference between "predestination" and "determinism." Predestination only concerns God's initiating the free gift necessary for overcoming the impairment of sin. It has nothing to do with free choice in all other areas of life such as family, work, and politics. In his early writings, Augustine rejected any form of predeterminism that would ascribe to God or to fate direct, detailed control over all areas of human life, so that free choice would be an illusion. *De Libero Arbitrio*, it must be said, is not about the same issue as his later writings on predestination, especially his controversy with Pelagius concerning the efficacy of works in salvation.

According to Augustine, evil is the result of Adam's sinful act of free will in which he disobediently ate of the forbidden fruit. By so doing he and Eve lost their innocence and became shamefully aware of their sexuality. Augustine referred to this act of disobedience as the Fall, meaning the fall from grace. The progeny of the primal pair inherited the inclination to evil. Consequently, all human beings since the time of the Fall have been sinners. No amount of good works chosen by man could make up for this propensity for evil; only God's grace could undo the original sin. Grace *(karis)* means the disposition to show favor. In Pauline thought, God's unrestrained kindness is offered by Him even though it is in no way deserved or earned by the beings to whom it is given. Beginning with Paul, and as reiterated by Augustine, grace was central to Christian theology. In Paul's terms, to be justified by God means to be righteous before God. For humankind, the possibility of eternal damnation was the price of moral freedom. Divine foreknowledge does not obliterate human freedom. God simply foresees the choice that free moral agents will make.[17] In Augustine's own words: "God . . . made all natures, not only those which were to abide in virtue and justice, but also those that were to sin. He did not make them in order that they might sin, but that whether they willed to sin or not to sin they might be ornaments of his universe. . . . God knows beforehand that they will sin."[18]

The basis of authority for Augustine, and, during medieval times, for Thomas Aquinas and other scholastic philosophers, was *natural theology.* Based on Aristotle's metaphysics, natural theology was what could be known of the divine through natural reason. Presuming the authority of revelation in the Scriptures, natural theologians attempted to use reason to discern truth. The theory, derived from Plato and Aristotle, was that if one's reasoning is logically consistent, it is also true in objective fact. Thus God's existence could be proven by logic, as Aquinas claimed to do in *Summa Contra Gentiles* and *Summa Theologica* during the twelfth century.

Augustine argued that God is rational and that there are logical reasons for His actions. God must be omnipotent and omniscient, or else He is not deity. It was inconceivable to the Patristic Fathers and to Augustine that God was in any way limited. Being omniscient, He necessarily knows beforehand all that is to come even though He has allowed free will to human beings.

In his later years Augustine was challenged by the Celtic British monk Pelagius (d. 418). Shocked by the gross decadence of culture accompanying the disintegration of the Western Roman Empire, Pelagius asserted the need for individual and collective moral responsibility. He maintained, as did the Jews, that Adam sinned only for himself and not for all of humanity, and that all human beings are able to behave rightly if they so choose without the need for New Birth. Humanity has *not* been impaired by the Fall. Instead, human beings have the inherent capacity for moral achievement. This was not only a revival of the Jewish ethic, but a harbinger of modern humanism. Pelagius asserted that human beings could save themselves by their righteousness: every person has the potential to attain salvation by his or her good works, and bliss in the life to come is a matter of just deserts. Pelagius attracted a considerable following of enthusiastic disciples. His doctrines were later embraced by Julian, the bishop of Eclanum. The latter was Augustine's chief opponent during his later years.[19]

In all of his polemical writings, Augustine struck out most aggressively against Pelagianism. Indeed, when Pelagius visited North Africa and wrote to Augustine, wishing to meet him, the latter evasively refused since, to him, Pelagius struck at the very heart of the Christian gospel by reviving the view that man could merit salvation by his own moral behavior. Augustine finally succeeded in having Pelagius and his teachings suppressed in C.E. 431.[20]

Augustine answered Pelagius in fifteen works of which two of the most important were *De Spiritu et littera* (On the Spirit and the Letter) and later *De Natura et Gratia* (On Nature and Grace). He confronted Julius of Eclanum in *Contra Julianum*. His purpose was to combat a heresy that threatened the Pauline doctrine of justification by faith; that is to say, the precept that human beings can only be saved by trusting (believing) in the grace of God revealed in Jesus Christ. According to Wilhelm Pauck, Augustine was the only early Christian theologian who revived the original Pauline teaching concerning justification, and developed it further. Augustine began with the assertion that the will is wholly bound by sin and incapable of doing anything meritorious in God's sight. All salvation (the attainment of goodness) depends on God. As "prevenient grace," a new spirit is infused into the human soul. As "cooperating grace," the divine spirit is subsequently present in all human "works," making them acceptable to God. According to Pauck, "All this is understood as justification which is identical with the inspiration of the Holy Spirit (or of love) into the sinful heart of man. In full consistency with this view [Augustine] advanced his doctrine of predestination."[21]

In *De Gratia et libero Arbitrio* (On Grace and Free Will), Augustine asserted, "No man, therefore, when he sins, can in his heart blame God for it, but every man must impute the fault to himself. Nor does it detract at all from a man's own will when he performs any act in accordance with God."[22] In *Contra Julianum* (Against Julian), Augustine railed against the Pelagian bishop, writing: "Know that good will, that good works, without the grace of God . . . can be granted to no one."[23]

At the risk of overgeneralization, it can perhaps be said that the entire history of the Western Christian Church can be reduced to a conflict between Augustine and Pelagius; between the prime importance of either faith or works.

During the fifth century C.E., most theologians, though impressed by Augustine, did not accept the whole of his doctrines of predestination and election, the absolute absence of freedom of the will to do good in the unconverted, and the irresistible power of grace. Instead, they preferred the older views of the earlier Patristic Writers, which, though far less precise than Augustine, and in some ways less consistent, were more acceptable to them.

It is interesting to note that an important aspect of Jung's "confrontation with the unconscious" during and just after World War I involved a recognition by him of the resemblance of his psychological system to that of the Church Fathers and Augustine. Jung argued that he had rediscovered their symbolic way of ferreting out what he called the "archetypes." He adopted this term from Irenaeus, Dionysius the Areopagite, and other early Christian writers, and especially Augustine, who though not actually using the term, referred to it by other words.[24] Thus, the allegorical way of studying Scripture was symbolic in ways that have been revived during the modern age. The point is vital because it is the way that Protestants in general, and Puritans in particular, read their Bibles. Every book, chapter, and verse of Scripture has immediate relevance to events in the present, a concept explored in considerable depth by recent scholars in the field of religion such as Mircea Eliade and Joseph Campbell. The essential thesis in this method is that myths, including biblical texts, as well as rites, which are their enactment and realization in the present, hold revelations of deep significance. The point is important, because there is a popular misconception that the Puritans were biblical literalists like the modern fundamentalists. To the contrary, they interpreted Scripture as the "Great Code," a term coined by the English poet of the eighteenth century William Blake, and expounded upon at considerable length by the Canadian literary scholar Northrop Frye, in his *Anatomy of Criticism.*[25] Thus, Augustine's allegorical system of biblical interpretation (which he learned from Ambrose) anticipated the archetypal school of literary criticism, as expounded by Frye, and was also one of the sources that Jung drew upon during the formative stages of his analytical psychology.[26]

PURITANS IN THE SEVENTEENTH CENTURY

We know the inner side of English Puritanism from its literature. Very devout Puritans kept daybooks and journals in which they recorded their inner experiences. These they carefully scrutinized in the constant search for evidences of divine grace and guidance. Some were very strict in their observances and lifestyle. Margaret Lady Hoby of the North Riding of Yorkshire, for instance, prayed three or four times a day, and when she was not at prayer, it seems she was poring over her Bible. John Bruen of Cheshire rose at three or four in the morning every day and spent two hours in solitary prayer. Later he would lead the family and servants in prayer, and in the singing of psalms, and repeat the same devotions at nightfall. He did virtually nothing but work and worship. In ways such as this, some Puritans made the disciplines of medieval monasticism the basis of their lifestyles—and of that of every member of their households.[27]

Whereas there was considerable variation among Puritan divines where doctrine was concerned, most probably agreed with William Perkins: "There is no virtue or gift of God in us, without our wills; and every good act God's grace and man's will renewed as the instrument of God. And in all good things, industry and labour and invocation on our parts is required."[28]

The education of Puritan ministers stressed the mastery of Greek, Latin, and Hebrew so that, ideally, the minister could read the Scriptures in the original tongues rather than in translation. Clerical education also included rigorous courses in logic to aid in the exegesis of the text.

The typical Puritan minister preached the Gospel in simple terms comprehensible to the common people. Most preachers used familiar and homely similes and illustrations. Their purpose was to make Christianity relevant to everyday life. Their focus was on the Bible which, in Augustinian fashion, was interpreted allegorically. They shared Augustine's belief that the Bible had been given to humanity by God as a code which must be deciphered and applied to even the most incidental aspects of daily life. Every sentence and phrase offered a clue concerning God's intention at the very moment when the Christian pondered the text. To some, even turning to passages at random was a way of discovering God's will in an immediate situation.

Learned Puritans shared the Augustinian-Calvinist view that reason must be used to the utmost in order to discover the hidden meaning of scriptural verse, since, while reason was impaired by the Fall, it was not wholly ruined. The learned regarded philosophy as the handmaiden of theology. The Christian scholar discovered the divine will both in nature and through the exercise of logic.

Many Puritans, those of a more Arminian bent, were wary of emotional experiences, which were called *enthusiasm:* the possession of the mind by a false spirit. *Enthusiasm* was a term derived from Greek classical studies. It was applied to the extreme forms of the conversion experience. It was acknowledged that some ardent souls might undergo dramatic religious experiences, but gradual infusions of divine grace were preferred. These were entirely the work of God, in this view, but it was advisable to study the Scriptures, pray, attend church, and meditate to encourage the Holy Spirit to work salvation in the human soul.

Appendix II: Chronology of Evangelicalism

1675   Jacob Spener publishes *Pia Desideria* (Earnest Desires for a Reform of the Evangelical Church), marking the beginning of Pietism.

1679   Solomon Stoddard of Northampton, Massachusetts stirs the first of five "harvests."

1683   Solomon Stoddard's second "harvest."

1696   Solomon Stoddard's third "harvest."

1705   Francke founds Pietist orphanage in Halle.

1712   Solomon Stoddard's fourth "harvest."

1718   William Tennent, Sr., arrives in America and is settled as Presbyterian minister of Eastchester, New York.

The fifth and last of Stoddard's "harvests."

1721   January: Theodorus J. Frelinghuysen begins preaching "soul-searching" sermons in Dutch Reformed churches of the Raritan River valley in New Jersey.

1725   William Tennent, Sr., founds the "Log College" at Neshaminy, Pennsylvania.

1726   Tennant, Sr., settled as minister of the Presbyterian Church in Neshaminy.

Revivalism peaks among the Dutch of the Raritan River valley.

Gilbert Tennent settles as Presbyterian pastor in New Brunswick, adopts Frelinghuysen's fervent style of preaching.

Jonathan Edwards accepts call to Northampton as Associate Pastor.

1727   Apocalyptic terrors briefly roused in New England by an earthquake.

1729   John Tennent settles in Freehold, New Jersey, and begins preaching in an emotional style which rouses his congregation.

Stoddard dies and Edwards becomes sole pastor in Northampton.

1732   John Tennent dies.

1734   Jonathan Edwards stirs a revival in Northampton.

1735   Edwards goes to New York where he learns about the revivalist activities of Frelinghuysen and the Tennents.

May: Edwards describes the Northampton revival to Colman in a personal letter and is encouraged to expand on it for publication.

1736   The first version of Edwards' *Faithful Narrative.*

Expanded version of Edwards' *Faithful Narrative* is published in London by Isaac Watts and John Guyse and is widely read in both Britain and the colonies.

1738   George Whitefield makes his first visit to America, at Savannah, Georgia.

1739   January 14: Whitefield is ordained at Oxford.

October 30: Whitefield arrives in Lewis Town, Delaware, and proceeds to Philadelphia, preaching to excited crowds in towns along way.

November 3–11: Whitefield preaches to large throngs in Philadelphia and to chiefly Scotch-Irish Presbyterians in and around Philadelphia.

November 13: Whitefield meets Gilbert Tennent in New Brunswick.

November 16–19: Whitefield and Gilbert Tennent travel together to New York City, where Whitefield is refused the pulpit of the Anglican Church. He and Tennent preach out-of-doors to small crowds.

November 23: Whitefield returns to Pennsylvania and meets William Tennent, Sr., at Neshaminy.

November 24: Whitefield preaches once more in the Anglican Church in Pennsylvania, and, with companions, travels south to northeast Maryland, arriving December 3.

1739–40   November 24: Whitefield and companions begin traveling south on horseback through Virginia, North Carolina, and South Carolina, arriving in Georgia January 10.

1740   March 8: Gilbert Tennent preaches "The Danger of an

Unconverted Ministry" to the Nottingham, Pennsylvania, Presbyterian congregation.

March 25: Whitefield begins construction of Bethesda, the orphanage in Savannah, Georgia.

April 13: Whitefield arrives in New Castle, Delaware.

April 14: Whitefield preaches in Wilmington and Philadelphia.

April 17–24: Whitefield preaches in and around Philadelphia, visits Tennent, Sr., again in Neshaminy.

April 26–28: Whitefield preaches in New Jersey, meets Gilbert Tennent again (April 26), Jonathan Dickinson in Elizabeth Town (April 28).

April 29–May 2, Whitefield preaches in New York and western Long Island.

May 6: Whitefield preaches in Freehold, New Jersey.

May 8–11: Whitefield preaches to large crowds in and around Philadelphia.

May 13: Whitefield preaches in Nottingham, Pennsylvania, in company with Gilbert Tennent and Samuel Blair.

May 16: Sails from New Castle for Savannah.

August 25: Whitefield sails for New England in response to an invitation from Benjamin Colman.

September 14: Whitefield arrives in Newport, Rhode Island, appoints Jonathan Barber as superintendent of the orphanage.

September 19–October 12: Whitefield preaches in Boston and surrounding towns and makes his way west to Northampton.

October 17: Whitefield arrives in Northampton, meets Edwards.

October 20–October 29: Whitefield preaches on the way from Northampton to New York.

November 4: Whitefield meets Gilbert Tennent on Staten Island and persuades him to make a preaching tour of New England. He also meets James Davenport of Southhold, Long Island, who accompanies him to Philadelphia.

November 9–November 23: Whitefield, Davenport, and Samuel Blair preach in and around Philadelphia.

December 14: Whitefield arrives back in Savannah.

December 20: Gilbert Tennent arrives in Boston to begin a three-month preaching tour in New England.

1740–41 Edwards stirs up a second wave of revivalism in thirty-five communities in the Connecticut River valley.

1741 January 16: Whitefield sails for England.

Edwards publishes *Distinguishing Marks of a Work of God*.

July 14–late August: James Davenport makes a revival tour of Connecticut towns from Stonington to New Haven.

1742 Whitefield's *Journal* published.

Charles Chauncy of First Church publishes *Enthusiasm Described and Caution'd Against*.

June 2: Davenport is arrested and deported from Hartford, Connecticut.

September 26: Davenport is deported from Boston.

1743 Charles Chauncy publishes *Seasonable Thoughts on the State of Religion in New England*.

Davenport and Timothy Allen found Shepherd's Tent in New London, Connecticut.

March 6: Davenport's New London episode.

1743–45 Thomas Prince publishes *Christian History*.

1744 Davenport publishes *Confessions and Retractions*.

Whitefield returns to Boston from England. After four more trips, dies in America in 1770.

1746 Gilbert Tennent speaks of the "late revival" in New Jersey and the Middle Colonies.

1748 Founding of Strict Congregational Churches in Connecticut and Long Island. By 1770, most in Connecticut have become Baptist.

1750 Jonathan Edwards dismissed from Northampton because of his opposition to the Half-Way Covenant.

1757 Davenport dies.

1758 Jonathan Edwards dies.

1750–70 The beginnings of Evangelicalism in Virginia and other southern colonies; proliferation of Baptist churches.

1841 Joseph Tracy publishes *The Great Awakening*, the first historical account of the revivals of the early eighteenth century.

Notes

PREFACE

1. Perry Miller, *Jonathan Edwards* (1949; reprint, Cleveland and New York: World Publishing, 1965), 133.

2. Charles Chauncy, *Enthusiasm Described and Caution'd Against . . . With a Letter to the Reverend Mr. James Davenport* (Boston: J. Draper, 1742).

3. Joseph Tracy, *The Great Awakening: A History of the Revival of Religion in the Time of Edwards and Whitefield* (1841; reprint, Boston: Charles Tappan Press, 1845).

4. Joseph Conforti, *Jonathan Edwards: Religious Tradition and American Culture* (Chapel Hill: University of North Carolina Press, 1995), 12.

5. Tracy, *The Great Awakening*, xvii–xviii.

6. Herbert I. Osgood, *The American Colonies in the Eighteenth Century*, vol. 3 (New York: Columbia University Press, 1924; reprint, Gloucester, Mass.: Peter Smith, 1958).

7. Charles Hartshorne Maxson, *The Great Awakening in the Middle Colonies* (1920; reprint, Gloucester: Peter Smith, 1958).

8. Ibid., 5–7.

9. Ibid., 9.

10. Ibid., 33–34.

11. Ibid., 112–38.

12. Wesley Gewehr, *The Great Awakening in Virginia, 1740–1790* (Durham: Duke University Press, 1930).

13. Leonard J. Trinterud, *The Forming of an American Tradition: A Re-Examination of Colonial American Presbyterianism* (Philadelphia: Westminster Press, 1949; reprint, Freeport, N.Y.: Books for Libraries Press, 1970).

14. Miller, *Jonathan Edwards*, 133–34.

15. Ibid., 133.

16. Perry Miller, *Errand in the Wilderness* (New York: Harper and Row, 1956).

17. Alan Heimert, *Religion and the American Mind: From the Great Awakening to the Revolution* (Cambridge: Harvard University Press, 1966).

18. Cedric Cowing, *The Great Awakening and the American Revolution: Colonial Thought in the Eighteenth Century* (Chicago: Rand-McNally, 1971).

19. Gary B. Nash, *The Urban Crucible: Social Change, Political Consciousness and the Origins of the American Revolution* (Cambridge: Harvard University Press, 1979).

20. Harry S. Stout, "Religion, Communications, and the Ideological Origins of the American Revolution," *William and Mary Quarterly* 34 (October 1977): 519–41.

21. John F. Berens, "Religion and Revolution Reconsidered: Recent Litera-

ture on Religion and Nationalism in Eighteenth-Century America," *Canadian Review of the Study of Nationalism* 10 (fall 1979): 233–45.

22. Jon Butler, "Enthusiasm Described and Decried: The Great Awakening as Interpretative Fiction," *Journal of American History* 69 (September 1982): 305–25.

23. Conforti, *Jonathan Edwards*, 12–13.

24. Frank Lambert, *Inventing the "Great Awakening"* (Princeton: Princeton University Press, 1999).

25. Ibid., 6.

26. George M. Marsden, "Evangelical and Fundamental Christianity," in *The Encyclopedia of Religion,* vol. 5, ed. Mircea Eliade (New York: Macmillan, 1986), 190–97.

27. Conrad Wright,*The Beginnings of Unitarianism in America* (Boston: Beacon Press, Starr King, 1956).

28. Frank Lambert, *"Pedlar in Divinity": George Whitefield and the Transatlantic Revivals, 1737–1770* (Princeton: Princeton University Press, 1994).

29. See Rhys Isaac, *The Transformation of Virginia, 1740–1790* (Chapel Hill: University of North Carolina Press, 1982).

30. John C. Miller, "Religion, Finance, and Democracy in Massachusetts," *New England Quarterly* 6 (March 1933): 29–58.

31. John M. Bumstead, "Religion, Finance, and Democracy in Massachusetts: The Town of Norton as a Case Study," *Journal of American History* 58 (March 1971): 817–31.

32. Clarence C. Goen, *Revivalism and Separatism in New England: Strict Congregationalists and Separate Baptists in the Great Awakening* (New Haven: Yale University Press, 1962).

33. Stout, "Religion, Communications," 519–41; see also his *The New England Soul: Preaching and Religious Culture in Colonial New England* (New York: Oxford University Press, 1986) and *The Divine Dramatist: George Whitefield and the Rise of Modern Evangelicalism* (Grand Rapids: William B. Eerdmans, 1991).

34. Patricia Bonomi, *Under the Cope of Heaven: Religion, Society, and Politics in Colonial America* (New York: Oxford University Press, 1986).

CHAPTER ONE: THE AUGUSTAN AGE

1. Robert Penfield, *The Quest for Security, 1715–1740* (New York: Harper Brothers, 1947), 1.

2. Frank Lambert, *"Pedlar in Divinity": George Whitefield and the Transatlantic Revivals, 1737–1770* (Princeton: Princeton University Press, 1994), 26–37.

3. Michael Kraus, *The Atlantic Civilization: Eighteenth-Century Origins* (New York: Russell and Russell, 1961), 1–23.

4. Lambert, *"Pedlar in Divinity,"* ch. 1.

5. Ibid., 48–49.

6. Quoted in Lambert, *"Pedlar in Divinity,"* 28.

7. Gary Nash, *The Urban Crucible: Social Change, Political Consciousness and the Origins of the American Revolution* (Cambridge: Harvard University Press, 1979), 3–25.

8. Lawrence Henry Gipson, *The British Isles and the American Colonies,*

vol. 3, *The Northern Colonies: The Northern Plantations, 1748–1754* (New York: Alfred A. Knopf, 1960), 4–6.

9. Ibid., 149–51; see also James A. Henretta and Gregory H. Nobles, *Evolution and Revolution: American Society, 1600–1820* (Lexington: D. C. Heath, 1987), 72–76.

10. Gipson, *The British Isles and the American Colonies*, 4.

11. Henretta and Nobles, *Evolution and Revolution*, 79–101.

12. Gipson, *British Isles and American Colonies*, 136–39; Henretta and Nobles, *Evolution and Revolution*, 48.

13. See Alan Heimert, *Religion and the American Mind: From the Great Awakening to the Revolution* (Cambridge: Harvard University Press, 1966).

14. See Frank Lambert, *Inventing the "Great Awakening"* (Princeton: Princeton University Press, 1999).

15. William G. McLoughlin, "Enthusiasm for Liberty: The Great Awakening as the Key to Revolution," in Jack P. Greene and William G. McLoughlin, *Preachers and Politicians* (Worcester, Mass.: American Antiquarian Society, 1977), 57.

16. Jack P. Greene and William G. McLoughlin, *Preachers and Politicians* (Worcester, Mass.: American Antiquarian Society, 1977), 58.

17. Richard Middleton, *Colonial America: A History, 1607–1760* (Cambridge: Blackwell Publishers, 1992), 51.

18. Greene and McLoughlin, *Preachers and Politicians*, 57.

19. Ibid., 61–62.

20. See Lambert, *Inventing the "Great Awakening,"* ch.1.

21. Jon Butler, "Enthusiasm Described and Decried: The Great Awakening as Interpretive Fiction," *Journal of American History* 69 (September 1982): 310–11.

CHAPTER TWO: THE STATE OF RELIGION IN COLONIAL AMERICA

1. Intensive studies of churches throughout New England are the bases of these conclusions. See, for example, John M. Bumstead, "Religion, Finance, and Democracy in Massachusetts: The Town of Norton as a Case Study," *Journal of American History* 58 (March 1971): 817–31.

2. Lawrence Henry Gipson, *The British Isles and the American Colonies*, vol. 3, *The Northern Colonies: The Northern Plantations, 1748–1754* (New York: Alfred A. Knopf, 1960), 21–24.

3. See Kenneth Lockridge, *A New England Town: The First Hundred Years* (New York: W. W. Norton, 1970); see also Jack P. Greene, *Interpreting Early America: Historiographical Essays* (Charlottesville: University Press of Virginia, 1996), 129.

4. In 1691, Massachusetts was given a new charter as a royal colony. The franchise was no longer based upon religious experience.

5. Greene, *Interpreting Early America*, 129–33.

6. See Michael Zuckerman, *Peaceable Kingdoms: New England Towns in the Eighteenth Century* (New York: Alfred A. Knopf, 1970), vii.

7. Edwin Scott Gaustad, *The Great Awakening in New England* (1957; reprint, Gloucester, Mass.: Peter Smith, 1965), 9.

8. Robert G. Pope, *The Half-Way Covenant: Church Membership in Puritan New England* (Princeton: Princeton University Press, 1969), 43–74.

9. E. Brooks Holifield, "The Intellectual Sources of Stoddardeanism," *New England Quarterly* 45 (September 1972): 373–92; Perry Miller, "Solomon Stoddard, 1643–1729," *Harvard Theological Review* 34 (October 1941): 277–320; James B. Walsh, "Solomon Stoddard's Open Communion: A Re-examination," *New England Quarterly* 43 (March 1970): 97–114.

10. Holifield, "Intellectual Sources of Stoddardeanism," 12–13.

11. Gipson, *British Isles and American Colonies*, 22–23.

12. Ibid., 26–27.

13. James A. Henretta and Gregory H. Nobles, *Evolution and Revolution: American Society, 1600–1820* (Lexington, Mass.: D. C. Heath, 1987), 79–101.

14. Leonard J. Trinterud, *The Forming of an American Tradition: A Re-Examination of Colonial American Presbyterianism* (Philadelphia: Westminster Press, 1949), 18–19.

15. Ibid., 34. This is the classic study of colonial Presbyterianism. Some of Trinterud's premises have been challenged, however, during the 1980s and 1990s by other historians.

16. Ibid., 63–64.

17. Ibid., 39–40.

18. Gaustad, *Great Awakening in New England*, 7–8.

19. Trinterud, *Forming of an American Tradition*, 170.

20. Ibid., 171.

21. Leonard J. Trinterud, ed., *Elizabethan Puritanism* (New York: Oxford University Press, 1971), 311–12.

22. Trinterud, *Forming of an American Tradition*, 172–73.

23. Gaustad, *Great Awakening in New England*, 8–9.

24. *Encyclopaedia Britannica*, 14th ed., s.v. "Arminius, Jacobus." See also Carl Bangs, *Arminius: A Study in the Dutch Reformation*, 2nd ed. (Grand Rapids: William B. Eerdmans, 1985).

25. *Encyclopaedia Britannica*, 11th ed., s.v. "Remonstrants." See also *"The Five Articles of the Remonstrants,"* in *Documents of the Christian Church*, ed. Henry Bettenson (London: Oxford University Press, 1963), 377–79.

26. Vergilius Ferm, ed., *An Encyclopedia of Religion* (New York: The Philosophical Library, 1945), 114.

27. Ibid., 38.

28. Joseph Ellis, "Anglicans in Connecticut, 1725–1750; The Conversion of the Missionaries," *New England Quarterly* 44 (March 1971): 66–81; Louise Greene, *The Development of Religious Liberty in Connecticut* (Boston: Houghton Mifflin, 1905), 154–92. See also Carl Bridenbaugh, *Mitre and Sceptre:Transatlantic Faiths, Ideas, Personalities, and Politics, 1689–1775* (New York: Oxford University Press, 1962). The latter is the fullest account of the role of the Anglican Church in America.

29. Quoted in Patrick Collinson, *The Religion of Protestants: The Church of English Society* (Oxford: Clarendon Press, 1982), 251.

30. John T. McNeill, *The History and Character of Calvinism* (New York: Oxford University Press, 1954), 263–65.

31. Samuel Eliot Morison, *The Intellectual Life of Colonial New England* (New York: New York University Press, 1956), 159. This view is also held by Edwin Morgan; see his "The American Revolution Considered as an Intellectual Movement" in *Paths of American Thought*, ed. Arthur M. Schlesinger, Jr., and Morton White (Boston: Houghton Mifflin, 1963), 11–15.

32. Gerald Goodwin, "The Myth of 'Arminian-Calvinism' in Eighteenth Century New England," *New England Quarterly* 41 (March 1968): 213–37.

33. Ibid., 216–17.

34. Perry Miller, *Jonathan Edwards* (1949; reprint, Cleveland and New York: World Publishing, 1965), 101–26.

35. Goodwin, "Myth of 'Arminian-Calvinism,'" 218.

36. John Checkley, *Choice Dialogues Between a Godly Minister, And an Honest Country-Man, Concerning Election & Predestination* (Boston, 1720), in Goodwin, "Myth of 'Arminian-Calvinism,'" 223.

37. Goodwin, "Myth of 'Arminian-Calvinism,'" 223.

38. Cotton Mather, *Ratio Disciplinae Fratrum Nova-Anglorum. A Faithful Account of the Discipline Professed and Practised In the Churches of New England* (Boston, 1726), quoted in Goodwin, "Myth of 'Arminian-Calvinism,'" 225.

39. Westminster Assembly of Divines, *The Confession of Faith, Together with the Larger Catechism* (Boston, 1723), 19–20.

40. William Cooper, "To the Reader," *The Doctrine of Predestination unto Life, Explained and Vindicated* (Boston, 1740), cited in Goodwin, "Myth of 'Arminian-Calvinism,'" 234.

41. Goodwin, "Myth of 'Arminian-Calvinism,'" 235.

42. Those who take this position include Joseph Tracy, Edwin Scott Gaustad, and Perry Miller. See Joseph Tracy, *The Great Awakening: A History of the Revival of Religion in the Time of Edwards and Whitefield* (1841; reprint, Boston: Charles Tappan Press, 1845), 8–9; Gaustad, *Great Awakening in New England,* 83–84; and Miller, *Jonathan Edwards,* 101–26.

43. See Appendix I for a more detailed discussion of the antecedents of Puritanism.

44. F. Ernst Stouffler, "Pietism," in *The Encyclopedia of Religion,* vol. 11, ed. Mircea Eliade (New York: Macmillan, 1986), 324–26. See also his *The Rise of Evangelical Pietism* (Leyden: Brill, 1965) and *German Pietism During the Eighteenth Century* (Leyden: Brill, 1973); and August Hermann Francke, "On Christian Reflection" (1690), "Autobiography" (1692), and "A Letter to a Friend Concerning the Most Useful Way of Preaching" (1725), in *Pietists: Selected Writings,* ed. Peter C. Erb, (New York: Missionary Society of St. Paul the Apostle in New York, 1983).

45. Philip Jacob Spener, *Pia Desideria* (1675), "The Spiritual Priesthood" (1677), "On Hindrances to Theological Studies" (1680), and "The Necessary and Useful Reading of the Holy Scriptures" (1694), in Erb, *Pietists: Selected Writings,* 31–75; for Count Zinzendorf and the rise of the renewed Moravian Church see Stoeffler, *German Pietism,* 217–65.

46. Charles Hartshorne Maxson, *The Great Awakening in the Middle Colonies* (Chicago: University of Chicago Press, 1920), 1–10.

47. Ibid., 6–7.

48. John B. Frantz, "The Awakening of Religion Among the German Settlers in the Middle Colonies," *William and Mary Quarterly* 34 (October 1977): 266–88.

49. Maxson, *The Great Awakening,* 8–10.

50. Gipson, *British Isles and American Colonies,* 109–28.

51. Frantz, "The Awakening of Religion," 275.

52. Frank Lambert, *"Pedlar in Divinity": George Whitefield and the Transatlantic Revivals, 1737–1770* (Princeton: Princeton University Press, 1994), 203.

53. George Marsden, "Evangelical and Fundamental Christianity," in *The Encyclopedia of Religion,* vol. 5, ed. Mircea Eliade, 190.

54. Ibid., 191.

55. William James, *The Varieties of Religious Experience* (1902; reprint, London: Longmans, Green, 1914), 217–58.

56. Hugh Kerr and John M. Mulder, eds., *Conversions in Christian Experience* (Grand Rapids, Mich.: William B. Eerdmans, 1983), ix.

57. James, *Varieties of Religious Experience,* 189.

58. Acts 9:1–9; 22:1–21; 26:1–23.

59. Frank Lambert, *Inventing the "Great Awakening"* (Princeton: Princeton University Press, 1999), 27.

60. Lambert, *Inventing the "Great Awakening,"* 26–27.

61. Ibid., 26–29.

62. Jonathan Edwards, *A Treatise Concerning Religious Affections* (Boston: Kneeland and Green, 1746).

63. Susan O'Brien, "A Transatlantic Community of Saints: The Great Awakening and the First Evangelical Network, 1735–1755," *American Historical Review* 91(October 1986): 817–19.

64. Ibid., 820.

65. Ibid., 811–19.

CHAPTER THREE: TRANSATLANTIC REVIVALS

1. Quotations from George Whitefield's *Journals* are cited in the text in this chapter using the following abbreviation: *GW: Whitefield's Journals, to Which is Prefixed His "Short Account" and "Further Account,"* ed. William Wale (1905; reprint, London: The Banner of Truth Trust, 1965).

2. Quoted in Stuart C. Henry, *George Whitefield: Wayfaring Witness* (New York: Abingdon Press, 1957), 23.

3. Henry, *George Whitefield,* 22.

4. Among Roman Catholics, Anglican, and Eastern Orthodox, a deacon is an ordained clergyman ranking just below a priest.

5. Henry, *George Whitefield,* 35–36.

6. Charles Hartshorne Maxson, *The Great Awakening in the Middle Colonies* (1920; reprint, Gloucester, Mass.: Peter Smith, 1958), 42–43.

7. It may be wondered whether so many people could hear an unamplified speaker. Ben Franklin conducted an experiment on this point later in Philadelphia. Whitefield was preaching to a large crowd from the Courthouse steps. Franklin walked away until Whitefield's voice became obscured. He then calculated that more than thirty thousand listeners could be fitted into the area covered by his voice, because of his perfect articulation, clarity of voice, and volume. *Memoirs of the Life & Writings of Benjamin Franklin* (London & Toronto: J. M. Dent & Sons, 1908), 168.

8. Henry, *George Whitefield,* 42–50. See also *Whitefield's Journals* for a day-by-day account of his evangelism.

9. Jon Butler, "Enthusiasm Described and Decried: The Great Awakening as Interpretative Fiction," *Journal of American History* 69 (September 1982): 305–25.

10. Maxson, *The Great Awakening,* 11–20; Leonard J. Trinterud, *The Forming of an American Tradition: A Re-Examination of Colonial American Presbyterianism* (1949; reprint, Freeport, N.Y.: Books for Libraries Press, 1970), 53–57.

11. Cedric Cowing, *The Great Awakening and the American Revolution: Colonial Thought in the Eighteenth Century* (Chicago: Rand-McNally, 1971), 51–53. Webster's Third New International Dictionary defines antinomianism as follows: "The theological doctrine that by faith and God's gifts of grace through the gospel a Christian is freed not only from the Old Testament law of Moses [Torah] and all forms of legalism but also from all law including the generally accepted standards of morality." *Webster's Third New International Dictionary*, unabridged (Springfield, Mass.: G. & C. Merriam Co., 1976), s.v. "Antinomianism." In common usage, antinomianism implies license, and emotionalism was at the time interpreted as one form of this license.

12. Maxson, *The Great Awakening,* 11–20; Trinterud, *Forming of an American Tradition,* 54–57; see also James Tanis, *Dutch Calvinistic Pietism in the Middle Colonies: A Study in the Life and Theology of Theodorus Jacobus Frelinghuysen* (The Hague: Brill, 1967).

13. Maxson, *The Great Awakening,* 14.

14. Ibid., 23–24.

15. Trinterud, *Forming of an American Tradition,* 63–64.

16. Quoted in Russell T. Hitt, "Gilbert Tennent, Gadfly for Righteousness," in *Heroic Colonial Christians,* ed. Russell T. Hitt (Philadelphia: J. B. Lippincott, 1966), 107–49.

17. Ibid., 112–13.

18. Trinterud, *Forming of an American Tradition,* 56–57.

19. Ibid., 59–60.

CHAPTER FOUR: JONATHAN EDWARDS

1. Edwin Scott Gaustad, *The Great Awakening in New England* (1957; reprint, Gloucester, Mass.: Peter Smith, 1965), 16–17.

2. Ibid.

3. Edward H. Davidson, *Jonathan Edwards: The Narrative of a Puritan Mind* (Boston: Houghton Mifflin, 1966), 2–3.

4. Quotations from Jonathan Edwards' early works are cited in the text in this chapter using the following abbreviation: *JE: Jonathan Edwards: Representative Selections, with Introduction, Bibliography, and Notes,* rev. ed., ed. Clarence H. Faust and Thomas H. Johnson (New York: Hill and Wang, 1967).

5. See my *Young Carl Jung* (Wilmette, Ill.: Chiron Publications, 1996).

6. Ibid., ch. 2.

7. Davidson, *Jonathan Edwards,* 8.

8. Ibid., 8–29.

9. Patricia Tracy, *Jonathan Edwards, Pastor: Religion and Society in Eighteenth-Century Northampton* (New York: Hill and Wang, 1980), ch. 1.

10. Herbert Wallace Schneider, *The Puritan Mind* (Ann Arbor: University of Michigan Press, 1958), 105–6.

11. Ibid., 105–8.

12. Davidson, *Jonathan Edwards,* 58–60.

13. Sereno E. Dwight, ed., *The Works of President Edwards* (Worcester, Mass., 1808), 65.

14. Perry Miller, *Jonathan Edwards* (1949; reprint, Cleveland and New York: World Publishing, 1965), 137.

15. Ibid., 139.

Chapter Five: George Whitefield in America

1. Frank Lambert, *"Pedlar in Divinity": George Whitefield and the Transatlantic Revivals, 1737-1770* (Princeton: Princeton University Press, 1994), 8–9.

2. Ibid., 104–5.

3. Ibid., 105.

4. *Pennsylvania Gazette,* 19 November 1739.

5. Quotations from George Whitefield's *Journals* are cited in the text in this chapter using the following abbreviation: *GW: Whitefield's Journals, to Which is Prefixed His "Short Account" and Further Account,"* ed. *William Wale* (1905; reprint, London: The Banner of Truth Trust, 1965).

6. *Memoirs of the Life & Writings of Benjamin Franklin* (London and Toronto: J. M. Dent & Sons, 1908), 125.

7. Quoted in Stuart C. Henry, *George Whitefield: Wayfaring Witness* (New York: Abingdon Press, 1957), 51.

8. Lambert, *"Pedlar in Divinity,"* 101.

9. Henry, *George Whitefield,* 53.

10. *Memoirs of Benjamin Franklin,* 127.

11. Ibid., 128.

12. Ibid., 129.

13. Quoted in Henry, *George Whitefield,* 105.

14. Henry, *George Whitefield,* 95–114.

15. Quoted in Gaustad, *Great Awakening in New England,* 34.

16. Gaustad, *Great Awakening in New England,* 33.

17. Ibid.

18. Ibid.

19. Quoted in Gausted, *Great Awakening in New England,* 30. It is interesting to note that this quote is not to be found in Whitefield's Journals under the entry for 29 October 1740, as reprinted by The Banner of Truth Trust.

20. Ibid., 30–31.

21. Ibid., 31–32.

Chapter Six: The Mad Enthusiast

1. Franklin Bowditch Dexter, *Biographical Sketches of the Graduates of Yale College, October 1701-May 1745* (New Haven: Yale University Press, 1885), 447.

2. Amzi Benedict Davenport, *Supplement to the History and Genealogy of the Davenport Family* (Stamford, Conn., 1876), 186–87, 192.

3. Samuel Cook, "Funeral Sermon for John Davenport," quoted in Davenport, *Supplement to the History,* 190–91.

4. Davenport, *Supplement to the History,* 198–205.

5. Ibid., 198.

6. *The Memoirs of the Life of David Ferris, an Approved Minister of the Society of Friends, Written by Himself* (1821; reprint, Philadelphia: Merrihew and Thompson, 1855), 15–19.

7. "Daniel Boardman to Charles Chauncy," in Charles Chauncy, *Seasonable Thoughts on the State of Religion in New England, A Treatise in Five Parts* (1743; reprint, Hicksville, N.Y.: Regina Press, 1975), 208–9.

8. Chauncy, *Seasonable Thoughts,* 210.

9. Ibid.

10. "Timothy Allen to Charles Chauncy," in Chauncy, *Seasonable Thoughts,* 211.

11. Ibid., 209–12.

12. Timothy Allen to Eleazar Wheelock, 26 November 1744, Archives, Dartmouth University Library, Hanover, N.H.

13. "Timothy Allen," in Chauncy, *Seasonable Thoughts,* 212–13.

14. Eleazar Wheelock to Charles Chauncy, 13 March 1769, Archives, Dartmouth University Library, Hanover, N.H.

15. "James Davenport to Stephen Williams," 1734, in William B. Sprague, *Annals of the American Pulpit,* vol. 3 (New York: R. Carter and Brothers, 1858), 81.

16. W. R. Bett, *A Short History of Some Common Diseases* (Oxford: Oxford University Press, 1934), 154.

17. "James Davenport to Stephen Williams," 80.

18. Dexter, *Biographical Sketches,* 447.

19. William Chalmers, Historical Sketch of Associated Congregationalism in Suffolk County, 1891, MS, Easthampton [N.Y.] Public Library, 26.

20. *Diary of Joshua Hempstead,* vol. 1 (New London, Conn.: New London County Historical Society, 1911), 342.

21. "Letter to Charles Chauncy from an Anonymous Friend in Long Island," in Chauncy, *Seasonable Thoughts,* 183.

22. Ibid., 187.

23. Ibid.

24. Ibid., 187–88.

25. Ibid., 190–91.

26. Quotations from George Whitefield's *Journals* are cited in the text in this chapter using the following abbreviation: *GW: Whitefield's Journals, to Which is Prefixed His "Short Account" and "Further Account,"* ed. William Wale (1905; reprint, London: The Banner of Truth Trust, 1965).

27. Quoted in Stuart C. Henry, *George Whitefield: Wayfaring Witness* (New York: Abingdon Press, 1957), 51.

28. *Memoirs of the Life & Writings of Benjamin Franklin* (London and Toronto: J. M. Dent & Sons, 1908), 126.

29. James Davenport to "Very Dear Brother," 1740, MS, Historical Society of Pennsylvania, Philadelphia.

30. Henry, *George Whitefield,* 118.

31. "Letter from an Anonymous Friend," 196–97.

32. *Boston Weekly Post-Boy,* 23 September 1741.

33. Ibid.

34. *Diary of Joshua Hempstead,* 380.

35. Benjamin Trumbull, *A Complete History of Connecticut, Civil and Ecclesiastical,* vol. 2 (New Haven, Conn.: Maltby, Goldsmith, 1818), 145.

36. *Diary of Joshua Hempstead,* 451.

37. Chauncy, *Seasonable Thoughts,* 155.

38. Ibid., 98–99.

39. Andrew Croswell, *A Letter from the Reverend Mr. Andrew Croswell to the Reverend Mr. Turell* (Boston: Massachusetts Historical Society, 1742).

40. "George Griswold to Thomas Prince," 14 July 1744, in *The Christian History, Containing Accounts of the Revival and Propagation of Religion in*

Great-Britain & America. For the Years 1743 and 1744, 2 vols., ed. Thomas Prince, (Boston: Kneeland and Green, 1744–45).

41. Jonathan Parsons, *Wisdom Justified of her Children* (Boston, 1742).

42. "Samuel Lynde, William Worthington, Abraham Not, George Beckwith, William Hart, and others," in Chauncy, *Seasonable Thoughts,* 153–54.

43. Chauncy, *Seasonable Thoughts,* 155.

44. Ibid., 156.

45. Ibid., 192–93.

46. "Thomas Clap et al.," in Chauncy, *Seasonable Thoughts,* 161.

47. *Public Records of the Colony of Connecticut,* October 1735–October 1743, vol. 8, ed. Charles Hoadley, (Hartford, Conn.: Case, Lockwood and Brainard, 1874), 438–39.

48. *Boston Weekly News-Letter,* 1 July 1742.

49. Ibid.

50. Ibid.

51. Ibid.

CHAPTER SEVEN: A RADICAL EVANGELICAL

1. Jonathan Dickinson, "Result of the Council of Ministers Convened at Southold," 5 October 1742, in William B. Sprague, *Annals of the American Pulpit,* vol. 3 (New York: R. Carter and Brothers, 1858), 84.

2. Richard Warch, "The Shepherd's Tent: Education and Enthusiasm in the Great Awakening," *American Quarterly* 30 (summer 1978): 177–98.

3. Quoted in Warch, "The Shepherd's Tent," 181.

4. Ibid., 180–81.

5. Ibid., 181–82.

6. "Samuel Whittelsey to Charles Chauncy," in Chauncy, *Seasonable Thoughts,* 215.

7. *Diary of Joshua Hempstead,* vol. 1, 2 February 1743 (New London, Conn.: New London County Historical Society, 1911), 452–53.

8. "An Act Relating to the Regulation of Schools," in *Public Records of the Colony of Connecticut,* vol. 8, ed. Charles Hoadley (Hartford, Conn.: Case, Lockwood and Brainard, 1874), 502.

9. Benjamin Colman, *Declaration of a Number of the Associated Pastors of Boston and Charlestown Relating to the Rev. Mr. Davenport and his Conduct* (Boston, 1742), 4–5.

10. *The Reverend Mr. Pickering's Letter to the Reverend N. Rogers as also to the Reverend James Davenport of Long Island* (Boston: Rogers and Fowle, 1742).

11. Andrew Croswell, *A Reply to the Declaration of a Number of the Associated Ministers in Boston and Charlestown, with Regard to the Reverend James Davenport and His Conduct* (Boston: Rogers and Fowle, 1742).

12. Harry S. Stout and Peter S. Onuf, "James Davenport and the Great Awakening in New London," *Journal of American History* 70 (December 1983): 566.

13. Croswell, *Reply to the Declaration.*

14. Ibid.

15. *Boston Evening Post,* 5 July 1742.

16. Ibid.

17. James Davenport, "A Song of Praise," in *The Great Awakening: Documents Illustrating the Crisis and Its Consequences,* ed. Alan Heimert and Perry Miller (Indianapolis and New York: Bobbs-Merrill, 1967), 202–3.

18. Heimert, Alan, and Perry Miller, eds.,*The Great Awakening: Documents Illustrating the Crisis and Its Consequences* (Indianapolis and New York: Bobbs-Merrill, 1967), 202.

19. *Boston Evening Post,* 2 August 1742.

20. Some studies seem to indicate that far from attracting only idlers and those of the lower classes, Davenport could also number many members of the professional and merchant/farmer classes among his followers. See Stout and Onuf, "James Davenport."

21. *A Curious New Sonnet Dedicated to the Street Musicians,* Broadsheet (Boston, 1742).

22. *To the Reverend James Davenport on his Departure from Boston, by a "female friend"* (Boston, 1742).

23. John C. Miller, "Religion, Finance, and Democracy in Massachusetts," *New England Quarterly* 6 (March 1933): 43–49.

24. "Isaac Watts to Dr. Colman," 15 November 1742, in Massachusetts Historical Society *Proceedings* 10 (February 1895): 398–99.

25. *Boston Weekly News-Letter,* 19 August 1742.

26. *Boston Evening Post,* 5 September 1742.

27. *Boston Weekly News-Letter,* 26 August 1742.

28. Ibid., 26 September 1742.

29. Ibid.

30. *To the Reverend Davenport on his Departure.*

31. Conrad Wright, *The Beginnings of Unitarianism in America* (Boston: Beacon Press, Starr King 1956), 56–58.

32. Edwin Scott Gaustad, *The Great Awakening in New England* (1957; reprint, Gloucester, Mass.: Peter Smith, 1965), 118.

33. "Isaac Watts to Dr. Colman," 398.

34. Wright, *The Beginnings of Unitarianism,* 33–37.

35. Ibid., 50–53.

36. Gaustad, *Great Awakening in New England,* 93–97.

37. Chauncy, *Seasonable Thoughts,* 220.

38. Quoted in Stout and Onuf, "James Davenport," 575.

39. "An Act in Addition to a Law of this Colony Entitled An Act for Regulating Abuses and Correcting Disorders in Ecclesiastical Affairs," in *Public Records of the Colony of Connecticut,* vol. 8, 569.

40. Chauncy, *Seasonable Thoughts,* 220–21.

41. *Boston Evening Post,* 28 March 1743.

42. *Letter From the Reverend Mr. James Davenport to the Reverend Mr. Jonathan Barber,* 30 November 1743 (Philadelphia, 1744), 6–7.

43. Chauncy, *Seasonable Thoughts,* 220–21.

44. *Boston Weekly Post-Boy,* 28 March 1743.

45. Ibid.

46. Ibid.

47. Dr. Alexander Hamilton, "The Great Fire of New London," in *Religious Enthusiasm in the Great Awakening,* ed. David S. Lovejoy (Englewood Cliffs, N.J.: Prentice-Hall, 1969), 67–68.

48. *Diary of Joshua Hempstead,* 453.

49. *Boston Weekly Post-Boy,* 28 March 1743.

50. Ibid.

51. Warch, "The Shepherd's Tent," 194.

52. Stout and Onuf, "James Davenport," 576–77.

53. Wright,*The Beginnings of Unitarianism,* 28–58.

54. Richard L. Bushman, ed., *The Great Awakening: Documents on the Revival of Religion, 1740–1745* (New York: Atheneum, 1970), 53.

55. *From the Reverend Davenport to the Reverend Barber.*

56. *Two Letters From the Reverend Mr. Solomon Williams & Wheelock of Lebanon to the Reverend Mr. James Davenport which were the Principal Means of His Late Confession and Retractions, with a letter from Mr. Davenport, Desiring Their Publication, for the Good of Others. And His Explanation of Some Passages in His Late Confession* (Boston: Kneeland and Green, 1744).

57. Ibid.

58. Ibid.

59. Sprague, *Annals of the American Pulpit,* 88–89.

60. Thomas Prince, ed., *The Christian History, Containing Accounts of the Revival and Propagation of Religion in Great-Britain & America. For the Years 1743 and 1744,* vol. 2 (Boston: Kneeland and Green, 1744–45).

61. *The Reverend Mr. James Davenport's Confession and Retractions* (Boston: Kneeland and Green, 1744).

62. Letter from the Reverend Dr. Colman to the Reverend Mr. Williams of Lebanon, upon Reading the Confession and Retractions of the Reverend Mr. Davenport. Boston: Royers and Fowle, 1744.

63. *From the Reverend Davenport to the Reverend Barber,* 6–7.

64. Sprague, *Annals of the American Pulpit,* 88–89.

65. Ibid.

66. *Diary of Joshua Hempstead,* 528.

67. James Davenport to Eleazar Wheelock, 25 January 1750, MS, Dartmouth University Archives, Hanover, N.H.

68. Wesley M. Gewehr, *The Great Awakening in Virginia, 1740–1790* (Durham, N.C.: Duke University Press, 1930).

69. "James Davenport to Stephen Williams," 19 September 1752, in Sprague, *Annals of the American Pulpit,* 89.

70. Amzi Benedict Davenport, *Supplement to the History and Genealogy of the Davenport Family* (Stamford, Conn.,1876), 237–38.

71. Records of the New Brunswick Presbytery, 25 October 1752, MS, vol. I B, 1748–1758, New Brunswick, N.J.

72. James Davenport to Stephen Williams, 14 November 1754, MS, Dartmouth University Archives, Hanover, N.H.

73. "James Davenport to Stephen Williams," 11 July 1755, in Sprague, *Annals of the American Pulpit,* 90–91.

74. Davenport, *Supplement to the History,* 237–38.

75. Ibid.

76. Ibid.

77. Hamilton, "The Great Fire," 67.

78. *Diary of Joshua Hempstead,* 449.

79. Ibid., 452.

80. E. F. Scott, *The Varieties of New Testament Religion* (New York: Charles Scribner's Sons, 1947), 111.

81. Ibid., 114.

82. Ibid.

83. Stout and Onuf, "James Davenport," 567.

CHAPTER EIGHT: THE LEGACY

1. Cedric Cowing, *The Great Awakening and the American Revolution: Colonial Thought in the Eighteenth Century* (Chicago: Rand-McNally, 1971), 197.

2. Ibid., 193.

3. Ibid., 193–96.

4. Richard Warch, "New Introduction to the Reprint Edition," in Charles Chauncy, *Seasonable Thoughts on the State of Religion in New England, A Treatise in Five Parts* (1743; reprint, Hicksville, N.Y.: Regina Press, 1975), 5w.

5. *The Works of President Edwards in Four Volumes,* vol. 3 (New York, 1843), 194–95.

6. Warch, "New Introduction," 4w.

7. Jonathan Edwards, *Some Thoughts Concerning the Present Revival of Religion in New England* (Boston, 1742), reprinted in *Jonathan Edwards on Revivals* (New York, 1832), 335.

8. Perry Miller, *Jonathan Edwards* (1949; reprint, Cleveland and New York: World Publishing, 1965), 144.

9. Gilbert Tennent, "The Danger of an Unconverted Ministry, Considered in a Sermon on Mark VI.34," 1742, in *Religious Enthusiasm in the Great Awakening,* ed. David S. Lovejoy, 48–54 (Englewood Cliffs, N.J.: Prentice-Hall, 1969).

10. Gilbert Tennent, quoted in Edwin Scott Gaustad, *The Great Awakening in New England* (1957; reprint, Gloucester, Mass.: Peter Smith, 1965), 67.

11. Edwards castigates enthusiasts as "those who falsely pretend to be inspired by the Holy Ghost as the prophets were." Lovejoy, *Religious Enthusiasm,* 1.

12. Gaustad, *Great Awakening in New England,* 91–92.

13. Conrad Wright, *The Beginnings of Unitarianism in America* (Boston: Beacon Press, Starr King, 1956), 187.

14. Frank Lambert, *Inventing the "Great Awakening"* (Princeton: Princeton University Press, 1999), 251–54; Jon Butler, "Enthusiasm Described and Decried: The Great Awakening as Interpretative Fiction," *Journal of American History* 69 (September 1982): 305–25.

15. William Chalmers, Historical Sketch of Associated Congregationalism in Suffolk County, 1891, MS, Easthampton [N.Y.] Public Library, 32.

16. Stephen A. Marini, *Radical Sects of Revolutionary New England* (Cambridge: Harvard University Press, 1982), 19.

17. Ibid., 20.

18. Quoted in Marini, *Radical Sects,* 19.

19. Ibid., 20.

20. Minutes of the Suffolk County Presbytery, 1747–1811, MS, Easthampton [N.Y.] Public Library, 43.

21. William Chalmers, A History of the Congregational Church in Aqueboque, 1910, MS, Congregational Church, Aqueboque, N.Y., 10.

22. *Confession of Faith and Form of Government of the Strict Congregationalist Churches* (Brooklyn, N.Y., 1823).

23. Minutes of the Suffolk Presbytery, 11–12.

24. Christopher Youngs, *Brief History of the Strict Congregational Convention of Long Island* (Brooklyn, N.Y.,1839), 34–39.

25. Baiting Hollow Church Records, MS, Baiting Hollow Congregational Church, Baiting Hollow, Long Island, N.Y. (n.d.)

26. Wading River Church Records, MS, Wading River Congregational Church, Wading River, N.Y. Easthampton [N.Y.] Public Library. (n.d.)

27. Youngs, *Brief History,* 34–39.

28. Ibid., 6.

29. Solomon Paine, *A Short View of the Differences between the Church of Christ, and the Established Churches in the Colony of Connecticut in Their Foundation and Practice* . . . (Newport, R.I.: James Franklin, 1752), 1–6.

30. Ibid.

31. Ibid.

32. *Public Records of the Colony of Connecticut,* vol. 13, ed. Charles Hoadley (Hartford, Conn.: Case, Lockwood and Brainard, 1874), 360. Freedom of assembly was finally granted in Connecticut in 1770.

33. *Extracts from the Itineraries and Other Miscellanies of Ezra Stiles,1755–1794,* ed. Franklin B. Dexter (New Haven: Yale University Press, 1916), 283.

34. Louise Greene, *The Development of Religious Liberty in Connecticut* (Boston: Houghton Mifflin, 1905), 242–43.

35. Marini, *Radical Sects,* 20–21.

36. Ibid., 21.

37. See Rhys Isaac, *The Transformation of Virginia, 1740–1790* (Chapel Hill: University of North Carolina Press, 1982).

38. Rhys Isaac, "Evangelical Revolt: The Nature of the Baptist Challenge to the Traditional Order in Virginia, 1765–1775," *William and Mary Quarterly* 31 (July 1974): 345–68.

39. Antitrinitarianism, based on biblical grounds since the trinity is not mentioned anywhere in the Scriptures, originated during the Renaissance and Reformation among continental European Protestants. Because they believed in the unity of the godhead, they were sometimes called Unitarians. Reformers, such as the Italian Faustus Socinus, founded a movement which was called either Socinianism or Unitarianism. It flourished in Poland, Transylvania, Holland, and England during the late sixteenth and early seventeenth centuries. The Socinians believed that Jesus was of natural birth, and that God chose him to be his Messiah at the time of his baptism. The miracles proved his special relationship to God, as did his resurrection. However, while there were many Socinians in Britain and Northern Ireland during the early eighteenth century, there were very few in the American colonies at that time. It is difficult to know what effect Socinian thought had on American ministers, but it was probably very little. The rise of American Unitarianism appears to have been a colonial phenomenon which occurred among those ministers in New England accused of "Arminianism" by their critics. By 1750, a few such as Charles Chauncy and Jonathan Mayhew actually held that theological position. However, because of their strong emphasis on works, they abandoned justification by faith altogether and secretly held the view that all human beings are saved (Universalism) and that they attain salvation by moral effort. This process continues after death. Therefore, the ministers who later became Unitarians and Universalists also rejected belief in the devil and hell. At the same time, they also embraced the Socinian view concerning the simple humanity of Jesus and rejected the doctrine of the trinity. Most of this appears to have been a result of their own reasoning rather than because of the direct influence of British and continental Unitarians. Because the ministers who espoused Unitarianism were highly discreet pastors of rather conservative congregations hostile to controversy of any kind, these new ideas were very carefully introduced. Nevertheless, nearly all

ministers and congregations in Boston were effectively Unitarian by the end of the eighteenth century. Their tendency to be evasive about this infuriated orthodox Congregationalists, who insisted that the Unitarians declare themselves openly, which they refused to do. The dispute finally surfaced when a Boston minister, William Ellery Channing, preached a sermon in Baltimore, Maryland, in 1819 in which he openly acknowledged the name "Unitarian," and proclaimed the theological position. Soon after, other small "u" unitarian ministers in New England did the same. By then, Unitarians made up 125 of the congregations of the Standing Order, soon after abolished. The ministers and people of these churches founded the American Unitarian Association in 1825 as a distinct denomination.

Appendix I

1. According to Perry Miller, in the theology of Jonathan Edwards there were two ways of asserting the "imputation" of Adam's guilt to his descendants. One of them was based on Augustine and Calvin. The other, however, was original with New England Puritans. See Perry Miller, *Jonathan Edwards* (1949; reprint, Cleveland and New York: World Publishing, 1965), 277. Augustine argued that Adam's sin was inherited like a disease. This concept was disturbing to New England divines, who were steeped in English common law. Inherited sin seemed to them to be an unfair concept, lacking in justice. It was for this reason that they were drawn to the Federal Theology that Miller attributes to New England Puritanism, but that actually originated among adherents of the Reformed or Calvinist Church in Switzerland and Germany after Calvin's time. According to this argument, Adam broke a contract and his guilt was transferred to his heirs as a liability. Miller argues that during the seventeenth century this forensic interpretation of the Fall took precedence over the Augustinian interpretation.

2. John Knox, *Chapters in a Life of Paul* (New York: Abington-Cokesbury Press, 1940), 114–16.

3. Quotations from the Bible in this chapter are taken from the Authorized (King James) Version.

4. Robert Jewett, "Paul the Apostle," in *The Encyclopedia of Religion,* vol. 11, ed. Mircea Eliade (New York: Macmillan, 1986), 212–13. There is by no means consensus among biblical scholars on this point.

5. Jewett, "Paul the Apostle," 213.

6. Daniel Whitby, *Discourses* (London, 1701), 80.

7. See *The Library of Christian Classics,* ed. John Baillie et al., vols. 6–8 (Philadelphia: Westminster Press, 1953–58).

8. The followers of Arius were successful in their missionary work among Germanic tribes such as the Visigoths prior to the migration of the latter into the Roman Empire. Consequently, during the fourth century C.E., the Arians constituted a powerful ethnic and political force which the Emperor Constantine regarded as a threat. The outcome of the Council of Nicaea was less determined by theological argument than by the powerful support given the Athanasian (trinitarian) camp by Constantine. The emperor was primarily concerned with the unity of the church for political reasons. Arianism was subsequently suppressed as a heresy. However, the scriptural basis of this position, such as John 1, was at least as strong as that of the trinitarians. There is no

214 A WONDERFUL WORK OF GOD

mention whatsoever of the trinity in the New Testament, nor any clear indication concerning the relationship of Jesus to God save that he is the Messiah, or Christ, the latter being the Greek translation. During the eighteenth century, Arianism was revived by certain divines such as Samuel Clark in his *Scripture-Doctrine of the Trinity* (London, 1737), and Thomas Emlyn in his *An Humble Enquiry into the Scripture-Account of Jesus Christ* (London, 1702). Both of these works were read by Arminians in New England. One such reader was Jonathan Mayhew, the pastor of West Church, Boston. Mayhew also corresponded with English antitrinitarians such as George Benson, Nathaniel Lardner, and James Foster. Mayhew was one of the earliest Arminian ministers in New England to become a small "u" unitarian. See Conrad Wright, *The Beginnings of Unitarianism in America* (Boston: Beacon Press, Starr King, 1955), 9–27.

9. Wright, *The Beginnings of Unitarianism*, 201–2.

10. Étienne Gilson's *The Christian Philosophy of Saint Augustine* (New York: Random House, 1960) deals with Augustine's thought and therefore with his concept of predestination in considerable detail. The best biographies of Augustine in English include Peter Brown, *Augustine of Hippo* (Berkeley: University of California Press, 1967). For a brief and relatively recent article on Augustine see Warren Thomas Smith's "Augustine of Hippo" in *The Encyclopedia of Religion*, vol. 1, ed. Mircea Eliade, 354–430 (New York: Macmillan, 1986). Smith states that, second only to the Bible, Augustine was the most quoted source in John Calvin's *Institutes of the Christian Religion*. My comments concerning Augustine are mainly based on Smith's article.

11. See "The Thirteen Books of the Confessions of Saint Augustine," in *Basic Writings of St. Augustine,* vol. 1, ed. Whitney J. Oates (New York: Random House, 1948), 126.

12. Smith, "Augustine of Hippo," 522.

13. Those works of Augustine that deal primarily with predestination and election include: *De Spiritu et littera* (On the Spirit and the Letter), *De Gratia et libero Arbitrio* (On Grace and Free Will), *De praedestinatione sanctorum* (On the Predestination of the Saints), *De dono persevereantiae* (On the Perseverance of the Saints), and *Contra Julianum* (Against Julius). These writings were anti-Pelagian, based on the proposition "that good will, that good works, without the grace of God . . . can be granted to no one." Smith, "Augustine of Hippo," 524.

14. Augustine of Hippo, "On Free Will" in *Augustine: Earlier Writings,* selected by John H. S. Burleigh (Philadelphia: Westminster Press, 1953), 113.

15. Ibid., 203.

16. Ibid.

17. Ibid., 177.

18. Ibid., 190–91.

19. Smith, "Augustine of Hippo," 523.

20. Ibid., 524.

21. Wilhelm Pauck, "Justification," in *An Encyclopedia of Religion,* ed. Vergilius Ferm (New York: The Philosophical Library, 1945), 410.

22. Augustine, "On Grace and Free Will," in Oates, *Basic Writings of St. Augustine,* 736–37.

23. Smith, "Augustine of Hippo," 523.

24. Carl Jung, "Archetypes of the Collective Unconscious" [1954], in *The Collected Works of C. G. Jung,* vol. 9.1 (Princeton: Princeton University Press, 1959), 4.

25. Northrop Frye, *The Great Code: The Bible and Literature* (Toronto: Academic Press Canada, 1981).

26. Jung, *Collected Works,* 4–5.

27. Walter Notestein, *The English People on the Eve of Colonization, 1603–1630* (New York: Harper Press, 1954), 151–52.

28. Patrick Collinson, *The Religion of Protestants: The Church of English Society* (Oxford: Clarendon Press, 1982), 251.

Select Bibliography

THIS BIBLIOGRAPHY IS A PARTIAL LIST OF THE SOURCES CONSULTED. It is by no means a complete record of all of them. It does, however, indicate the range of reading on the basis of which I have formed my ideas. I have used both primary and secondary sources. Printed pamphlets, sermons, and books by both Friends of Revival and Opposers are very numerous for the period 1735–1745, and there are also several excellent collections of documents, such as the Proceedings of the Massachusetts Historical Society. Colonial newspapers are another rich source for the Great Awakening. Unpublished sources include letters and papers to be found in the archives of institutions of higher learning such as Dartmouth and Yale, as well as in public libraries and church records.

The secondary sources include classical works such as Joseph Tracy's *The Great Awakening: A History of the Revival of Religion in the Time of Edwards and Whitefield* (1841), standard works in the field such as Edwin Gaustad's *The Great Awakening in New England* (1957), and revisionist studies such as Frank Lambert's *Inventing "The Great Awakening"* (1999) and Jon Butler's "Enthusiasm Described and Decried: The Great Awakening as Interpretative Fiction" (1982).

PRIMARY DOCUMENTS

Acquittal of James Pomeroy. MS. Connecticut State Library, Hartford, 1742.

Adams, James Truslow. *History of the Town of Southampton.* Southampton, N.Y., 1918.

Agents to Present Charges Against James Davenport. MS. Connecticut State Library, Hartford, 1742.

Allen, Timothy. Letter to Eleazar Wheelock, 26 November 1744.Archives, Dartmouth University Library, Hanover, N.H.

Assembly's Judgment Against James Davenport. MS. Connecticut State Library, Hartford, 1742.

Augustine: Earlier Writings. Selected by John H. S. Burleigh. Philadelphia: Westminster Press, 1953.

Backus, Isaac. *Church History of New England, from 1620 to 1804.* Philadelphia: Baptist Tract Depository, 1839.

Baillie, John, et. al., eds. *The Library of Christian Classics.* Vols. 6–8. Philadelphia: Westminster Press, 1953–58.

Baiting Hollow Church Records. MS. Baiting Hollow Congregational Church, Baiting Hollow, Long Island, N.Y. (n.d.)

Bettenson, Henry, ed. *Documents of the Christian Church.* London: Oxford University Press, 1963.

Boston Evening Post. 23 September 1741; 5 July; 2, 8, 30 August; 5 September 1742; 28 March 1743.

Boston Weekly News-Letter. 24 June; 19, 26 August; 26 September 1742; 25 March and 8, 12 December 1743.

Boston Weekly Post-Boy. 23, 25 September; 5 October 1741; 1 July; 23 August 1742; 28 March 1743.

Burleigh, John H. S., ed. *Augustine: Earlier Writings.* Philadelphia: Westminster Press, 1953.

Bushman, Richard L., ed. *The Great Awakening: Documents on the Revival of Religion, 1740–1745.* New York: Atheneum, 1970.

Chalmers, William. Historical Sketch of Associated Congregationalism in Suffolk County. MS. Easthampton [N.Y.] Public Library, 1891.

———. A History of the Congregational Church in Aqueboque. MS. Congregational Church, Aqueboque, N.Y., 1910.

Chauncy, Charles. *The New Creature Describ'd, and consider'd as the sure Characteristick of a Man's being in Christ.* Boston, 1741.

———. *Enthusiasm Described and Caution'd Against . . . With a Letter to the Reverend Mr. James Davenport.* Boston: J. Draper, 1742.

———. *The Gifts of the Spirit to Ministers consider'd in their Diversity.* Boston, 1742.

———. *The Late Religious Commotions in New-England Considered. An Answer to the Reverend Mr. Jonathan Edwards's Sermon, Entitled, The Distinguishing Marks of a Work of the Spirit of God. . . . By a Lover of Truth and Peace.* Boston: Green, Bushell, and Allen, 1743.

———. *Seasonable Thoughts on the State of Religion in New England, A Treatise in Five Parts.* Boston: Rogers and Fowle, 1743. Reprint, Hicksville, N.Y.: Regina Press, 1975.

———. *Ministers cautioned against Occasions of Contempt.* Boston, 1744.

———. *Ministers exhorted and encouraged to take heed to themselves, and to their Doctrine.* Boston, 1744.

———. *Twelve Sermons.* Boston, 1765.

———. *The Benevolence of the Deity Fairly and Impartially Considered, in Three Parts.* Boston, 1784.

[Chauncy, Charles] *A Letter from a Gentleman of Boston, to Mr. George Wishart, One of the Ministers of Edinburgh, Concerning the State of Religion in New-England.* Edinburgh, 1742.

———. *A Letter to the Reverend George Whitefield, Vindicating certain Passages he has excepted against.* Boston, 1745.

Clap, Thomas. *A Brief History and Vindication of the Doctrines Received and Established in the Churches of New England*. New Haven, 1755.

Clark, Samuel. *Scripture-Doctrine of the Trinity*. London, 1737.

Colman, Benjamin. *Sermon on the General Court*. Boston, 1741.

———. *Declaration of a Number of the Associated Pastors of Boston and Charlestown Relating to the Rev. Mr. Davenport and his Conduct*. Boston, 1742.

———. *The Great God has magnified his Word to the Children of Men*. Boston, 1742.

———. Complaint Against James Davenport for Extravagant Conduct. MS. Connecticut State Library, Hartford, 1742.

———. *Letter From the Reverend Dr. Colman to the Reverend Mr. Williams of Lebanon, upon Reading the Confession and Retractions of the Reverend Mr. Davenport*. Boston: Rogers and Fowle, 1744.

Confession of Faith and Form of Government of the Strict Congregationalist Churches. Brooklyn, N.Y., 1823.

Croswell, Andrew. *A Reply to the Declaration of a Number of the Associated Ministers in Boston and Charlestown, with Regard to the Reverend James Davenport and His Conduct*. Boston: Rogers and Fowle, 1742.

———. *A Letter From the Reverend Mr. Andrew Croswell to the Reverend Mr. Turell*. Boston: Massachusetts Historical Society, 1742.

A Curious New Sonnet Dedicated to the Street Musicians. Broadsheet. Boston, 1742.

Davenport, Amzi Benedict. *Supplement to the History and Genealogy of the Davenport Family*. Stamford, Conn., 1876.

Davenport, James. Letter to "Very Dear Brother." MS. Historical Society of Pennsylvania, Philadelphia, 1740.

———. Letter to Eleazar Wheelock. Dartmouth University Archives, Hanover, N.H., 5 October 1740.

———. *The Reverend Mr. James Davenport's Confession and Retractions*. Boston: Kneeland and Green, 1744.

———. *Letter From the Reverend Mr. James Davenport to the Reverend Mr. Jonathan Barber* (30 November 1743). Philadelphia, 1744.

———. Letter to Eleazar Wheelock. MS. Dartmouth University Archives, Hanover, N.H., 25 January 1750.

———. Letter to Stephen Williams. Rare book collection, Yale University Library, New Haven, 14 November 1754.

Davenport, James, and Daniel Tuthill. Letter to Eleazar Wheelock. Dartmouth University Archives, Hanover, N.H., 25 January 1750.

Dexter, Franklin B., ed. *Extracts from the Itineraries and Other Miscellanies of Ezra Stiles, 1755–1794*. New Haven: Yale University Press, 1916.

Dickinson, Jonathan. "The Witness of the Spirit." 1740. In *The Great Awakening: Documents Illustrating the Crisis and Its Consequences*. Edited by Alan Heimert and Perry Miller. Indianapolis and New York: Bobbs-Merrill, 1967.

———. *A Defence of the Dialogue Entitled a Display of God's Special Grace Against the Exceptions Made to it by the Reverend Andrew Croswell*. Boston, 1743.

Edwards, Jonathan. *God A Divine and Supernatural Light*. Boston, 1734.

———. *A Faithful Narrative of the Surprising Work of God in the Conversion of Many Hundred Souls in Northampton and the Neighboring Towns and Villages*. London, 1737.

———. *The Distinguishing Marks of a Work of the Spirit of God*. New Haven, 1741.

———. *Some Thoughts Concerning the Present Revival of Religion in New England*. Boston, 1742.

———. *A Treatise Concerning Religious Affections*. Boston: Kneeland and Green, 1746.

———. *Jonathan Edwards on Revivals*. New York, 1832.

———. *The Works of President Edwards in Four Volumes*. Vol. 3. New York, 1843.

Eells, Nathaniel. "The State of Religion in North America." In *American Magazine and Historical Chronicle*. Boston, 1743.

Emlyn, Thomas. *An Humble Enquiry into the Scripture-Account of Jesus Christ*. London, 1742.

Faust, Clarence H., and Thomas H. Johnson, eds. *Jonathan Edwards: Representative Selections, with Introduction, Bibliography, and Notes*. 1935. Reprint, New York: Hill and Wang, 1962.

Ferris, David. *The Memoirs of the Life of David Ferris, an Approved Minister of the Society of Friends, Written by Himself*. 1821. Reprint, Philadelphia: Merrihew and Thompson, 1855.

Franklin, Benjamin. *Memoirs of the Life & Writings of Benjamin Franklin*. London and Toronto: J. M. Dent & Sons, 1908.

Gee, Joshua. *Letter From the Reverend Joshua Gee to the Reverend Nathaniel Eells*. Boston: Rogers and Fowle, 1743.

Greene, Louise. *The Development of Religious Liberty in Connecticut*. Boston: Houghton Mifflin, 1905.

Heimert, Alan, and Perry Miller, eds. *The Great Awakening: Documents Illustrating the Crisis and Its Consequences*. Indianapolis and New York: Bobbs-Merrill, 1967.

Hempstead, Joshua. *Diary of Joshua Hempstead*. Vol. 1. New London, Conn.: New London County Historical Society, 1911.

Historical Narrative of the Connecticut Strict Congregational Convention. 1781. Revised. Brooklyn, N.Y., 1823.

Hooper, William. Apostles Neither Enthusiasts nor Imposters. MS. Boston, 1742. Long Island, 1839. Easthampton [N.Y.] Public Library.

Minutes of the Suffolk County Presbytery, 1747–1811. MS. Easthampton [N.Y.] Public Library.

Oates, Whitney J., ed. *Basic Writings of St. Augustine*. Vol. 1. New York: Random House, 1948.

Paine, Solomon. *A Short View of the Differences between the Church of Christ, and the Established Churches in the Colony of Connecticut in Their Foundation and Practice, with Their Ends: Being Discovered by the Word of God and Certain Laws of Said Colony, Called Ecclesiastical, With a Word of Warning to Several Ranks of Professors; and Likewise of Comfort to the Minister Members of the Church of Christ*. Newport, R.I.: James Franklin, 1752.

Parsons, Jonathan. *Wisdom Justified of her Children.* Boston, 1742.

Peirpoint, Sarah. Davenport Deserted: A Letter. 30 May 1743. MS. Archives, Dartmouth College Library, Hanover, N.H.

Pickering, Rev. Mr. *The Reverend Mr. Pickering's Letter to the Reverend N. Rogers as also to the Reverend James Davenport of Long Island.* Boston: Rogers and Fowle, 1742.

Prince, Thomas, ed. *The Christian History, Containing Accounts of the Revival and Propagation of Religion in Great-Britain & America. For the Years 1743 and 1744.* 2 vols. Boston: Kneeland and Green, 1744–45.

———. *The History of Boston.* Boston, 1744.

Public Records of the Colony of Connecticut. Vols. 8 and 13. Edited by Charles Hoadley. Hartford, Conn.: Case, Lockwood and Brainard, 1874.

Records of the New Brunswick Presbytery. Vol. I B. 1748–1758. 25 October 1752. MS. New Brunswick, N.J.

Sprague, William B. *Annals of the American Pulpit.* Vol. 3. New York: R. Carter and Brothers, 1858.

Stewart, Gordon. Introduction to *Documents Relating to the Great Awakening in Nova Scotia, 1760–1791.* Vol. 52. In *Publications of the Champlain Society.* Toronto: Champlain Society, 1982.

Tennent, Gilbert. *A Solemn warning to the secure world.* 1735.

———. *The Danger of an Unconverted Ministry, Considered in a Sermon on Mark VI.34.* Boston: Rogers and Fowle, 1742.

———. *The Necessity of holding fast the Truth With an Appendix, Relating to Errors lately vented by some Moravians in those Parts.* Boston, 1743.

The Testimonies and Advice of a Number of Laymen Respecting Religion. Boston, 1743.

To the Reverend James Davenport on his Departure from Boston, by a "female friend." Boston, 1742.

Trumbull, Benjamin. *A Complete History of Connecticut, Civil and Ecclesiastical.* Vol. 2. New Haven, Conn.: Maltby, Goldsmith, 1818.

Turell, Ebenezer. *Mr. Turell's Dialogue Between a Minister and His Neighbor About the Times.* Boston, 1742.

Wading River Church Records. MS. Wading River Congregational Church, Wading River, N.Y. Easthampton [N.Y.] Public Library. (n.d.)

Watts, Isaac. "Isaac Watts to Dr. Colman." 15 November 1742. Reprinted in Massachusetts Historical Society *Proceedings* 10 (February 1895): 398–99.

Westminster Assembly of Divines. *The Confession of Faith, Together with the Larger Catechism.* Boston, 1723.

Wheelock, Eleazar. Letter to James Davenport, 15 November 1756. Archives, Dartmouth University Library, Hanover, N.H.

———. Letter to Mr. Lord, 16 March 1759. Archives, Dartmouth University Library, Hanover, N.H.

———. Letter to Charles Chauncy, 13 March 1769. Dartmouth University Archives, Hanover, N.H.

Whitby, Daniel. *Discourses.* London, 1701.

Whitefield, George. *Whitefield's Journals, to Which is Prefixed His "Short Ac-*

count" and "Further Account." Edited by William Wale. London: Henry J. Drane, 1905. Reprint, London: The Banner of Truth Trust, 1965.

Willard, Samuel, et al. *A Compleat Body of Divinity*. Boston, 1726.

Williams, Solomon. *Letter to the Reverend Mr. James Davenport*. Boston: Kneeland and Green, 1744.

————. *Letter From the Reverend Mr. Solomon Williams of Lebanon to the Reverend Mr. Prince of Boston enclosing the Reverend Mr. Davenport's Humble and Ingenious Confession and Retractions*. Boston: Kneeland and Green, 1744.

Williams, Solomon, Eleazar Wheelock, and James Davenport. *Two Letters From the Reverend Solomon Williams & Wheelock of Lebanon to the Reverend Mr. Davenport which were the Principal Means of His Late Confession and Retractions, with a letter from Mr. Davenport, Desiring Their Publication, for the Good of Others. And His Explanation of Some Passages in His Late Confession*. Boston: Kneeland and Green, 1744.

The Wonderful Narrative or an Account of the French Prophets and Others of Like Spirit. Boston, 1742.

Youngs, Christopher. *Brief History of the Strict Congregational Convention of Long Island*. Brooklyn, N.Y., 1839.

SECONDARY SOURCES

Adams, James Truslow. *Provincial Society, 1690–1763*. New York: Macmillan, 1934.

Aldridge, Alfred Owen. *Jonathan Edwards*. New York: Washington Square Press, 1964.

Bangs, Carl. *Arminius: A Study in the Dutch Reformation*, 2nd. ed. Grand Rapids, Mich.: William B. Eerdmans, 1985.

Berens, John F. "Religion and Revolution Reconsidered: Recent Literature on Religion and Nationalism in Eighteenth-Century America." *Canadian Review of the Study of Nationalism* 10 (fall 1979): 233–45.

Bett, W. R. *A Short History of Some Common Diseases*. Oxford: Oxford University Press, 1934.

Blake, Leroy Stiles. *The Separates, or Strict Congregationalists of New England*. Boston: Pilgrim Press, 1902.

Bonomi, Patricia. *Under the Cope of Heaven: Religion, Society, and Politics in Colonial America*. New York: Oxford University Press, 1986.

Bridenbaugh, Carl. *Cities in the Wilderness*. New York: Alfred A. Knopf, 1960.

————. *Mitre and Sceptre: Transatlantic Faiths, Ideas, Personalities, and Politics, 1689–1775*. New York: Oxford University Press, 1962.

Brockway, Robert W. "The Significance of James Davenport in the Great Awakening." Ph.D. diss., Columbia University, 1951.

————. *Young Carl Jung*. Wilmette, Ill.: Chiron Publications, 1996.

————. "The Significance of James Davenport in the Great Awakening." *Journal of Religious Thought* 24, no. 2 (1967–68): 86–94.

————. "Theological Parties in New England and the Middle Colonies." *Crane Review* (spring 1967): 125–35.

Brown, Peter. *Augustine of Hippo*. Berkeley: University of California Press, 1967.

Brown, Ralph. *Historical Geography of the United States*. New York: Harcourt, Brace and World, 1948.

Bumstead, John M. "Religion, Finance, and Democracy in Massachusetts: The Town of Norton as a Case Study." *Journal of American History* 58 (March 1971): 817–31.

Butler, Jon. "Enthusiasm Described and Decried: The Great Awakening as Interpretative Fiction." *Journal of American History* 69 (September 1982): 305–25.

————. *Awash in a Sea of Faith: Christianizing the American People*. Cambridge: Harvard University Press, 1990.

————. *The Huguenots in America: A Refugee People in New World Society*. Cambridge: Harvard University Press, 1983.

Butterfield, Herbert. *The Origins of Modern Science, 1300–1800*. Toronto: Clarke Irwin, 1968.

Carse, James. *Jonathan Edwards on the Visibility of God*. New York: Charles Scribner's Sons, 1967.

Cheney, Sheldon. *A World History of Art*. New York: Viking Press, 1944.

Clark, Charles E. "Boston and the Nurturing of Newspapers: Dimensions of the Cradle, 1690–1741." *New England Quarterly* 44 (June 1991): 243–71.

Collinson, Patrick. *The Religion of Protestants: The Church of English Society*. Oxford: Clarendon Press, 1982.

Conforti, Joseph. *Jonathan Edwards: Religious Tradition and American Culture*. Chapel Hill: University of North Carolina Press, 1995.

Cowing, Cedric. *The Great Awakening and the American Revolution: Colonial Thought in the Eighteenth Century*. Chicago: Rand-McNally, 1971.

Davidson, Edward H. *Jonathan Edwards: The Narrative of a Puritan Mind*. Boston: Houghton Mifflin, 1966.

Dexter, Franklin Bowditch. *Biographical Sketches of the Graduates of Yale College, October 1701—May 1745*. New Haven: Yale University Press, 1885.

Eliade, Mircea, ed. *The Encyclopedia of Religion*. 15 vols. New York: Macmillan, 1986.

Ellis, Joseph. "Anglicans in Connecticut, 1725–1750: The Conversion of the Missionaries." *New England Quarterly* 44 (March 1971): 66–81.

Erb, Peter C., ed. *Pietists: Selected Writings*. New York: Missionary Society of St. Paul the Apostle in New York, 1983.

Ferm, Vergilius, ed. *An Encyclopedia of Religion*. New York: The Philosophical Library, 1945.

Frantz, John B. "The Awakening of Religion Among the German Settlers in the Middle Colonies." *William and Mary Quarterly* 34 (October 1977): 266–88.

Frye, Northrop. *The Great Code: The Bible and Literature*. Toronto: Academic Press Canada, 1981.

Gaustad, Edwin Scott. *The Great Awakening in New England*. 1957. Reprint, Gloucester, Mass.: Peter Smith, 1965.

Gewehr, Wesley M. *The Great Awakening in Virginia, 1740–1790*. Durham, N.C.: Duke University Press, 1930.

Gilson, Étienne. *The Christian Philosophy of St. Augustine.* New York: Random House, 1960.

Gipson, Lawrence Henry. *The British Isles and the American Colonies.* Vol. 3, *The Northern Colonies: The Northern Plantations, 1748–1754.* New York: Alfred A. Knopf, 1960.

Goen, Clarence C. *Revivalism and Separatism in New England: Strict Congregationalists and Separate Baptists in the Great Awakening.* New Haven: Yale University Press, 1962.

Gollin, Gillian Lindt. *Moravians in Two Worlds: A Study of Changing Communities.* New York: Columbia University Press, 1967.

Goodwin, Gerald. "The Myth of 'Arminian-Calvinism' in Eighteenth Century New England." *New England Quarterly* 41 (March 1968): 213–37.

Greene, Jack P. *Interpreting Early America: Historiographical Essays.* Charlottesville: University Press of Virginia, 1996.

Greene, Jack P., and William G. McLoughlin. *Preachers and Politicians.* Worcester, Mass.: American Antiquarian Society, 1977.

Greene, Louise. *The Development of Religious Liberty in Connecticut.* Boston: Houghton Mifflin, 1905.

Grout, Donald Jay. *A History of Western Music.* New York: W. W. Norton, 1987.

Harkness, Georgia. *John Calvin, the Man and His Ethics.* New York: Abingdon Press, 1991.

Harper, George W. "Clericalism and Revival: The Great Awakening in Boston as a Pastoral Phenomenon." *New England Quarterly* 57 (December 1984): 554–66.

Heimert, Alan. *Religion and the American Mind: From the Great Awakening to the Revolution.* Cambridge: Harvard University Press, 1966.

Henretta, James A., and Gregory H. Nobles. *Evolution and Revolution: American Society, 1600–1820.* Lexington, Mass.: D. C. Heath, 1987.

Henry, Stuart C. *George Whitefield: Wayfaring Witness.* New York: Abingdon Press, 1957.

Hitt, Russell T. "Gilbert Tennent, Gadfly for Righteousness." In *Heroic Colonial Christians.* Edited by Russell T. Hitt. 107–49. Philadelphia: J. B. Lippincott Press, 1966.

Hofstadter, Richard. *America at 1750: A Social Portrait.* New York: Alfred A. Knopf, 1976.

———. *Anti-Intellectualism in American Life.* New York: Alfred A. Knopf, 1963.

Holifield, E. Brooks. "The Intellectual Sources of Stoddardeanism." *New England Quarterly* 45 (September 1972): 373–92.

Hutchison, William R. *Errand to the World.* Chicago: University of Chicago Press, 1987.

Isaac, Rhys. "Evangelical Revolt: The Nature of the Baptist Challenge to the Traditional Order in Virginia, 1765–1775." *William and Mary Quarterly* 31 (July 1974): 345–68.

———. *The Transformation of Virginia, 1740–1790.* Chapel Hill: University of North Carolina Press, 1982.

James, William. *The Varieties of Religious Experience.* 1902. Reprint, London: Longmans, Green, 1914.

Jung, Carl. *The Collected Works of C. G. Jung*. Vol 9.1. Princeton: Princeton University Press, 1959.

Keller, Charles Roy. *The Second Great Awakening in Connecticut*. New York: Anchor Books, 1968.

Kerr, Hugh, and John M. Mulder, eds. *Conversions in Christian Experience*. Grand Rapids, Mich.: William B. Eerdmans, 1983.

Knox, John. *Chapters in a Life of Paul*. New York: Abington-Cokesbury Press, 1940.

Kraus, Michael. *The Atlantic Civilization: Eighteenth-Century Origins*. New York: Russell and Russell, 1961.

Kucklick, Bruce. *Churchmen and Philosophers: From Jonathan Edwards to John Dewey*. New Haven: Yale University Press, 1985.

Labaree, Benjamin. *Colonial Massachusetts*. Millwood, N.Y.: KTO Press, 1973.

Labaree, Leonard. *Conservatism in Early American History*. Ithaca: Cornell University Press, 1947.

Lambert, Frank. *Inventing the "Great Awakening."* Princeton: Princeton University Press, 1999.

————. *"Pedlar in Divinity": George Whitefield and the Transatlantic Revivals, 1737–1770*. Princeton: Princeton University Press, 1994.

Langdon, Edward. *History of the Moravian Church*. London: George Allen and Unwin, 1956.

Langer, William L., ed. *Encyclopedia of World History*. Boston: Houghton Mifflin, 1972.

Lockridge, Kenneth. *A New England Town: The First Hundred Years*. New York: W. W. Norton, 1970.

Lockwood, Rose. "The Scientific Revolution in Seventeenth-Century New England." *New England Quarterly* 53 (March 1980): 76–95.

Lodge, Martin E. "The Crisis of Churches in the Middle Colonies, 1720–1750." *Pennsylvania Magazine of History and Biography* 95 (April 1971): 195–220.

Lovejoy, David S., ed. *Religious Enthusiasm in the Great Awakening*. Englewood Cliffs, N.J.: Prentice-Hall, 1969.

Marini, Stephen A. *Radical Sects of Revolutionary New England*. Cambridge: Harvard University Press, 1982.

Maxson, Charles Hartshorne. *The Great Awakening in the Middle Colonies*. Chicago: University of Chicago Press, 1920. Reprint, Gloucester, Mass.: Peter Smith, 1958.

McNeill, John T. *The History and Character of Calvinism*. New York: Oxford University Press, 1954.

McNeill, William. *The Rise of the West: A History of the Human Community*. New York: W. W. Norton, 1964.

Middleton, Richard. *Colonial America: A History, 1607–1760*. Cambridge, Mass.: Blackwell Publishers, 1992.

Miller, John C. "Religion, Finance, and Democracy in Massachusetts." *New England Quarterly* 6 (March 1933): 29–58.

Miller, Perry. *Jonathan Edwards*. New York: William Sloane Associates, 1949. Reprint, Cleveland and New York: World Publishing, 1965.

———. *Orthodoxy in Massachusetts*. Cambridge: Harvard University Press, 1933.

———. "Solomon Stoddard, 1643–1729." *Harvard Theological Review* 34 (October 1941): 277–320.

———. *Errand in the Wilderness*. New York: Harper and Row, 1956.

———. *The New England Mind in the Seventeenth Century*. Cambridge: Harvard University Press, 1967.

———. *The New England Mind: From Colony to Province*. 1953. Reprint, Boston: The Beacon Press, 1961.

Morgan, Edwin. "The American Revolution Considered as an Intellectual Movement." In *Paths of American Thought*. Edited by Arthur M. Schlesinger, Jr., and Morton White. Boston: Houghton Mifflin, 1963.

Morison, Samuel Eliot. *The Intellectual Life of Colonial New England*. New York: New York University Press, 1956.

———. *The Oxford History of the American People*. New York: Oxford University Press, 1965.

Nash, Gary B. *The Urban Crucible: Social Change, Political Consciousness and the Origins of the American Revolution*. Cambridge: Harvard University Press, 1979.

Notestein, Walter. *The English People on the Eve of Colonization, 1603–1630*. New York: Harper Press, 1954.

Nybakken, Elizabeth. "New Light on the Old Side: Irish Influences on Colonial Presbyterianism." *Journal of American History* 69 (March 1982): 813–32.

O'Brien, Susan. "A Transatlantic Community of Saints: The Great Awakening and the First Evangelical Network, 1735–1755." *American Historical Review* 91 (October 1986): 811–32.

Onuf, Peter S. "New Lights in London: A Group Portrait of the Separatists." *William and Mary Quarterly* 37 (October 1980): 627–43.

Opie, John. *Jonathan Edwards and the Enlightenment*. Lexington, Mass.: D. C. Heath, 1969.

Osgood, Herbert I. *The American Colonies in the Eighteenth Century*. Vol. 3. New York: Columbia University Press, 1924. Reprint, Gloucester, Mass.: Peter Smith, 1958.

Penfield, Robert. *The Quest for Security, 1715–1740*. New York: Harper Brothers, 1947.

Petit, Norman. "Prelude to Mission: Brainerd's Expulsion from Yale." *New England Quarterly* 59 (March 1986): 28–50.

Pierce, David C. "Jonathan Edwards and the 'New Sense of Glory.'" *New England Quarterly* 41 (March 1968): 82–95.

Pope, Robert G. *The Half-Way Covenant: Church Membership in Colonial New England*. Princeton: Princeton University Press, 1969.

Rowel, Robert. "The Great Awakening: An Historical Anaysis." *American Journal of Sociology* 75 (May 1979): 907–25.

Rutman, Darrett B. *American Puritanism*. New York: W. W. Norton, 1977.

———, ed. *The Great Awakening: Event and Exegesis*. New York: John Wiley and Sons, 1970.

Savelle, Max, and Robert Middlekauff. *A History of Colonial America.* New York: Holt, Rinehart and Winston, 1964.

Schneider, Herbert Wallace. *The Puritan Mind.* Ann Arbor: University of Michigan Press, 1958.

Scott, E. F. *The Varieties of New Testament Religion.* New York: Charles Scribner's Sons, 1947.

Sklar, Robert. "The Great Awakening and Colonial Politics: Connecticut's Revolution in the Minds of Men." *Connecticut Historical Society* 5 (spring 1963): 81–95.

Stouffler, F. Ernst. *The Rise of Evangelical Pietism.* Leyden: Brill, 1965.

————. *German Pietism During the Eighteenth Century.* Leyden: Brill, 1973.

Stout, Harry S. "Religion, Communications, and the Ideological Origins of the American Revolution." *William and Mary Quarterly* 34 (October 1977): 519–41.

————. *The New England Soul: Preaching and Religious Culture in Colonial New England.* New York: Oxford University Press, 1886.

————. *The Divine Dramatist: George Whitefield and the Rise of Modern Evangelicalism.* Grand Rapids, Mich.: William B. Eerdmans, 1991.

Stout, Harry S., and Peter S. Onuf. "James Davenport and the Great Awakening in New London." *Journal of American History* 70 (December 1983): 556–78.

Sweet, William Warren. *Religion in America.* 1930. Reprint, New York: *New York Times* and Arno Press, 1950.

Tanis, James. *Dutch Calvinistic Pietism in the Middle Colonies: A Study in the Life and Theology of Theodorus Jacobus Frelinghuysen.* The Hague: Brill, 1967.

Tracy, Joseph. *The Great Awakening: A History of the Revival of Religion in the Time of Edwards and Whitefield.* 1841. Reprint, Boston: Charles Tappan Press, 1845.

Tracy, Patricia. *Jonathan Edwards, Pastor: Religion and Society in Eighteenth-Century Northampton.* New York: Hill and Wang, 1980.

Trinterud, Leonard J. *The Forming of an American Tradition: A Re-Examination of Colonial American Presbyterianism.* Philadelphia: Westminster Press, 1949. Reprint, Freeport, N.Y.: Books for Libraries Press, 1970.

————, ed. *Elizabethan Puritanism.* New York: Oxford University Press, 1971.

Trumbull, Benjamin. *A Complete History of Connecticut, Civil and Ecclesiastical.* Vol. 2. New Haven, Conn.: Maltby, Goldsmith, 1818.

Wainwright, William. *Reason and the Heart: A Prolegomenon to a Critique of Personal Reason.* Ithaca: Cornell University Press, 1995.

Walsh, James B. "Solomon Stoddard's Open Communion: A Re-examination." *New England Quarterly* 43 (March 1970): 97–114.

————. "The Great Awakening in the First Congregational Church of Woodbury, Connecticut." *William and Mary Quarterly* 28 (October 1971): 543–62.

Walzer, Michael. "Puritanism as a Revolutionary Ideology." In *Essays in American Colonial History.* Edited by Paul Goodman. New York: Holt, Rinehart and Winston, 1967.

Warch, Richard. "The Shepherd's Tent: Education and Enthusiasm in the Great Awakening." *American Quarterly* 30 (summer 1978): 177–98.

Ward, Harry M. *Colonial America, 1607–1763.* Englewood Cliffs, N.J.: Prentice-Hall, 1991.

White, Eugene E. "The Decline of the Great Awakening in New England, 1741–1746." *New England Quarterly* 34 (March 1961): 35–52.

Whitehead, Walter Muir. *Boston: A Topographical History.* Cambridge: Harvard University Press, Belknap Press, 1968.

Winslow, Ola. *Jonathan Edwards, 1703–1758.* New York: Crowell-Colliers, 1961.

Wright, Conrad. *The Beginnings of Unitarianism in America.* Boston: Beacon Press, Starr King, 1955.

Zuckerman, Michael. *Peaceable Kingdoms: New England Towns in the Eighteenth Century.* New York: Alfrd A. Knopf, 1970.

Index